FROM MANAGEMENT THEORY
TO BUSINESS SENSE

FROM MANAGEMENT THEORY TO BUSINESS SENSE

The Myths and Realities
of People at Work

David A. Whitsett
Lyle Yorks

American Management Associations

This book is available at a special discount when ordered in bulk quantities. For information, contact AMACOM, Special Sales Department, 135 West 50th Street, New York, NY 10020.

Library of Congress Cataloging in Publication Data

Whitsett, David A.
    From management theory to business sense.

    Includes bibliography and index.
    1. Management literature—United States—History.
I. Yorks, Lyle. II. Title.
HD30.5.W48 1983   809'.935658   82-73830
ISBN 0-8144-5765-7

First Printing

To
Laurel and Lisa Whitsett
and
Joanne, Lyle, Tracy, and Russell Yorks
They make our world special for us.

Preface and Acknowledgments

This book grew out of an interest in what appeared to be significant distortions of events that have served as the basis for management theories. In 1975, when we began our research, we were aware of two sources pointing to such distortions. The first was the rare but apparently well-researched articles in professional journals questioning some of the popular interpretations of landmark studies, especially Taylor's work and the Hawthorne research. Despite the implications of these articles, they have remained outside the mainstream of textbook literature. Second, we were well aware that some of the emerging lore surrounding contemporary management techniques, especially work-restructuring methods, had often been packaged in ways that provided a skewed picture of events. The process of distortion was subtle and was contributed to by respected professionals with solid credentials.

Interesting questions suggested themselves. To what extent were actual events at variance with popular beliefs about what had happened? How might the landscape of management theory look different if these possible discrepancies were taken into account? To what extent were the adversarial postures between some schools of management practice exaggerated? What was myth and what was reality? What are the implications of such distortions for the ways in which managers use the results of field investigations?

A preliminary investigation suggested that the problem was indeed very complex. We found that the distortion process was somehow caught up with how management studies were used to promote change in organizations. As we worked through this issue it became clearer to both of us that the project was an assessment of our craft—the application of behavioral science knowledge.

While we were working on this book, a series of critical articles appeared in the journal *Public Interest* dealing with how social science has been used in the development of public policy. James Lee wrote an intriguing book, *The Gold and the Garbage in Management Theory.* A body of literature that addressed the issue of distortion began appearing in *American Psychologist.* This material was both encouraging and helpful. It indicated that others were interested in these issues and provided us with additional ideas.

The final product is twofold. In Parts One through Three, which describe Taylorism, the Hawthorne studies, and the General Foods Topeka dog food plant findings, we attempt to present these studies thoroughly and from an integrated perspective. In the last chapter of each of these sections, judgments are made on the basis of available historical evidence about how alternative interpretations came to be popularized. In Part Four, dealing with the application of management theories, we discuss issues that arose during our research and place them within the context of our own experiences in organizations. We believe these issues are pertinent both to researchers in field settings and to practitioners.

Undoubtedly, some will read this book as an attempted indictment of the management literature. This is not our intent. For us the exercise of researching and writing this book was one of coming to a better understanding of the nature and dynamics of the knowledge base with which we work in the field of organizational management. Personally we have developed a deep respect for both the usefulness and the limitations of the theories and concepts involved.

Our efforts were facilitated by the work of several scholars. Indeed, in the case of Taylorism and the Hawthorne studies, such work provided the basis for our initial curiosity. We readily acknowledge such intellectual debts. With regard to Taylor, Donald Nelson and Charles Wrege have done rare and invaluable research. Similarly, A. J. M. Sykes's and Alex Carey's analyses of the Hawthorne studies were highly insightful. During the course of our work, the publication of a reanalysis of the Hawthorne data from the relay assembly test room by Richard Franke and James Kaul provided substantial support for Carey's earlier analysis.

The resources of the Taylor Collection of the Stevens Institute, The Baker Library at the Harvard Business School, and the Rockefeller Foundation provided documents indispensable to our research on Taylorism and the Hawthorne studies. Mrs. Jane Hartye, curator of the Taylor Collection, was especially helpful, as were the members of the readers' service staff of the University of Northern Iowa Library. The research at Stevens Institute was supported, in part, by a grant from the University of Northern Iowa Graduate College, for which we are grateful. We thank George F. F. Lombard of the Harvard Business School for sharing his experience as a colleague of Elton Mayo and Fritz Roethlisberger.

We are grateful to Philip Simshauser and Donald La Fond for their comments on initial drafts of the chapters on the General Foods Topeka plant. Both played important roles in the design and administration of the facility. Their support in providing access to original documents from Topeka is appreciated.

Steve Morris of Drake Beam Morin was helpful in commenting on early versions of the manuscript and referring us to specific resources. We thank him for his support and interest. Special thanks go to Jay Carroll, who originally encouraged us to write this book. Eric Valentine's editorial comments were insightful and encouraging, and helped make this a better book. Finally, Pat Devlin of Drake Beam Morin provided important administrative support and the staff of the word processing group at the University of Northern Iowa gave us invaluable typing help.

In this book we have sought to integrate much independent work previously done and extend the earlier analyses by providing additional information on the context in which the studies were completed. We have also tried to suggest a perspective for understanding how management knowledge is generated and applied. This latter purpose is, we believe, of crucial importance to the way future research findings in organizational settings are utilized.

David A. Whitsett
Lyle Yorks

Contents

FROM MANAGEMENT THEORY TO BUSINESS SENSE

Introduction

Perspectives on the Problem of Managing Others

"The Management Theory Jungle" is the title of a classic article on management theory,[1] a title as appropriate today as it was in 1961 when it was published. The field of management is as divided now as it was then, and perhaps more so. There are the traditional divisions of the classic administrative science school, the behavioral science school, and the mathematically oriented management science school. There are also debates over the need for American history to return to the basics of production management, the desirability of our learning Japanese management methods, and the long-range implications of extensive bargaining in labor relations.

Further, many of the "classic" studies in the field are being reevaluated, with some researchers suggesting that the results of these studies have been seriously misrepresented. The famous Hawthorne studies are but one example of this phenomenon. Within organizations the lines between engineers and psychologists often appear as combative as ever. A newcomer to the field could easily be confused.

Jungles are notoriously dangerous places. The management theory jungle is no exception. Better for the manager to enter that jungle skeptical of the existing guides than to place too much trust in them, since the economic stakes are high. He or she should be well prepared to assess what the guides proclaim.

This book examines three major sets of studies: Taylor's scientific management experiments, the Hawthorne studies, and the Experimental General Foods dog food plant in Topeka, Kansas. Each has been controversial; each has been distorted in the literature and yet has been a major landmark for people trying to penetrate the management theory jungle.

The material on each of these studies is presented in considerable detail. This detail is not superfluous, but is fundamental to understanding the history of the studies and how they came to be interpreted as they were. One common denominator of the three sets of studies is that each represents an attempt to reform, even revolutionize how organizations are managed. The theorists associated with each—Taylor, Mayo, and Walton—were conducting scientific investigations but were perhaps even more committed to the potential consequences of their studies. As much as any economist, they fit the characterization of "worldly philosophers." Although each is coming to be viewed from the perspective of his historical context, the methods they advocated continue to be widely utilized.

Lordstown: Perspectives in Conflict

Lordstown. For people interested in productivity improvement, the name of this small Ohio town is infamous.

In February 1972, the United Auto Workers walked out of the Lordstown General Motors Vega plant to begin a bitter wildcat strike. For three weeks production halted. Management specialists championing the cause of job enrichment, work redesign, and quality-of-work-life improvements seized upon the walkout as symbolic of the problems created by dull, monotonous jobs. The Health, Education, and Welfare report *Work in America*, published in 1973, warned that "increased industrial sabotage and sudden wildcat strikes, like the one at Lordstown, portend something more fundamental than the desire for money." The national media took up the theme that Lordstown was a rebellion against the "mindless system of mass production." The term "Lordstown syndrome" was coined to identify this apparently powerful source of worker discontent.

Representatives of a more traditional perspective on managing work railed against the publicity given to this position. The issue at Lordstown, they asserted, was a speedup. Management was running the assembly line faster than was the case at any other plant, with no additional wages.

In reality, this latter position was closer to the truth. General Motors had placed the plant under the jurisdiction of the General Motors Assembly Division (GMAD). Created as a centralized corporate production authority charged with increasing the efficiency of assembly operations, GMAD had a reputation for taking tough stands on job elimination and production standards.

At Lordstown, GMAD was eliminating 700 jobs that it maintained were no longer needed once the startup on the new Vega was completed. The union wasn't buying, arguing that the bottom line was loss of jobs and more pressure on production workers. The confrontation was over classic issues: job security and work standards.[2]

Once production resumed, workers claimed that G.M. was so productivity-conscious that they were being forced to make cars that were junk. The company charged that the assembly workers were sabotaging the product. Behavioral scientists took the position that regardless of the specific issues that triggered the walkout, the point was clear: scientific management, pressed to its ultimate end, is not an effective way of achieving productivity gains. Rather, it reduces pride in workmanship and generates labor unrest.

Lordstown represents something significant to different camps of management thought. Like many symbolic events in management–labor relations history, it has become anecdotal data for a number of theoretical positions. One thing is certain: Lordstown became a rallying point around which two perspectives on management confronted each other.

The "Engineering" and "Behavioral" Views

Managing both the technical and the human elements of the organizations has posed continuing problems for practicing managers and management theorists alike. Increasing productivity, reducing employee errors, cutting absenteeism, maintaining good labor relations, and improving job satisfaction—these are but some of the issues with which managers have grappled while striving to improve organizational performance. In their thinking about strategies for attacking such questions, many managers have adopted either an "engineering" or a "behavioral" view of the management process.

In actuality neither point of view encompasses a cohesive school of thought or practice. Rather, each is a loosely grouped set of assumptions and beliefs. Indeed, the distinctions "engineering" and "behavioral" are misleading, since many industrial and production engineers have vigorously championed the introduction of behavioral science principles into the practice of their discipline. Likewise, not all behavioral scientists are of the same theoretical ilk. Some are more closely aligned with the positions of classic management theory than with the humanistic psychologists who have had great visibility in the management literature during recent decades.

While these terms cannot readily be used to identify particular professions or schools of thought, many people have used the labels "engineering" and "behavioral" as shorthand for expressing two conflicting perspectives on the world of work. These labels are regularly referred to during the verbal battles fought in corporations over what constitutes proper management practice. The distinction between the two has become quite real in the minds of practitioners.

Generally speaking, the *engineering* view argues that efficiency is the principal measure of management effectiveness. People holding this view are sympathetic to mechanical and electronic revolution in the workplace. Large-scale organization and its accompanying economies of scale are good, contributing to the progress of society.

The practical assumptions underlying this view are reflected in such principles as:

1. Get the work done at the appropriate level. Simple tasks should be assigned to lesser-paid individuals.
2. Reduce the number of separate tasks being performed in any one work unit. Departments and work units should specialize.
3. Simplify and streamline. Simple means easy, and easy means lower costs.
4. Batch the work wherever possible, giving each employee a measured volume of work to do.[3]

The engineering view assumes that workers are primarily motivated by money and employment benefits. Managing the people side of the business is seen as a problem of alternately using carrots and sticks to control the behavior of workers.

This view, then, gives primacy to the formal, technological system of the organization. The emphasis is on task specialization and differentiation. It comes closest to the formal schools of management thought that are commonly labeled "classical" and "scientific" management.

Conversely, the *behavioral* view emphasizes the human variable as the solution to obtaining organizational effectiveness. Interpersonal cooperation replaces efficiency as the dominant organizational problem. While maintaining that they are not opposed to efficiency measures, proponents of this view frequently point out that overemphasis on efficiency distorts the picture of organizational performance: it masks worker discontent, management's resistance to change, and the problem of low commitment to the organization. The positive development of these factors, it is argued, is crucial to long-term high organizational performances. Some assumptions underlying the behavioral view are that:

1. Employee job satisfaction is a strong determinant of organizational performance and causes workers to be more resilient in a time of challenges and crises.

2. Conflict and change should be managed so as to elicit mutual cooperation from the organization members involved. This requires trust and openness on the part of management.
3. Well-managed organizations strive to satisfy the psychological needs of their employees while trying to meet organizational goals.
4. Full utilization of employee skills and talents, including employees' abilities to exercise discretion and make decisions, will result in improved organizational effectiveness.

Those sympathetic to this view emphasize programs that improve the interpersonal competence of managers, increase the involvement of subordinates in decisions affecting their work and lifestyle, and more fully utilize the skills of employees. Economic needs are seen as less significant than psychological ones in motivating employees. In the management literature this perspective approximates a mixture of theoretical positions, most of which are traditionally grouped as either personalistic, human relations, or human resource models.

These two views support specific management strategies and practices that are often formalized in staff departments. An example is work-measurement departments, found in many commercial and industrial organizations. Essentially, the work-measurement strategy emphasizes systematic collection of data through the use of flowcharts, task lists, work-distribution charts, and similar tools for analyzing procedures. The data collected are analyzed to determine whether a given change might produce measurable cost reductions and increased productivity. This analysis is combined with a time measurement of the tasks involved to create a specific standard for staffing control. The organizational unit carrying out this analysis is typically called Operations Improvement, Operations Analysis, Systems and Methods, Office Management Systems, or Industrial Engineering.

The staff delivering this service is usually said to have an "engineering" view of management. Most work-measurement analysts view themselves as pragmatists responding to the current realities they see expressed by their data. Their principal goal is to identify opportunities for immediate cost reduction through trial-and-error manipulation of data.

The analysis process is illustrated by the following description by a work-measurement analyst:

In the [clerical] area there were six jobs at the start of the study which are combined into three jobs. The reason was that there was a lot of passing items back and forth within the department. Further, when measured, each job could not support a full person. So, we combined work. The prime objective was to fill up the jobs. We looked first for logically related tasks, but we might also combine apples and oranges if it meant a further reduction in staff.[4]

During such an analysis process, with its "engineering" view, line managers are generally most cooperative if they hold a similar view and agree with the justifications given for the changes.

Work simplification, a cousin of work measurement with a dose of human relations, also strikes a responsive chord with individuals who subscribe to the engineering view. Likewise, most piecework and group-incentive systems are designed and willingly utilized by managers who share the engineering view of the management process.

Subscribers to the behavioral view believe that people perform better when the work situation encourages their involvement in shaping the tasks they carry out and when management expresses active interest in the advancement aspirations of individual employees. Behaviorally oriented programs include communication skills training, participative management, team-building, job enrichment, and sensitivity training. Managers are able to choose from a wide variety of people-oriented programs, including some developed by those with an engineering stance.

As with the engineering view, this perspective is represented by staff departments serving the organization. Personnel Research, Organizational Development, and Human Resources Development are some labels that identify departments providing people-oriented advice and programs. Their best clients within the organization are managers who hold similar views.

As we have discussed, the grouping of management techniques as "engineering" or "behavioral" is somewhat artificial. However, many managers do hold a loosely constructed view of the world of work that closely corresponds to one of these descriptions. A manager with an "engineering" view is likely to be sympathetic to a range of techniques aimed at operational efficiencies; a manager with "behavioral" leanings is likely to favor methods based on the social sciences.

The clash between the two views was brought clearly into focus by the popularity of job enrichment in the early 1970s. The behavioral point of view now invaded the traditional turf of the industrial engineer, the design of jobs. The conflict thus generated was inevitable and direct.

Illustrative of this conflict is the work of Mitchell Fein, a prominent consulting engineer, who in his critiques of job enrichment rails against "behavioralists" who insist that "they know better what workers want than do workers themselves." Fein states the engineering view quite plainly:

Most workers do not come to work for fulfillment from work itself. They come to work to eat, to exchange their time, effort, and skills for what they can buy outside of the workplace. They want more of the good things in life that they see paraded in front of them in living color on T.V. They want to satisfy their material aspirations.[5]

This is coupled with:

[The behavioralists'] key proposal calls for autonomy at the workplace and the redesign of jobs to permit decisions by workers. But this idealized version just is not possible. Few decisions are needed on what to do in mass production. A piece is put into press and hit; two pieces or 50 are assembled in a given manner, simply because the pieces would not fit together in any [other] way. In typing a letter or keypunching, the operators are required to strike certain keys, not any keys they wish; and so it goes.

Fein states the engineering view articulately: economic man is integrated into the relatively inflexible demands of the technological system through mutual financial exchange. When hearing Fein speak on the subject, we have been struck by how his comments generated strong reactions from the audience, both positive and negative.

Origins of the Two Views

Although job enrichment has recently brought into sharp focus the battle between the engineering and behavioral views, both views—and the conflict between them—have existed for a long time. Neither viewpoint can be attributed to a single individual or group of individuals.

The engineering view of management is a cultural belief system spawned from the classic tradition of management theory. With its emphasis on formal structure, span of control, the functions of management, formal control systems, and measurement of performance, this school of thought remains influential in standard management texts. The behavioral view originally grew out of the psychoanalytical orientation of the early human relations researchers. Today the view is expressed in the work of sociologists and psychologists who study organizations and the behavior of people who work in them. In the case of both orientations, practitioners, consultants, and even researchers have blended theory, objective data, and myth to generate particular belief systems that support a type of managerial action.

Although the influences have been diverse, two pieces of research can be identified that have had a disproportionate impact on the evolution of management thought. Both were cornerstones for what emerged as major schools of thought and management practice. These are the scientific management studies of Frederick Taylor and the Hawthorne studies.

The intellectual origins of the management strategies associated with the engineering view are generally traced to the work of Frederick Taylor. Often referred to as the father of scientific management, Taylor made repeated reference to his study of how pig iron was loaded at the Bethlehem Iron (later Steel) Company. This study was to become Taylor's principal illustrations of the practicality of scientific management. It was a significant part of his *Principles of Scientific Management*, published in 1911.

A brilliant man with seemingly endless energy, Taylor became one of the dominant mechanical engineers of his time. Through the Taylor Society, which evolved from his work on management, his principles cast a long influence over the early development of industrial engineering and management theory alike. For Taylor the problem of motivation was essentially one of economics. The opportunity to increase one's income was the vehicle for marrying the worker to Taylor's system of industrial organization.

The major beginnings of the behavioral view are found in the writings of Elton Mayo and Fritz Roethlisberger of the Harvard Business School. More than anyone else, these two men shaped the early years of the human relations movement in industry. In so doing they forged the principal path for research in the area of organization behavior. From studies conducted in the Hawthorne plant of the Western Electric Company, Mayo and Roethlisberger were to directly challenge many of the principles of scientific management. Among them was the idea that economic interest was the primary motivator of worker behavior.

For years, scientific management and the human relations orientation were regarded as opposites. Managers believed they had to choose between a hard (scientific management) and a soft (human relations) approach toward their subordinates. Then, in 1960, Douglas McGregor stated that the choice was irrelevant for the contemporary manager.[6]

Basing his reasoning on Abraham Maslow's hierarchy of needs, McGregor found both the hard and the soft approach "useless methods of motivating people whose physiological and safety needs are reasonably satisfied and whose social, egotistic, and self-fulfillment needs are predominant." Presumably a hard or soft approach was a meaningful choice for managers whose workers' physical and security needs were unsatisfied. McGregor therefore developed a new set of assumptions about human nature, which he labeled Theory Y. This theory reflected an essentially positive view of human nature and assumed that mature adults found meaningful work inherently satisfying. He contrasted Theory Y assumptions with a more negative view of human nature, which he labeled Theory X, and he suggested that Theory X represented the thinking of many traditional managers.

When McGregor recommended Theory Y assumptions, he did not intend them to be merely another name for the traditional human resources view. Most managers, however, misread Theory X and Theory Y as representing the traditional hard/soft choice. This interpretation shows the continued strength of the dualistic orientation in management thinking, and today the belief systems of managers still tend to split along these lines.

Management Theory: How Much Legend, How Much Science?

This book initially grew out of the authors' experiences in a wide range of industries—experiences that led us increasingly to feel that the techniques and strategies managers use differ more in stated ideology than in actual practice. To be sure, substantive differences exist between such methods as work measurement and job enrichment. Yet even when techniques from the different orientations have seemed obviously complementary, opportunities to try new methods have been actively resisted.

Our interest in these phenomena led us to consider another intriguing possibility: that the data on which many management techniques are based have been significantly misreported or misrepresented in the evolution of management theory and practice. The more one examines the events surrounding the landmark research studies, the more one realizes that popular interpretations are often better characterized by the term legend than science.

Members of the academic community have commonly accused commercial consultants of oversimplifying and misrepresenting research data in their eagerness to promote their services. The legends of management theory, however, are not so easily explained.

The principal assertion to be made in this book is that much of what managers frequently state with regard to the "engineering" or "behavioral" views is based on myth rather than on the events that actually characterized the studies on which the views traditionally rest. Further, the myths are in many instances traceable back to the principal figures in the studies themselves.

The explanation of myths in management theory is interwoven with the complexities of generating applied knowledge in the social sciences. The management researcher is not only a generator of knowledge but a person seeking to show how the knowledge can be utilized. No matter how pure the research orientation, the question of "How could people use it?" looms large over the researcher. This is particularly true when the researcher initially defines his or her audience as including not only the academic community but the world of the practicing manager.

It might be tempting, but is simplistically misleading, to attribute the misinterpretation of management research to ulterior motives or scientific incompetence on the part of the researchers or their close associates. It is more pertinent to look at the ways in which managerial practice is continually being influenced by academic work, and vice versa. A clearer understanding of the process through which management knowledge is generated and translated into practice is needed. Without such an understanding, management will remain a field chasing itself.

In order to explore this issue we invite the reader to examine the two landmark studies referred to earlier, Taylor's scientific management research and the Hawthorne studies. We also invite the reader to consider more closely the schools of thought that emerged from this work: scientific management and human relations, respectively. The causes of the misinterpretations of these studies are very much relevant to contemporary workplace experiments. To provide a recent example, we will make a similar analysis of the General Foods experimental plant at Topeka. These three sets of studies have been very visible—and controversial—in the management literature, and so can serve as prototypes of the phenomena we are discussing. Of course, many other such studies exist, and will be drawn upon when appropriate.

NOTES

1. Harold Koontz, "The Management Theory Jungle," *Academy of Management Journal*, December 1961, pp. 174–188.
2. A brief account of the strike is found in J. Patrick Wright, *On a Clear Day You Can See General Motors* (Grosse Pointe, Mich.: Wright Enterprises, 1979). Interviews with workers who were in the plant support this position.
3. These principles emerged, for example, during a study of work-measurement practices. See Lyle Yorks, Marti Kaplar, and Richard Ochs, "Job Enrichment and Operations Involvement," *Journal of Systems Management*, March 1978, pp. 17–25.
4. Ibid., p. 18.
5. Mitchell Fein, "Job Enrichment Does Not Work," *Atlanta Economic Review*, Vol. 25, No. 6 (November–December 1975), pp. 50–54.
6. Douglas McGregor, *The Human Side of Enterprise* (New York: McGraw-Hill, 1960).

PART ONE

Frederick Taylor and the Rise of Scientific Management

1

Frederick Taylor: An Introduction to the Man and the System

Frederick Winslow Taylor was born on March 20, 1856, in Germantown, near Philadelphia. He was the second of three children of Quaker parents, Franklin Taylor and Emily Winslow Taylor.

Franklin Taylor was a lawyer and planned to have young Fred follow in his footsteps. At the age of sixteen Fred was sent to Phillips Exeter Academy to prepare for Harvard Law School. He then passed the Harvard entrance exams, but he was advised by his physician that his eyes had become badly weakened from his extended nighttime studying and that continuation of an academic education was inadvisable.

Extremely disappointed and restless, the young man seized an opportunity to learn the trades of pattern-maker and machinist in a small pump manufacturing company. Taylor spent four years there as an apprentice. His parents were quite upset by this decision to join a manufacturing organization. Fred was from a well-to-do Quaker family, and becoming a laborer was not something expected from people of his station.

Taylor's biographer, Frank Copley, reports that during his years at this company, Taylor "had [his] eye on the bad industrial conditions which prevailed at the time, and gave a good deal of time and thought to some possible remedy for them."[1] To today's reader, this quotation implies a concern with "bad industrial conditions" such as exploitation of workers and poor physical surroundings. However, the context in which Copley couches this comment makes it clear that Taylor actually was referring to workers' practice of restricting production—or, as he called it, "soldiering."

Fred's personality development as a young adult can be linked quite clearly with the personalities of his parents. Throughout his life, Franklin Taylor conveyed to his children a gentleness combined with strength and inner resolve. He was a devoted, though somewhat distant and aloof, father. In the Quaker tradition, he had led a life of service to others, including fifty-seven years of work with the Pennsylvania Training School for feeble-minded children. Franklin had a clear sense of one's duties and obligations, placing a very high value on the development of inner control and conscience. But Taylor's mother seems to have been the "stronger character" of the parents.

Emily Winslow Taylor descended from a family line of both New England Puritans and Quakers. She was an extremely demanding parent, which was a function of her own personality and of prevailing beliefs concerning child-rearing during most of the nineteenth century. Most books on child-rearing during this period imparted the message that an infant's nature was depraved, willful, and intensely selfish, and must therefore be suppressed by strict obediance training. It was believed that, in order to form Christian habits of mind, the child must submit to the parents' will and any obstinacy must be severely punished.

If we add to this philosophy the power of Emily Taylor's own determination and strong will, we can form a picture of the "ruled and regular" household she commanded. Her system of child training consisted of "work and drill and discipline."[2]

Emily Taylor possessed one other particularly relevant characteristic. "She never set much store on tact. Tact she was inclined to associate with hypocrisy. She knew her mind, and in reason she spoke it plainly and to the point. Hers was the Quaker ideal of language stripped of all flattery and purged of all dross."[3] Fred was later to be very outspoken himself.

As might be expected from such an atmosphere, Fred developed a somewhat rigid and compulsive personality. Numerous incidents in his early life demonstrate this trait. As a child, he was much concerned that the games in which he played conform exactly to their rules and regulations. He often arrived early for ball games to lay out the field in exact distances. When playing croquet, he carefully worked out the angles of strokes and the force of impact. Later, when attending dances, he would prepare detailed lists of all the girls he regarded as attractive and unattractive, and then carefully divide his time equally among them.

Taylor's young life was full of repetitive, ritualistic acts that are the hallmark of the developing obsessive-compulsive personality. This characteristic was combined with a Puritan intolerance for anything less than one's best effort (in either himself or others) and a highly intense nature. Taken together, these attributes formed a man with "a whale of a New England conscience," who set exceptionally high and rigid standards for himself and everyone around him and who reacted strongly to any failure to measure up to these standards.

As we will see, this constellation of characteristics greatly affected the content of Taylor's work and theories. In 1878, Taylor moved on to the Midvale Steel Works, which was the setting of an experience that launched his lifelong quest for a system of management based on facts and data rather than on guesses and opinions. At Midvale, at age twenty-three, he was given his first chance at supervision when he was made gang boss of the lathe hands alongside whom he had previously been working.

Taylor had become familiar with the practice of workers restricting their production, and had done so himself as a lathe hand. Later he was to write that under a system of piece-rate pay, workers felt it was to their advantage to restrict their production, since production at an "all-out" pace would result in management raising its expectations of output. They would then have had to work harder for the same amount of money. Taylor sympathized with this position and remained opposed to straight piecework systems throughout his life.

But when made gang boss, he perceived himself as "on the other side of the fence" and therefore responsible for increasing output if at all possible. Taylor announced his intentions to his men, and they believed he was about to become a "damn piecework hog." The battle lines were thus drawn between a young, committed gang boss who was determined to raise what he knew to be artificially low rates of output, and an older, just as determined work force that was prepared to resist his efforts.

The battle lasted three years. According to Taylor, the first was a bitter one that escalated into threats and intentional sabotage of equipment on the part of the workers. Taylor retaliated with firings and assessments of large fines. Finally, the men gave in. Victory, however, apparently found Taylor deeply hurt and upset by the conflicts and resulting loss of friendships.

The only detailed account of this series of events comes from Taylor himself. The account was delivered almost twenty-five years later, in 1912, during a series of congressional hearings in which Taylor testified before the Special House Committee to Investigate the Taylor and Other Systems of Shop Management. The picture presented of these events may be partially inaccurate, since features of the story might have become distorted in Taylor's mind as a result of the time lapse and through repeated retelling. Taylor was at this point an accomplished, mature, and somewhat embattled man, justifying a major part of his life's work. His recollection of his motives twenty-five years earlier was likely to be somewhat distorted.

There is no doubt that the experience had a profound effect on the shape of Taylor's future career. Two of his principal personal characteristics had come head-to-head in his battle in increase output. One was his very strong distaste for conflict. Taylor disliked arguments and often tried to be the peacemaker in such situations. The other was perhaps his strongest characteristic, which he himself described as a tendency to "hold on tight with the teeth." Frank Copley reports that this tenacity is "the only quality for which he ever publicly gave himself credit."[4] Thus, although experiencing great discomfort during his fight with the workers, Taylor was governed by his powerful and compulsive determination to finish whatever he started.

From his experience, Taylor concluded that the primary cause of this type of conflict between management and workers is that managers, without really knowing what constitutes a fair day's work, try to secure increased output by pressuring workers for more productivity. Taylor decided that if managers could scientifically determine how much production was possible in a day on a given job, they could then get a high level of output by demonstration rather than through coercion. Management could *show* that a worker could reasonably achieve a given level of productivity instead of simply insisting on it.

This viewpoint can be seen, in part, as a rationalization of the conflict Taylor had experienced during this period of his life. He felt that the anger of his workers was not directed at him personally, but was rooted in an inadequate system of managing.

Taylor set out to develop an approach for increasing productivity that would avoid the type of conflict he had personally experienced. He wanted to substitute "science" for rule-of-thumb guesswork. His concern is more clearly placed in perspective against the backdrop of the typical authority pattern that existed in nineteenth century factories.[5]

Prior to World War I the foreman's job was largely undefined. What constituted effective foremanship was sometimes discussed at trade association and technical society meetings, but beyond that little had been done to develop a clear description of the foreman's position. As a result, the actual power and function of any particular foreman were often determined as much by the technology involved as anything else. The foreman's power was likely to be greatest in factories using a unit or small batch production process (for example, machine shops) and slightly less in "mass" production type facilities. In general, the foreman was lord of the shop floor, workers having little recourse for appeal of his decisions.[6]

At his most powerful, a foreman might determine both the manner of production (including tools, materials, work sequences, and methods) and personnel matters (including hiring, training, supervising, motivating, paying, and disciplining).

In mass production shops (for example, textiles), the foreman determined less about the tools and materials used but was still in charge of many "personnel" matters. He was responsible for making sure that production was maintained, and he used whatever methods were required, including threats, shouting, profanity, and discharge.

Taylor, of course, had used just such methods in his fight to increase production at Midvale, and he was in search of an alternative. He decided to experiment to discover what a proper day's work was for every operation in the shop over which he had control. (Later in his years at Midvale, this encompassed almost the whole shop.) These extremely meticulous and long experiments continued throughout his time at Midvale, and during subsequent years at Bethlehem Steel and as an independent consultant, for a total of more than twenty-five years.

During his eight years at Midvale, Taylor progressed to chief engineer for the entire plant. His eyes improved significantly, and he completed a mechanical engineering degree at Stevens Institute.

In the course of his work as a foreman and a manager, Taylor developed what he called the "task system." His associates referred to it as the "Taylor system," and in the early 1900s it became known as scientific management.

Taylor's System

Taylor had begun his system by simply trying to solve the problem of "soldiering" on the part of workers. Years later, he described his subsequent efforts as a search for a system of management that would achieve maximum gains for both management and workers through establishment of an atmosphere of cooperation. His goal, throughout his working life, was to establish a method of eliminating the conflict, ignorance, and deceit that he felt characterized the management–worker relationship. Along the way, he discovered that in order to gain the cooperation of both groups it was necessary to develop a system in which both realized geniune gains.

Years later, he summarized his system in the following words. It involved, he said:

> Science, not rule of thumb
> Harmony, not discord
> Cooperation, not individualism
> Maximum output, in place of restricted output
> Development of each man to his greatest efficiency and prosperity

Taylor acknowledged that for his system of management to succeed, a massive change in thinking was necessary on the part of all
concerned. Both management and labor had to come to believe what
Taylor believed: their interests were really mutual and not antagonistic. Developing this belief was the first step of what Taylor came to
call the great "mental revolution" that he considered the essence of
scientific management.

Two assumptions were fundamental to this revolution. First, it
would be necessary for management and workers to cease fighting
about how large a share of the "pie" each should get and to realize that
both their interests were served best by concentrating on how to
make the pie bigger. Second, both would have to realize that the best
route to maximizing the size of the pie was through the substitution of
science for what he called rule-of-thumb management.

Taylor felt that all the techniques and mechanics of scientific management which emerged—such as time study, motion study, and routing systems—were useless and sometimes even dangerous if changes
were not made in these basic ways of thinking. Unfortunately, Taylor
had no idea how to achieve this "mental revolution" in the minds of
those with whom he worked. Thus he had no choice but to try to
persuade managers to stand aside and let him install the mechanics of
scientific management, hoping that they would be patient enough to
allow his techniques time to produce results that would make them
believers. Management almost never allowed him that much time, so
there were frequent failures and, perhaps, ample demonstration that
the mental revolution *did* have to come first.

Nevertheless, Taylor put together what may be the most comprehensive and detailed system of management ever developed. In order to
assess the extent to which this system has become distorted and misused,
we need to understand how it evolved. In Taylor's system, the burden of
behavior change fell mostly on the shoulders of management. He described four basic types of duties that management needed to accept in
order to use his system.

The first one was the development of the "science" involved in doing
the work. This required management to assemble all the knowledge that
was in the heads of the workers concerning the best ways of doing the
work, record this information, tabulate it, and reduce it to rules, laws, or
even mathematical formulas. Taylor believed that "among the various
methods and implements used in each element of each trade there is
always one method and one implement which is quicker and better than
any of the rest. And this one best method and best implement can only be
discovered or developed through a scientific study and analysis of all of
the methods and implements in use, together with accurate, minute,
motion and time study."[8]

The second responsibility of management involved the systematic selection, training, and development of workers. In Taylor's time, there were no very highly developed approaches to worker selection. However, Taylor often referred generally to "classes" of workers and their suitability for various types of work. Although he did not use the word "scientific" in this regard, his approach seems consistent with his objective of substituting science for rule-of-thumb decision-making.

With respect to training, Taylor was no more specific. He wrote about the importance of demonstrating the best ways of working and of giving employees "object lessons" in trying scientifically developed work methods, but he offered few other thoughts in this regard. Nevertheless, he recognized that some kind of improved information transmittal was needed.

Taylor described management's third task as "heartily cooperating with the men so as to insure all of the work being done in accordance with principles of the science which has been developed."[9] Here Taylor was advocating the provision of a monetary incentive (a "differential" piece rate) as well as the help and support of management. He wrote:

> . . . each man should daily be taught by and receive the most friendly help from those who are over him instead of being, at the one extreme, driven or coerced by his bosses, and at the other left to his own unaided devices.
>
> This close, intimate, personal cooperation between the management and the men is of the essence of modern scientific or task management.[10]

During the installation of Taylor's systems, there was often a period of struggle between management and workers, with *both* groups sometimes substantially resisting the changeover to his methods. "Hearty cooperation" was an ideal, seldom attained.

Finally, Taylor said, it was management's responsibility to "take over all work for which they are better fitted than the workmen," by which he meant provision of support systems that would allow workers to get on with their work. For example, management should ensure the availability of the appropriate tools, materials, equipment, and information so that the workers' progress in using the new methods was not held up. Taylor emphasized that every worker's duties should be fully planned out by management at least one day in advance. Each worker was to receive complete written instructions, describing in detail the tasks to be accomplished and the means to be used.

Taylor used these four management responsibilities as the basis of his most comprehensive paper, "The Principles of Scientific Management." Nevertheless, calling them "principles" is somewhat misleading in that they do not represent four distinct responsibilities of management. There are significant overlap and duplication involved among the four.

Taylor invariably gave the impression that each principle was to be implemented in sequence, but in actual practice he accomplished the fourth step before any of the others. Although Taylor himself never did so, one of his followers, H. K. Hathaway, published a series of articles in which he described the actual steps involved in converting a management system over to Taylor's methods. Since Hathaway became one of Taylor's "inner circle" of approved consultants, his description of the steps can be accepted as accurate. The following material is drawn in substantial part from Hathaway's articles.[11]

Hathaway pointed out that the actual order of implementation was seldom, if ever, carried out completely as prescribed. He discussed the need to "do stunts" of a spectacular nature in order to bolster management's faith or to appease its clamor for results. Between these "stunts," he said, the real work of implementation was done in the following eleven-point order. It is significant that those aspects of scientific management most commonly discussed in the literature, namely, time and motion studies, were a small part of the total process and were meant to be implemented *last.* Taylor's approach involved a complete restructuring of the organizational system. According to Hathaway, the desired, logical course of events was as follows.

1. *Development of a general plan of organization, including the design of departments and subdivisions.* This plan would include a definition of the nature and scope of departmental activities, an explanation of departments' authorities with regard to those activities, and a statement of interdepartmental relations and responsibilities. From this plan, model accounting and cost systems, as well as a file of "standing orders," could be developed. Hathaway noted that as work progressed, modifications would be made in the plan, but a beginning plan was needed as an ideal toward which to work.

2. *Development of a plan for the physical rearrangement of departments and equipment in accordance with the prospective general plan of the organization.* This often took the form of proposals for consolidation of what had been decentralized functions. For example, it might include plans for one common drafting department, and almost always included provision of common space for repair, toolroom, storeroom, cost-keeping, and timekeeping functions.

3. *Collection and classification of data relating to products.* This step included the gathering of product specifications, working samples, gauges, drawings, and so on. Mnemonic classifications of products were also prepared, to be used later in connection with the routing of work and in store- and cost-keeping.

4. *Collection and classification of data relating to machinery and equipment.* Included were all data that would be used in the planning process, the standardization of machines and tools, the maintenance system, and the establishment of machine rates.

5. *Standardization of machines and tools, development of the maintenance system, and establishment of a toolroom.* Hathaway reported that this work was often begun in a preliminary way at this point, and was further developed as a result of time study in Step 10 below.

6. *Development of the stores and order systems.* This was a complex, comprehensive, and time-consuming step in the installation of scientific management. It involved establishing the optimum physical arrangement of the storeroom, as well as setting up centralized administrative controls for both purchased and manufactured materials—including inventory control, purchasing systems, and all facets of accounts payable for these materials. In addition, at this point the system and forms for handling customer orders were revised to accommodate the stores systems and to provide a transition to the routing system discussed in Step 8.

7. *Modification of the timekeeping system.* The purpose was to provide data necessary for cost-keeping, payroll, analysis of indirect expenses, and the routing of work and orders carried out by the planning department.

8. *Development and installation of the routing system, including the complete planning in advance of work to be done and the provision of forms and materials necessary to maintain the work flow.* Hathaway was very emphatic about the importance of this step. He wrote that "neglect of this most important feature [routing] of scientific management—either from lack of knowledge or too hasty a desire to reap the benefits of time study—has been almost if not quite as prevalent a cause of unsuccessful or unsatisfactory attempts to apply Taylor's teachings as has been the failure to establish and maintain standardized conditions."[12]

9. *Establishment and use of a mechanism for follow-up and control of work in progress.* This "mechanism" consisted of bulletin boards for both the planning department and the shop; operation, inspection, and "move" orders (along with the means for their issue and return); and routing and progress sheets to control and record each successive step in the accomplishment of the work as planned. At this time a "balance-of-work" program, whose objective was the fullest possible utilization of plant facilities, was developed.

Hathaway pointed out that at this stage there was usually a need for cooperative effort by the sales department. He also noted that at this time the functional foremen known as the "gang boss" and the "inspector" should be established.

10. *Performance of time study, improvement and standardization*

of methods, and inauguration of a pay system based thereon. Hathaway emphasized that a system of pay involving a suitable reward for a given level of production under standard conditions during a given time period could not logically be established before this point. Until the prior steps had been implemented, no proper foundation existed for such a pay system.

Hathaway also noted that the functional foreman known as the "instruction card clerk" should be established. It was his duty to make clear the methods developed and prescribed by the planning department, giving special attention to the less skilled workers.

11. *Establishment of cost and accounting systems.* Once stores, timekeeping, and order and routing systems were established, the putting together of cost and accounting systems became logical. These systems were then used to calculate expenses for each lot of every product and to determine the monthly profits or losses incurred on each product. Any changes necessary in the general bookkeeping system were also made at this point.

Hathaway pointed out that the above order of installation was not rigid and that the steps often overlapped. But he emphasized that Step 10—time study—was *not* taken out of order but rather was postponed until other systems were in place.

An understanding of Taylor's system requires further elaboration on some of its features. One is the pay system referred to in Step 10.

Taylor favored (depending on the type of work involved) one or the other of two pay systems. One was developed by Henry Gantt and was called "task work with a bonus." Taylor felt that this was the best pay system to use when the work consisted of a variety of activities. He recommended that a "large daily task" be put together for each worker, which might consist of a combination of duties such as shoveling, loading, cleaning, and the like.

Taylor emphasized that people who did such task work should be required to start work at a regular hour but should be allowed to leave whenever they had completed the assigned daily tasks. No deduction in pay was to be made for those who finished early, and no extra pay allowed for those working late. Rather, he suggested that a bonus be paid for finishing the task within an expected time period.

Taylor recommended a different pay system for work of a highly repetitive nature. He called it the differential piece-rate system, and apparently implemented it as early as 1884 at Midvale Steel. The particular job involved was turning standard steel forgings on lathes. Prior to the installation of the differential piece rate, the men had been paid on a straight piece-rate system at the rate of $0.50 per forging. They were producing about four or five forgings a day, thus earning $2.00 to $2.50. In order to install the new pay system, Taylor first timed the job; determined the cutting tools, feeds, and speeds to be used; and established through experimentation that, using his methods, a worker could produce ten forgings a day. He then set a rate of $0.25 per forging if a worker produced fewer than ten forgings per day and $0.35 per forging if the worker succeeded in making ten or more. Taylor reported that the men were able to achieve a rate of ten forgings per day almost every day for many years.

The cost comparison between the old system and the new one is as follows: Under the old system the workers made about $2.50 a day and the machine cost was $3.37 for the day, so the total cost to management for the day was $5.87 for the five pieces produced, or about $1.17 per piece. Taylor's system allowed the worker to make about $3.50 a day, as opposed to the previous $2.00–$2.50. The machine cost was still $3.37, yielding a total cost of $6.87 for the day. Since about ten pieces per day were now produced, the cost per piece was reduced to about $0.69. Taylor felt that this perfectly illustrated his assertion that it was possible to effect a system in which the worker's desire for higher wages and management's desire for lower unit costs could be met simultaneously.

The figures given above were reported by Taylor in "Shop Management."[13] It should be noted that other factors might affect such a cost comparison—for example, material costs, machine maintenance costs, and the costs involved in determining the best methods to be used.

Another feature of the Taylor system requiring further explanation is the concept of "functional foremen" referred to in Steps 8 and 10 of Hathaway's discussion. Taylor said that "functional management consists in so dividing the work of management that each man from the assistant superintendent down shall have as few functions as possible to perform. If practicable, the work of each man in the management should be confined to the performance of a single leading function."[14]

Taylor recommended that each worker receive his daily orders and help directly from eight different foremen, each of whom performed a specialized function. Four of these people worked in a "planning room," and the other four were to be in the shop area. The titles and duties of each of these eight "bosses," as Taylor called them, were as follows.

The *gang boss* had charge of preparing the work; he made sure that each man had at least one piece of work ahead to do at his machine, with all materials ready to go when he finished the piece he was working on. The gang boss was to see that the set-up procedures went quicky and smoothly.

The *speed boss* made sure the work was done according to the prescribed methods—that the appropriate speeds, feeds, and depth of cut and tools were used. His work began after the piece was correctly placed in the machine and ended when the actual machining was completed.

The *inspector* was responsible for the quality of the work. Both the workmen and the speed boss were to see that the work was finished to suit the inspector.

The *repair boss* made sure that standards established for the care and maintenance of the machines and their accessories were adhered to.

The four bosses described above, or *shop bosses,* were to be present on the floor to work directly with the men. The remaining four bosses would have much less direct contact with the workers, since they would be situated in the planning room.

The *order of work and route clerk* prepared the exact route by which each piece of work was to travel through the shop. Using that plan, he prepared lists each day instructing workers and shop bosses as to the exact order in which all work should be done.

The *instruction card clerk* prepared cards containing all information regarding how work was to be done and what pay rates were to be received. The cards included such information as what drawings to refer to, special equipment needed, tools to use, and so on.

The *time and cost clerk* was responsible for supplying workers with the cards and information necessary to record their times and the costs of the work, and to secure the proper return of such information from them.

The *shop disciplinarian* handled cases involving insubordination, lateness, unexcused absences, or failure to do one's duty. Taylor says this person was to "apply the proper remedy" in such cases and to see that a complete record of each person's virtues and defects was kept. The shop disciplinarian was to be consulted when adjustments in a worker's wages were made and functioned as a "peacemaker."

Taylor advocated that in a large shop all the bosses performing the same function—for example, all the speed bosses—should have their own foreman over them. These "over-foremen" would teach their foremen the exact nature of their jobs and (at the start) "nerve and brace them up" to insist that the workers carry out their work exactly as specified on the instruction cards.

Another function of the over-foremen would be to smooth out difficulties that arose between the different types of bosses. Taylor recognized that the different functional foremen would "come in contact edgeways" and that at the start there would be quite a bit of friction between them.

At the next higher level, that of assistant superintendent, the strict functional basis of supervision would disappear. The assistant superintendent would function as an arbitrator, establishing what Taylor called "the unwritten code of laws" by which the shop was governed.

The planning department was central to Taylor's system. He felt that the shop, and indeed the entire company, should be managed not by line managers (that is, superintendents and shop foremen) but rather by the planning department. He advocated that "all possible brainwork" be removed from the shop and centered in the planning department. In this fashion, shop managers could be freed to do what he called "executive" work. For Taylor, executive work meant instruction, guidance of workers, enforcement of rules, and similar activities of a directly supervisory nature.

Taylor envisioned the planning department as a control center from which emanated all instructions and orders—a sort of command post from which the organization could be directed. He wrote:

> An elaborate timetable should be made out showing daily the time when each report is due. It should be the duty of the member of the planning room in charge of this function to find out at each time through the day when reports are due, whether they have been received, and if not, to keep bothering the man who is behindhand until he has done his duty.[15]

The planning room was to be to the plant what the brain is to the rest of the body, complete with a "conscience" to keep everybody honest.

This approach—born out of an attempt to avoid conflict between supervisor and worker over what constituted a fair day's production, developed into a broad, systemic approach to production management. It was a system Taylor never succeeded in implementing in its totality. Yet its legacy has been of overwhelming significance, as seen in such practices as method analysis, time and motion study, work measurement, and production planning.

Perhaps of more importance than the techniques which evolved from Taylorism was the management revolution that his work facilitated. Taylor's ideas had a revolutionary impact, although somewhat different from the one he had envisioned. His work helped to shape the "engineering view" of work.

In the process, Taylor obtained an intensely negative image among certain publics, an image that in some quarters persists to this day. During his life he was denounced by powerful politicians, organized labor, and social theorists. To some contemporary behavioral scientists and managers trained in humanistic psychology, the term "Taylorism" conjures up almost satanic imagery.

The major feature of Taylor's negative image was, and is, that he was an *anti-humanist*—that he advocated coercion and exploitation of workers, saw them as stupid and as requiring heavy control and guidance, and was opposed to their right to form and be active in unions. Among other things, Taylor is viewed as an advocate of the carrot-and-stick philosophy of management and of paying workers "for pieces." Sometimes even the very origin of the idea of piecework is attributed to Taylor.

Yet another anti-humanistic charge that has been made against Taylor is that he is responsible for the spread of authoritarian, controlling organization structures that preclude opportunities for self-expression and personal development. In this view, Taylor's anti-humanism is evident in his opposition to letting workers be involved in deciding how their work should be done.

Apart from the issue of anti-humanism, Taylor has been characterized by some as a man with a "bag of tricks" who had no conceptual framework underlying his work. A related charge is the suggestion that Taylor was reckless in how he initiated change in organizations, often creating hardships for the people involved.

Most biting of the charges made against Taylor is the idea that he was an obsessive-compulsive neurotic who through his work imposed his neurosis on generations of workers. This is the most personal of the criticisms, and suggests that more than his surface motivations were to be questioned. The charge questions the accuracy of Taylor's perception of human nature and of the work situation.

It is neither unique nor surprising that a man who had Taylor's impact on society's institutions should have critics, detractors, and opponents. However, the arguments that characterized the debate over scientific management in Taylor's time remain strikingly similar today. The positions of both sides have changed little, with myth and misunderstanding hindering progress toward resolution of issues important to management practice. The prevailing conceptions, both pro and con, require careful distillation.

NOTES

1. Frank B. Copley, *Frederick W. Taylor,* Vol. 1 (New York: Harper, 1923), p. 3.
2. Ibid., p. 52
3. Ibid., p. 53.
4. Ibid., p. 5.
5. Daniel Nelson, *Managers and Workers. Origins of the New Factory System in the United States, 1880–1920* (Madison: University of Wisconsin Press, 1975), Chapter 3.
6. Ibid., p. 42.

7. Frederick W. Taylor, "The Principles of Scientific Management." In *Scientific Management* (New York: Harper & Row, 1947), p. 40.

8. Ibid., p. 25.

9. Ibid., p. 36.

10. Ibid., p. 26.

11. H. K. Hathaway, "Logical Steps in Installing the Taylor System of Management," *Industrial Management,* August, September, and October 1920.

12. Ibid., October, p. a83.

13. Frederick W. Taylor, "Shop Management." In *Scientific Management* (New York: Harper & Row, 1947), pp. 81-83.

14. Ibid., p. 99.

15. Ibid., p. 117.

2

Taylor's Research
in Support of His System

An assessment of Taylor's work best begins with a review of the data on which he rested his arguments. In developing his system, Taylor conducted an impressive and meticulous group of studies, some of which have become part of the folklore of management. In illustrating the principles of scientific management, he repeatedly referred to certain studies that he felt supported his points in a vivid and conclusive fashion. As did later theorists, Taylor presented these studies in a manner calculated to move his audience to action.

The Pig-Iron Studies

Perhaps the best known of Taylor's experiments is the application of scientific management to the task of loading pig iron onto rail cars. What follows is based on Taylor's own account of these studies as he presented them in his article "The Principles of Scientific Management."[1] Later chapters will examine the implications, distortions, and controversies that have evolved from this now famous application of his methods.

Taylor reports that this was one of his first attempts to introduce scientific management at Bethlehem Steel. It involved a gang of some 75 men whose task it was to load some 80,000 tons of pig iron, which sat in small piles in a field near the plant, onto railroad flatcars. Because of low iron prices, management stored the iron until it could be sold at a profit. However, with the beginning of the Spanish-American War in 1898, the price of pig iron rose and the large accumulation was sold. This gave Taylor an opportunity to demonstrate the effectiveness of his ideas in a rather dramatic and visible way.

Prior to Taylor's involvement, the men had been loading the pigs, which weighed about 92 pounds each, at an average rate of 12½ tons per man per day. Each pig was picked up from a pile, carried a distance averaging about 36 feet across flat ground, and carried up an inclined plank onto the flatcar where it was dropped.

Some years earlier Taylor and one of his close associates, Carl Barth, had "discovered the law governing the tiring effect of heavy labor on the first-class man."[2] They now applied the law to the pig-iron loading situation. Their conclusion was that for maximum productivity a first-class laborer, suited to such work as handling pig iron, should be under load (that is, actually carrying the 92-pound pigs) only 42 percent of the working day and be free from load the remaining 58 percent of the day.

These figures had been worked out from a series of experiments in which two physically powerful, steadily working laborers were paid double wages with the provision that they work to the best of their ability consistently over an extended period of time. These men were then given a variety of tasks, which they performed while being closely observed and timed.

Taylor was seeking an answer to the question: "What fraction of a horsepower is a man able to exert, that is, how many foot-pounds of work a man could do in a day."[3] Besides this experiment, he later conducted two other sets of experiments, which were more thorough and exhaustive. However, Taylor could not find a direct relation between the foot-pounds of work a man does and the tiring effects on him.

He remained convinced, however, that there was *some* clear-cut law as to what constitutes a full day's work for a first-class laborer, and that his carefully kept data from the three sets of experiments contained the information necessary for establishing that law. Feeling that mathematical skill was necessary to extract the law from the accumulated data, he turned the task over to Carl Barth, whom he felt was the best mathematician among his colleagues.

Barth worked out a series of curves that showed, for different amounts of weight carried, what percentage of the day a "first-class laborer" could be under load. For a worker who was handling a half pig weighing about 46 pounds, Barth's calculations indicated that he could be under load 58 percent of the day and would have to rest 42 percent of the day to achieve maximum productivity. As the weight grew heavier, the man would have to be under load less of the time; as it grew lighter he could remain under load a larger percentage of the day. Taylor and Barth referred to this as the "law of heavy laboring."

Using the mathematical relationships Barth had worked out, Taylor concluded that for the handling of 92-pound pigs the men would be most productive if they were under load just 43 percent of the day. These calculations indicated that a first-class laborer should be able to handle 47½ tons per day, or about 1,156 pigs (increasing output approximately fourfold). Taylor decided to require that the men rest after loading 10 to 20 pigs.

From experience, Taylor anticipated resistance to such a substantial increase in output. Getting the workers to attempt the increase, he believed, required two things. One was the opportunity to make a great deal more money. The second was a clear demonstration that the increase could actually be accomplished.

Taylor felt that an increase in wages on the order of 60 percent was necessary to induce workmen's interest in such an effort. When loading 12½ tons, they were being paid at the rate of $1.15 per day. Under the concept of the differential piece rate, Taylor decided to offer a rate of $1.85 for loading the 47½ tons.

Taylor felt that an "object lesson" was needed to demonstrate that loading 47½ tons was possible. He chose a man whom he gave the pseudonym of "Schmidt." He described Schmidt as "a little Pennsylvania Dutchman who had been observed to trot back home for a mile or so after his work in the evening about as fresh as he was when he came trotting down to work in the morning."[4] Taylor explained the task and the new $1.85 pay rate to Schmidt, and the man agreed to try it. The next day Schmidt followed the directions regarding when to work and when to rest and, according to Taylor's report, by 5:30 that afternoon had loaded 47½ tons of pig iron. He continued to do so almost every day for a period of some three years.

Taylor also claims that following the training of Schmidt, several other men were picked out and successfully trained to handle the same amount of work. He stated that only about one man in eight of the original 75 pig-iron handlers was physically capable of loading the 47½ tons per day.

The Shoveling Studies

A second series of studies for which Taylor became widely known involved his development of the "science of shoveling." These were also carried out at Bethlehem Steel and involved an extended series of stopwatch observations to determine the most advantageous shovel load.

Using basically the same method as in the pig-iron studies, Taylor selected a small number of "first-class shovelers," paid them extra wages to do their very best work, and then systematically varied the shovel load. All conditions accompanying the work were observed and recorded as well. The optimum shovel load was found to be 21 pounds.

Utilizing this information, Taylor established at Bethlehem a procedure in which, instead of allowing each shoveler to select his own shovel, some eight to ten different types of shovels were kept on hand in a toolroom. Depending on the material to be shoveled, the most appropriate size of shovel would be issued to each man. In addition, thousands of stopwatch observations were conducted to determine just how quickly a shoveler, provided with the proper tool, could push his shovel into a pile of materials, withdraw it properly loaded, and then throw the load a given horizontal distance at a given height. These observations were made with variations in the surface being shoveled, the portion of pile (outer edge or middle) entered, the arc of the backward swing of the shovel, the horizontal distance the material was to be thrown, and the height at which it was thrown.

The resulting data were compiled, joined with the optimum load data and the "law of endurance" previously worked out with Barth, and then used in training and assigning work and tools to the some 600 shovelers and laborers in the Bethlehem Steel yards. These people were scattered in their work over a yard that was about two square miles in size. A detailed system was established for directing the men in their work, to replace the old system in which a few foremen handled the men in large gangs.

Taylor's system required each workman to report in the morning to a central labor office where the superintendent and the clerks in charge of the yard were housed. This was the "planning room," where each man's work was planned out and assigned. Large diagrams and maps were employed, and the men were placed and moved, much as chessmen are on a chessboard. A telephone and messenger system was installed to facilitate the movement of individuals. In this way, the time previously lost through improper distribution and movement of large gangs was substantially reduced.

As each workman entered the labor office he removed, from a pigeonhole bearing his number, two slips of paper. One slip told him what tools to get from the toolroom and where in the yard he was to report for work. The second slip told him exactly how much work he had accomplished the preceding day and how much he had earned for that work. To the extent possible, each workman was assigned a separate, individual task. For example, if ore was to be unloaded from rail cars, each man was assigned his own car. Usually no labor gangs larger than four men were permitted.

This system, Taylor reported, allowed the total number of laborers in the yard to be reduced from 600 to 140, increased the average number of tons handled per man per day from 16 to 59, increased the average daily earnings per man from $1.15 to $1.88, and reduced the average handling cost per ton of material from $0.072 to $0.033. The savings thus achieved were between $75,000 and $80,000 per year. Taylor reports as well that the effect on the workmen was substantial and positive. His manner of expressing this option gives an insight into his thinking:

> Perhaps the most important of all results attained was the effect on the workmen themselves. . . . Many, if not most of them, were saving money, and they all lived better than they had before. These men constituted the finest body of picked laborers that the writer has ever seen together, and they looked upon the men who were over them, their bosses and their teachers, as their very best friends; not as nigger [sic] drivers, forcing them to work extra hard for ordinary wages, but as friends who were teaching them and helping them to earn much higher wages than they have ever earned before. It would have been absolutely impossible for any one to have stirred up strife between these men and their employers. And this presents a very simple though effective illustration of what is meant by the words "prosperity for the employee, complete with prosperity for the employer," the two principal subjects of management.[5]

Whether the men actually felt this way is, of course, something we cannot know. However, the above quotation well illustrates Taylor's feeling that scientific management offered benefits to workers as well as management. True, the benefits are phrased in a paternalistic and condescending way, but Taylor's perceptions of workers and his language are representative of standard turn-of-the-century thinking.

Gilbreth's Bricklaying Studies

Another series of studies illustrating the application of Taylor's thinking was conducted by Frank B. Gilbreth, who undertook to apply Taylor's approach to the bricklaying trade. Making an extremely detailed study of the movements involved in the traditional method of bricklaying, Gilbreth discovered that the process of laying a single brick could be reduced from eighteen individual motions to just five.[6]

Gilbreth achieved this using four types of improvements. First, he entirely eliminated some movements that he had determined to be unnecessary. Second, he introduced the use of apparatuses such as an adjustable scaffold, a redesigned mortar box, and wooden packets to hold the bricks. Third, he transferred a few simple tasks, such as sorting bricks and placing them with the best side up, to a laborer who helped the bricklayer. Finally, he taught his bricklayers to do motions simultaneously with both hands rather than sequentially. Using these methods Gilbreth was able, in some instances, to almost triple the number of bricks laid per hour.

In reporting on Gilbreth's work, Taylor emphasized that this improvement could never have been achieved under the approach to management that he called "initiative and incentive" — that is, simply urging the men to do more. He pointed out that management had to develop the "science of bricklaying," select and train bricklayers who were amenable to the new methods, and see that they received quick and correct support from the laborers. In other words, Taylor felt that the productivity gains were due primarily to management's increased and expanded role rather than to a sheer increase in the workers' efforts.

Taylor's Studies of Bicycle-Ball-Bearing Inspectors

To illustrate his principle of "scientific selection of the workman," Taylor liked to describe an application of his thinking to the task of inspecting ball bearings for bicycle wheels.[7] His assignment had been to systematize a large bicycle-ball-bearing factory (a part of the Simonds Company) in which approximately 120 women performed the task of inspecting the steel balls. Each woman placed a row of the balls on the back of her left hand in the crease between her fingers, rolled the balls over, and examined them under intense light for defects. Defective balls were then picked out with a magnet held in the right hand. The defects were mostly minute, so the work required very close concentration and attention.

Observing that most of the women spent a good portion of their 10½-hour workday in idleness, Taylor concluded that the workday was too long for a task requiring such constant close attention. Therefore, the workday was shortened in successive steps down to 8½ hours, while pay was kept the same. With each shortening of the day, Taylor reported that production increased.

At this point, he turned the project over to one of his followers, Sanford E. Thompson, who continued the work with some direction from H. L. Gantt. Thompson was apparently familiar with some previous research that had been done on reaction times. He recognized that the quality most needed in ball-bearing inspectors was quick reaction time, meaning the ability to rapidly perceive the defects in the balls and then to react quickly by removing a defective ball.

Consequently, those women with slow reaction times were weeded out. Taylor reported that this "unfortunately . . . involved laying off many of the most intelligent, hardest working, and most trustworthy girls merely because they did not possess the quality of quick perception followed by quick action."[8]

Other changes included an "over-inspection" system to ensure against any drop-off in the quality of the inspection work. To check the checkers, there was an elaborate system of "blind" multiple inspections by the workers, as well as periodic "planted" lots of balls with a predetermined percentage of defects.

Once this system was in place, a careful time study was undertaken that highlighted the best methods to be used and the need for periodic breaks. A pattern involving four ten-minute breaks, in addition to the normal lunch break, was adopted. Finally, a differential piece-rate pay system was installed, along with a method of measuring the output of each worker as often as every hour. The practice was "to send a teacher to each individual who was found to be falling behind to find out what was wrong, to straighten her out, and to encourage and help her to catch up."[9]

The results of these changes were that 35 workers did the work previously requiring 120, with an accuracy rate two-thirds greater than had been achieved before. The women averaged 80–100 percent higher wages while working a two-hour-shorter workday, and having the additional breaks. Taylor's opinion was that, although numerous changes were involved, the most significant factor was the careful selection of women with quick perception.

Other Studies in the Pursuit of Scientific Management

Of all Taylor's experiments, those concerning the machining of metal were by far the most exhaustive. They best illustrate his tenacity and attention to detail. From the point of view of many people, they also represent his most valuable contribution to production management.[10]

When Taylor became a foreman at Midvale, he perceived his principal responsibility to be the maximization of output. Taylor came to define the problem of getting output in a machine shop as one of determining "how to remove chips fast from a casting or forging, and how to make the piece smooth and true in the shortest time."[11] He viewed the problem as consisting of two subproblems: (1) the mechanics of the shop's equipment (a purely technical matter), and (2) the workers' operation of that equipment (a personal matter). So far we have focused on Taylor's efforts concerning personnel. We turn now to his work on the technical issue. All of this work, however, was performed in the service of his basic objective: to discover "laws" by which maximum output could be attained.

Taylor began his studies at Midvale by examining what he then regarded as the most important variables affecting output on the jobs he supervised: the proper clearance angle, side slope, and back slope in positioning the tools. He told William Sellers, for whom he worked at Midvale, that by determining these angles he could establish the proper speed at which the cutting tools should run. Taylor estimated that he could complete his experiments within six months. As it turns out, he did not complete the studies until 24 years later, long after he had left Midvale.

Fortunately for Taylor, Midvale had a large supply of scrapped locomotive wheels on hand that could be cut up into chips, providing the almost inexhaustible supply of raw material he needed. In addition, a 66"-diameter vertical boring mill was available for his use.

After six months of work, Taylor had learned that the cutting angles made virtually no difference at all. But he felt that valuable information was being generated by the experiments, and, after convincing Sellers of this, he continued the work. Soon Taylor discovered that pouring a heavy stream of water directly on the point at which the metal was being cut permitted a significant increase in cutting speed (he reported 30–40 percent).

In late 1883, Sellers authorized Taylor to design and build a new shop that included facilities for supplying such streams of water to each machine. Probably the building of a new shop had already been planned, but Taylor's discovery contributed to the decision to move ahead. The new shop also enabled Taylor to launch a series of experiments on belting that extended over a nine-year period and culminated in his paper "Notes on Belting," which he presented to the American Society of Mechanical Engineers in 1893.

Taylor had observed that difficulties with belting often caused delays and interruptions in production. Specifically, in his metal-cutting experiments he was having trouble maintaining the tension of the belt that was used to drive the boring mill. After investigating, he concluded that the belt was probably too light and should be tightened at regular intervals with spring-loaded clamps. With his usual methodical approach, he conducted an extended series of experiments involving belts of different weights and different maintenance schedules (cleaning and repairing as well as tightening). His data gave him further insight into the original question of the best feeds and speeds to use in cutting metals.

He made substantial progress on this work during his remaining years at Midvale (through 1889), but he still had no quick way of determining the best feed and speed on any given machines. Then, during a six-month tenure at Cramp's shipyards in Philadelphia, where he was employed to systematize the shops, he was able to make a major stride forward.

Since his days at Midvale there had come into use a type of tool steel called Mushet steel. The discoverer of this steel, Robert Mushet, had found that adding tungsten and a substantial amount of manganese to ordinary carbon steel caused the tool to be almost as hard when cooled slowly in air as carbon tools became when cooled in water. For this reason, the Mushet tools were often referred to as air-hardening or self-hardening tools. Mushet tools were being used only on particularly hard forgings and castings that were difficult to cut with carbon tools.

Taylor decided to compare the attainable cutting speeds of carbon and Mushet tools. Using an electrically driven lathe at Cramp's shipyards, he determined that, with the Mushet steel, a speed gain of 41–47 percent was possible when cutting hard forgings but, more surprisingly, that an almost 90 percent gain could be achieved when cutting softer metals. Taylor had demonstrated the clear superiority of the self-hardening tools for the large percentage of softer metal usually cut.

There were several varieties of self-hardening steel on the market, and Taylor set out to determine which of them was the best. In a shop provided by William Sellers, who by this time had set up his own company, Taylor conducted a series of experiments and narrowed the best types of self-hardening steel down to two: Mushet steel and a steel made by Midvale. He remained unsure of which was superior, but his experiments with heating the tools before grinding brought him close to his most celebrated discovery in the field of metal cutting: the discovery of high-speed steel.

Later, while involved in systematizing the shop at Bethlehem, Taylor continued his experiments along these lines. In 1898, working with J. Maunsel White, a metallurgical engineer, he made the discovery that led to the development of high-speed steel. It had previously been believed that the temperature to which carbon tools should be heated to produce the best results in hardening was 1350° to 1500° Fahrenheit. Heating carbon tools beyond this point caused them to be permanently damaged. It was generally assumed that the critical temperature for the new steels was the same, and tool steelmakers commonly warned users against overheating their products.

Taylor and White, using chromium-tungsten tools in their experiments, found that heating the tools to slightly above 1500° did weaken them, but only if the heating was *stopped* at that point. If they were heated to just below their melting point (about 1850° Fahrenheit), the result was exceptionally strong and heat-resistant tools.

Next followed a long series of experiments testing various metal compositions and cooling processes to maximize the "retained hardness" characteristic. Ultimately Taylor and White were able to increase the speeds of the main lines of shafting in the Bethlehem shop from 96 rpm up to 225–300 rpm! The output of the shop more than doubled.[12]

Taylor and White achieved worldwide recognition for their discovery, but Taylor regarded the advance as just another step in his continuing quest to replace the rule-of-thumb approach with science in the field of management. Taylor had become involved in a time study to determine what a *man* could do and in experiments with metal cutting to determine what a *machine* could do. Each investigation was aimed at scientifically determining what constituted a full day's work and what system would best ensure that the work was accomplished.

In the service of these same ends, Taylor developed a mnemonic system of classification that he used to provide order and control in his system. This was helpful when he began analyzing work at Midvale but became increasingly essential in his later work involving the analysis, classification, storage, and issuance of tools and machine parts; the routing of work; the scheduling of plant and machine maintenance; and so on.

The Search for Control Systems

As Frank Copley pointed out, much of Taylor's work was aimed at achieving control over the processes with which he worked. His interest in accounting grew out of this motivation.

Taylor had become interested in cost accounting in the 1890s, when he saw that the method could help identify areas of inefficiency. Although he intensely disliked clerical work of all kinds, Taylor went about developing this aspect of his system in his usual careful, methodical manner. Eventually he decided that the post-mortem accounting reports that appeared annually or semiannually were of little value because they offered no improvement in control.

Therefore, in his early system of cost-keeping, Taylor instituted monthly reports presented in such a way as to focus the manager's attention on any unusual waste or costs. Ultimately he concluded that cost-accounting data were useful only if they could be generated *at the same time as* (not even monthly) and as a by-product of production records. To accomplish this, he recommended moving cost accounting out of the general accounting department and placing it in the "planning room." He then designed planning and control documents to include cost data, thereby generating information on costs coincidentally with that concerning operations. This made the information available promptly so that it could be used for Taylor's ultimate purpose—control.

Summary

This chapter has illustrated Taylor's methods as well as the breadth of his interests. The pig-iron, shoveling, bricklaying, and ball-bearing experiments were the classic studies that Taylor, and later his followers, used to support his principles of scientific management. However, his work in production scheduling, metal cutting, and cost accounting—as well as a variety of inventions—was equally important to his system and, in fact, consumed more of his energies.

Taylor's system of management generated considerable controversy and, as we have stated, was frequently distorted and misunderstood. In the next two chapters we will examine how scientific management spread as a system, and perhaps even as an ideology, of management.

NOTES

1. Frederick W. Taylor, "The Principles of Scientific Management." In *Scientific Management* (New York: Harper & Row, 1947), pp. 40–64.
2. Ibid., p. 57.
3. Ibid., p. 55.
4. Ibid., pp. 43–44.
5. Ibid., pp. 71–72.
6. F. B. Gilbreth, *Bricklaying System* (New York: Myron C. Clark Publishing, 1909).
7. Taylor, "Principles," pp. 77–86.
8. Ibid., p. 90.
9. Ibid., p. 94.
10. L. Rolt, *A Short History of Machine Tools* (Cambridge, Mass.: M.I.T. Press, 1965), pp. 197–201.
11. Taylor, "Principles," pp. 102–103.
12. Frank B. Copley, *Frederick W. Taylor,* Vol. 1 (New York: Harper, 1923), p. 112.

3

Taylor's System in Practice: The Great Debate

Taylor was an active promoter of his ideas, but his interest was in seeing them implemented, not discussed. He viewed himself as a pragmatist and a man of the world. In fact, throughout his life he remained suspicious of intellectuals. His system was spawned when he was a supervisor and grew to maturity as he advanced in the ranks of management. Later, Taylor founded a consulting practice.

Eventually, Taylor ceased personal implementation of his principles in order to devote full attention to the promotion of the system. His intended audience remained the owners and managers of industrial corporations. Taylor's accomplishments and charismatic personality attracted devoted disciples and a large number of proponents of his views. Enemies were attracted as well—who were usually vehement and often powerful.

Taylor's Own Contributions to Distortions of the System

Taylor's ideas were frequently distorted by supporters and adversaries alike. In addition, his system and his purposes experienced distortion from a more intimate source: Taylor himself.

Taylor's Style of Presentation

Taylor's particular style of presenting his ideas undoubtedly contributed to misunderstandings concerning his work. Sometimes his way of making a point—especially his choice of language—proved almost an invitation for attack.

A good example of this phenomenon is the famous story of "Schmidt," the pig-iron loader at Bethlehem Steel. In his article "The Principles of Scientific Management," Taylor gave a line-by-line dialogue that was supposed to have taken place between himself and Schmidt.*

"Schmidt, are you a high-priced man?"

"Vell, I don't know vat you mean."

"Oh yes, you do. What I want to know is whether you are a high-priced man or not."

"Vell, I don't know vat you mean."

"Oh, come now, you answer my questions. What I want to find out is whether you are a high-priced man or one of these cheap fellows here. What I want to find out is whether you want to earn $1.85 a day or whether you are satisfied with $1.15, just the same as all those cheap fellows are getting."

"Did I vant $1.85 a day? Vas dot a high-priced man? Vell, yes, I vas a high-priced man."

"Oh, you're aggravating me. Of course you want $1.85 a day—every one wants it! You know perfectly well that has very little to do with your being a high-priced man. For goodness' sake answer my questions, and don't waste any more of my time. Now come over here. You see that pile of pig iron?"

"Yes."

"You see that car?"

"Yes."

"Well, if you are a high-priced man, you will load that pig iron on that car to-morrow for $1.85. Now do wake up and answer my question. Tell me whether you are a high-priced man or not."

"Vell—did I got $1.85 for loading dot pig iron on dot car tomorrow?"

"Yes, of course you do, and you get $1.85 for loading a pile like that every day right through the year. That is what a high-priced man does, and you know it just as well as I do."

"Vell, dot's all right. I could load dot pig iron on the car tomorrow for $1.85, and I get it every day, don't I?"

"Certainly you do—certainly you do."

"Vell, den, I vas a high-priced man."

"Now, hold on, hold on. You know just as well as I do that a high-priced man has to do exactly as he's told from morning till night. You have seen this man here before, haven't you?"

"No, I never saw him."

"Well, if you are a high-priced man, you will do exactly as this man tells you to-morrow, from morning till night. When he tells you to pick up a pig and walk, you pick it up and walk, he tells you to sit down and rest, you sit down. You do that right straight through the day. And what's more, no back

---

* In this account Taylor never said that it was *he* who spoke to Schmidt, but the implication is certainly clear.

talk. Now a high-priced man does just what he's told to do, and no back talk. Do you understand that? When this man tells you to walk, you walk; when he tells you to sit down, you sit down, and you don't talk back at him. Now you come on to work here to-morrow morning and I'll know before night whether you are really a high-priced man or not."[1]

After presenting the dialogue, Taylor admitted that "this seems to be rather rough talk" and conceded that it would have been so if directed toward "an educated mechanic or even an intelligent laborer." However, he stated: "With a man of the mentally sluggish type of Schmidt it is appropriate and not unkind, since it is effective in fixing his attention on the high wages which he wants and away from what, if it were called to his attention, he would probably consider impossibly hard work."[2]

It is easy to see why such a presentation caused many people to conclude that Taylor was an insensitive and perhaps even cruel man who had little if any respect for workers. However, Taylor presented the story in this way to illustrate his assertion that the workman best suited to perform a job is precisely that person who is ill equipped to understand the science involved in the task. In the pig-iron story, Taylor was describing the application of his thinking to the simplest of all work—loading. Taylor wanted to demonstrate that even in this elementary task there is a science, and that the discovery of that science would not be made by people well suited to perform the loading job.

Taylor's intended point was that Schmidt was the best person to *perform* the work—that "simple" work requires "simple" minds—but not to design the best *method* of performing it. He portrayed Schmidt as "the type of the ox" to emphasize that "the man who is suited to handle pig iron cannot possibly understand it, nor even work in accordance with the laws of this science, without the help of those who are over him."[3]

The striking nature of the dialogue naturally led many authors to reprint it, without focusing at all on Taylor's reasons for the style of presentation.[4] In the original article, Taylor himself increased the likelihood of this happening by placing the Schmidt story first among a series of illustrations of his work and then taking a long and circuitous route to explain how the "science" of pig-iron loading was developed.

It appears that Taylor's real purpose in emphasizing the Schmidt story was to *illustrate the basic responsibilities of management.* The story demonstrated the necessity for managers to figure out the science of the work—that is, to plan work methods. Taylor then used the bricklaying example to illustrate management's task of providing support, help, and cooperation; the bicycle balls study was meant to show the importance of selecting the best people; and so on. In the pig-iron situation, Taylor was arguing for the development and teaching of a science, and *against* the older approach of simply "driving" workers to do more. He regarded the older approach as both inhumane and ineffective. Thus it is ironic that the Schmidt dialogue has so often been used to illustrate Taylor's anti-humanism.

Taylor's ways of making his points often placed him in a disadvantageous light. Recognizing this, H. H. Farquhar wrote, "Many of us feel that it is unfortunate that Mr. Taylor expressed himself so frequently and forceably on the question of soldiering and that he emphasized the profit motive on the part of the workmen almost to the exclusion of other instincts and motives in life in which at heart he knew every workman was interested."[5]

Taylor's repeated references to soldiering reinforced people's belief that he looked down on workmen and thought of them in a very negative way. His comments made him appear interested only in pushing workers to do more. Yet he also emphasized the earnings of employees, in such statements as: "Higher wages can come from the enormous difference between the amount of work which a first-class man can do under favorable circumstances and the work which is actually done by the average man."[6]

Misunderstandings arose concerning Taylor's use of the term "work." Frequently he was not simply referring to human effort but meant "output." A careful analysis of his writings shows that phrases such as "more output . . . under favorable circumstances" referred not to the workers' efforts alone but to the increased productivity possible through a new and highly developed combination of labor, equipment, and managerial techniques.

Taylor would have better conveyed his point if he had clearly stated that higher wages were to be drawn from the enormous difference in output resulting from the combination of capable workmen, proper equipment, and correct managerial organization—as compared to the output ordinarily produced by the usual workmen, equipment, and managerial organization. Unfortunately, he stated his case more curtly, and sometimes this made it sound as though he was trying to drive workers to higher productivity simply by standing over them in a more oppressive fashion.

The impression that Taylor wished to "drive" workers to higher productivity was also fostered by his choice of the label "speed boss" for one of his function foremen. Taylor's critics pictured a boss with a whip (at least a verbal one), exhorting people to more and more production. Use of the term "speed" made Taylor appear particularly oppressive and seemed to refute his oft-repeated contention that scientific management was not designed to coerce people to work harder.

In practice the role of the speed boss was to be an instructor in proper work methods. Taylor called him a speed boss because in a machine shop, where most of Taylor's early work took place, the correct use of cutting speeds and feeds was an important part of work methods. For a time, the speed boss was the acknowledged expert in such matters. Actually his role had nothing to do with the speed or pace of the workers' actions but rather was concerned with the speed at which the machines turned.

Taylor, in fact, would have been among the *last* to advocate a system that involved oppressive, sweatshop-type supervision. He had made that mistake at Midvale and sought to avoid repeating it. In a letter to his biographer, Taylor wrote:

> This is the most serious accusation which has been made against scientific management, namely, that it is a system for merely speeding up workmen, causing them to overwork, and finally leaving them with no more pay than they originally had. . . . It is the worst falsehood that has been told against scientific management because it is directly the opposite of the truth.[7]

Peter Drucker, an admitted admirer of Taylor, credits him with giving management the wherewithal to progress beyond techniques of simply exhorting workers to work faster. He says, "Without [scientific management] we could never, in managing workers and work, go beyond good intentions, exhortations or the 'speedup.' "[8] From Taylor's private correspondence, public testimony, and writings it is clear that he believed that it was not the workers but rather managers who needed to change first. Managers, before asking workmen to do anything differently, had to standardize tools and implements, develop the best ways of doing tasks, and provide proper working conditions and flow of materials. Only then, under these scientifically worked out circumstances, would it be reasonable to give an "object lesson" to the worker and explain that new methods would result in higher wages.

Another piece of terminology that has contributed to misunderstandings is Taylor's frequent use of the phrase "first-class man." Some have viewed this as indicative of Taylor's class consciousness and his awareness of his own well-to-do background as opposed to the origins of others. Although there may be some truth to this allegation, this was not unusual phraseology at the turn of the century and reflected the times as well as Taylor's personal beliefs.

What Taylor meant by the term is clarified by a portion of his testimony before the Special House Committee to Investigate the Taylor and Other Systems of Shop Management in 1912. The committee chairman was concerned that Taylor's system was designed to accommodate only "first-class men" in the sense of some kind of elite supermen, with all others pushed aside. Taylor testified as follows:

> What I want to make clear is that each type of man is "first-class" at some kind of work, and if you will hunt far enough you will find some kind of work that is especially suited to him. But if you insist, as some people in the community are insisting (to use the illustration of horses again), that a task—say a load of coal—shall be made so light that a pony can haul it, then you are doing a fool thing, for you are substituting a second-class animal (or man) to do work which manifestly should be done by a "first-class" animal (or man). And that is what I mean by the term "first-class man."[9]

Clearly, what Taylor meant by "first-class" was "well-suited" or "well-placed." His assumption that every worker could be matched perfectly with some kind of work is obviously unrealistic. The point is that he was simply talking about individual differences and the placement of workers in jobs that utilized their talents most effectively— hardly in itself an elitist notion. In fact, this is one of the basic premises of industrial psychology.

The term "first-class" also had another, entirely separate connotation to Taylor. He spoke of men who, though physically well able to work, "are simply lazy, and through no amount of teaching and instructing and through no amount of kindly treatment, can be brought into the 'first-class' . . . that is the man whom I call 'second-class.'"[10] Taylor's strong dislike of sloth is apparent here. But, once again, to describe an unenergetic employee as "second-class" could perhaps be considered insensitive but hardly elitist.

Taylor's use of animal analogies to illustrate his points also contributed greatly to his image as an elitist and to misunderstanding of his motives. These analogies do create the impression that he viewed workers as lesser beings and as basically interchangeable. Taylor's unfortunate use of such terminology stemmed from his belief that "every one of us knows a good deal about the capacity of horses, while there are very few people who have made a sufficient study of men to have the same kind of knowledge about men that we all have about horses."[11] Thus, in trying to illustrate his ideas of individual differences and appropriate placement of people, he chose terms that he felt would be widely understood. We may question his judgment, but his intent seems clear.

Taylor's Inability to Generalize

Taylor's manner of expression, which made him an easy target for critics who challenged his character and motivations, was a matter of form rather than substance. Taylor had, however, a more fundamental problem in trying to communicate his ideas: an inability to generalize. This trait contributed particularly to *misapplications* of his work.

Taylor usually expressed himself with an incredible amount of detail. Even in his paper titled "The Principles of Scientific Management," he still wrote in detail rather than generalizing. He knew that people often mistook the mechanical details of his papers for the true essence of his system. He may not have realized that this was partly because he was rather inarticulate when trying to describe the broader objectives of his work. Consequently, readers and listeners often came away with a narrow view of his ideas, not because of their own close-mindedness but because of Taylor's mode of expression.

Often, employers looked upon scientific management exactly as Taylor insisted that they should not: as an arsenal of devices designed to simplify and improve the current ways of managing labor. So, for example, it was common for companies to install Taylor's pay system but not to do the necessary work on unit times, or to perform the time studies but ignore his ideas on foremanship. As Reinhard Bendix points out:

> . . . these were all merely adjuncts of scientific management according to Taylor, for they could be adopted without the mental revolution he regarded as mandatory. And this is precisely what made scientific management popular among American employers. They could adopt any or all of Taylor's devices, and they could advocate cooperation between capital and labor, without accepting the idea that they must submit the management of their enterprises to the results of scientific study.[12]

The infrequency with which Taylor successfully clarified his general principles played into the hands of those who sought to achieve quick and easy results. But for Taylor the detailed techniques of scientific management were just indicators of the progress in installing the overall system. He saw the following points as the essence of the system:

1. The development of a true science—that is, a science that tells exactly what an adequate amount of work is on any given task
2. The scientific selection of workers
3. The scientific education and development of those workers
4. Intimate and friendly cooperation between management and employees

During his testimony before the Special House Committee, Taylor did succeed in generalizing more effectively in response to questioning than he had ever done in writing. For example, when asked how many companies were using the scientific management system in its entirety, Taylor responsed that there were "none, not one." He explained:

> Scientific management cannot be said to exist in any establishment until after a change has taken place in the mental attitude of both the management and the men. Both as to their duty to cooperate in producing the largest possible surplus and as to the necessity for substituting exact scientific knowledge for opinions or the old rule of thumb or individual knowledge. These are the two absolutely essential elements of scientific management.[13]

But it was rare for Taylor to speak in such terms, a factor which reinforced the notion that his work consisted of "a collection of techniques."

Taylor's Promotion of His System

Donald Nelson argues that scientific management as it was actually practiced by Taylor and his associates was quite different from the way Taylor's public pronouncements often made it sound. He describes Taylor's system as "a comprehensive answer to the problems of factory coordination, a refinement and extension of the earlier ideas known as systematic management."[14] Nelson, after reviewing documents concerning Taylor's work, concluded that those features of scientific management which directly affected labor (that is, time studies and the incentive wage) were incidental to Taylor's system and often were not even implemented.

The public perception that the central thrust of scientific management was the labor problem emerged in part because of the way Taylor often described his system. And, to some degree, he described it the way he did because he felt that this was what his audience wanted to hear. As Nelson explains: "Throughout his career as a promoter of scientific management, Taylor assumed that his greatest chance of success lay in emphasizing his answers to the labor problem. Thus, he stressed time study, the incentive wage, and the effects of his system on the workman rather than the system itself."[15]

Taylor was a clever marketer: he knew that company managers and owners were very concerned with worker productivity and would be interested in, for example, incentive wage systems as a possible means of improvement. In emphasizing these aspects of his system and deemphasizing the technical and organizational features, Taylor "indelibly fixed the popular conception of scientific management as a system of labor measures."[16]

This fixed conception probably did great damage to Taylor's cause in the long run by increasing the likelihood that attempts to implement his system would fail. When managers or company owners hired Taylor or one of his associates to systematize their organization, they often had unrealistic expectations. They would become impatient for what they perceived to be the central benefit of scientific management—improved output. Most had been attracted to Taylor's work in the first place because of his system's apparent impact on the behavior of workers. And, even though Taylor fully apprised prospective clients of all the steps that had to be taken *before* time study, management still tended to expect quick results. When these were not forthcoming, clients applied significant pressure for some early tangible evidence that their investment would pay off.

If such pressure was applied to Taylor himself, he usually became very rigid and insistent on following his careful, detailed procedures. This sometimes produced major disagreements between him and his clients, and in turn led to failures in implementation. When client pressure was applied in cases where his associates (Gantt, Barth, Cooke, Hathaway, and so on) were the principal consultants, they sometimes modified their approaches to accommodate the client's wishes. This tendency was even more pronounced among a rather large and growing group of "efficiency experts" who were in no way directly associated with Taylor but who took advantage of the market for efficiency improvements created by his prominence.

Robert Hoxie studied thirty-five companies where some form of Taylor's system was used and concluded that much of the application of the system was poorly done, particularly with respect to the task-setting step. Hoxie found that because of pressure from management for quick returns, task-setting was often quick and inadequate.[17] One of Taylor's most loyal followers, H. K. Hathaway, observed that: "Unfortunately [time study and the setting of incentive pay rates] is where in the past too many efforts to apply and profit by Taylor's teaching have commenced and have consequently either ended in failure or have fallen far short of the desired results."[18]

The entire history of implementation of scientific management is marked by frequent upheavals and failures. Some resulted from Taylor's personal style of consulting, some from his followers' reactions to client pressures, some from the "get rich quick" promotions of charlatans, some from honest misunderstandings in which managers mistook the mechanisms of Taylorism for its essence, and some, as we will see, from worker and union resistance. All of these problems were related to scientific management's public image as being "a partial solution of the labor problem."

Taylor's Personal Image

Another distorted image arose because, for many people, Taylor's own personal presence became fused with the content of this theory. During his lifetime, scientific management was synonymous with the name Taylor, and today his system and the school of thought it produced are often labeled Taylorism.

We have already seen how Taylor's compulsive nature manifested itself in a relentless search for the "one best way" to perform tasks, in the incredible twenty-six years of experimentation on metal cutting, in the remarkable detail that went into his plans for routing work and materials, and in his relentless efforts to seek out and eliminate all sources of variance in an industrial system. Both of Taylor's parents had taught him the importance of control, and his work and theory reflect an unending concern with this issue. His entire life's work might be viewed as a massive and intricately detailed attempt to achieve total control over all aspects (human and nonhuman) of production systems.

Taylor must have initially disliked the control exerted over him by his parents. Yet their emphasis on maintaining control became embedded in his values. He had a resulting ambivalence concerning the exercise of authority—both that which he exerted and that which others exerted over him. This ambivalence must have influenced his vehemence in asserting that "law" was the ultimate authority, and that when someone resisted the installation of his system, that person was in conflict with inexorable laws rather than with Taylor himself. His determination to enforce conformity with these "laws" was based not on any lack of concern for people but rather on his assumption that they, like he, were more comfortable when events were orderly and predictable. He felt that everyone must prefer a smooth-running, well-oiled, highly controlled system.

Taylor's rigidity, compulsivity, intolerance, and intensity naturally affected his manner of presenting his ideas and relating to others. Even Taylor's admiring biographer, Frank Copley, discussed Taylor's "monumental Puritan intolerance." The way this affected his work may be seen in Copley's comment that: "The charge may be appropriately leveled against Taylor that at Bethlehem he failed to allow his men sufficient time to get revolutionized mentally and that he repeatedly exhibited the old Puritan vice of intolerance."[19] As an example, Copley described an incident in which Taylor became involved in an "altercation" with an official of the Bethlehem plant. The argument concluded with Taylor saying, "Now look here, I don't want to hear anything more from you. You haven't got any brains, you haven't got any ability—you don't know anything. You owe your position entirely to your family pull, and you know it. Go on and work your pull if you want to, but keep out of my way, that's all."[20] This is, as Copley notes mildly, a "fairly intolerant speech."

Taylor was not completely oblivious to the personal image he projected. Occasionally he included references to his image in his writings, such as when he was describing his method of installing a change in working hours at the Simonds bicycle-ball-bearing factory. He wrote: "The writer had not been especially noted for his tact so he decided it would be wise for him to display a little more of this quality by having the girls vote on the new proposition."[21] He went on to say, however, that such tact turned out to be unjustified and was henceforth "thrown to the winds."

Taylor was often impatient and contentious when people disagreed with him or failed to comply with his directives. However, it was probably not necessary to challenge him in order to feel the effects of his demeanor. Taylor's public presentations were characterized by great attention to detail and were often delivered in a tone implying that they represented, as *he* felt they did, incontrovertible law.

Taylor's rigidity and tendency to see things as black and white were displayed in his writing by his frequent use of terms such as "all," "never," "invariably," "always," and "no." In one paper he asserted, "There is *no* class of work which cannot be profitably submitted to time study."[22] Both orally and in articles, he was fond of prefacing his statements with "Anyone can see," "No one doubts," "It is perfectly evident," and—his favorite—"There is no question . . . ." Taylor's way of expressing himself clearly suggested that anyone who failed to see the wisdom of his assertions was ignorant, stupid, or perhaps both.

Taylor's personal characteristics laid him open to charges that he was an autocratic, anti-humanistic obsessive whose purpose was to reduce workers to implements of the production system. For many people the man and the system were inseparable.

Taylor's Years at the Manufacturing Investment Company

Taylor's manner of relating to others had a particularly negative effect in his role as a consultant. Taylor's personal consulting record was nothing short of dismal. He repeatedly ran afoul of the owners and chief executives of the organizations for which he worked. In fact, this pattern was evident even before he set up his consulting practice.

Just prior to becoming a consultant, Taylor spent three years with the Manufacturing Investment Company, which had been formed to utilize a newly developed process for making paper out of forest products. The founding group invited Taylor to invest in the company, become the general manager, and run it according to his principles of management. In 1890 Taylor began his work at the new plant site in Madison, Maine. The next three years were, according to his biographer, the unhappiest of his life.

Taylor had his usual troubles with the workers, somewhat exacerbated by the north-woods, small-town, "work when you need some money" attitude he encountered. There was also some difficulty with the patents on the papermaking process and, to some extent, with the efficiency of the process itself. However, the largest problem was lack of harmony between Taylor's principles and methods and those of the chief owners of the business.

Taylor and the owners disagreed on many counts, but the most troublesome related to Taylor's tendency to "make money fly." Taylor tended to overbuild, in the sense that he constructed what would today be called back-up systems for protection against equipment failure. He eventually installed a complete alternate power plant, as well as duplicate line shafting for the entire mill. To Taylor the worst thing that could happen was for production to be disrupted. His sense of order and efficiency simply would not tolerate this prospect, so he would go to almost any lengths to avoid it.

The expenses involved were, of course, obvious to his financial backers; the savings resulting from avoidance of downtime were less evident. When they protested that Taylor's expenditures were devastating to the return on their investments, he labeled their concerns shortsighted and suggested that they "wait a few years" to see the benefits. Taylor and the owners wrangled constantly over what he came to regard as their aloof and aristocratic lack of concern for the concrete problems of managing the organization. They were, he felt, concerned only with making money quickly and he came to dislike them heartily for it. His relationship with them steadily deteriorated, and he left in 1893.

The Consulting Years

At this point Taylor decided to establish himself as an independent consultant. His major clients included Cramp's Shipyards in Philadelphia; the Johnson Company in Johnstown, Pennsylvania; the Simonds Company in Fitchburg, Massachusetts; and, of course, Bethlehem Steel. Though there were exceptions (for example, his work at the Johnson Company apparently went well), this was a period during which the pattern at the Manufacturing Investment Company repeated itself time and again. One source of the difficulty can be seen in this statement by Taylor: "I always insist that in all essential matters relating to the management, the company for which I am working must do as I tell them, and the only way in which I have been able to enforce this is that I hold myself free to withdraw from the work at any time in case they refuse to follow my directions."[23]

Taylor apparently carried through with this imperious attitude toward his clients. An example is Taylor's description of a disagreement he had with the owners of Bethlehem Steel. He reports that as his work progressed in the yards there, it became apparent to the owners that he was succeeding in his efforts to improve efficiencies and that the work force would ultimately be cut by about three-fourths. Since the owners also owned all the local houses and company stores, they decided that this was not in their overall best interests and ordered Taylor not to cut staff any further. He described the subsequent conversation as follows:

> I said: "You are going to have it whether you want it or not, as long as I am here. You employed me with the distinct understanding that that is what I was going to do. You agreed to it, and got me here for that purpose. You had a unanimous vote. I would not [have] come here if there was a single man that did not want what I was going to do."

> "Well, we did not think you could do it."

> I said: "I don't care what you thought. Your remedy is at hand. Tell me any night you want me to go, and I go tomorrow morning. On the other hand, Mr. President, just countermand one of my orders and I will go tomorrow morning, but while I am here I am going to do what I came to do, whether you like it or not. . . ."[24]

This was representative of the many encounters that came to pass between Taylor and Robert Linderman, the president of Bethlehem. Linderman's ultimate response was probably also representative of what happened in Taylor's consultations. When Taylor returned from a vacation in April of 1901, he found a letter on his desk that read:[25]

> Dear Sir,
>
> I beg to advise you that your services will not be required by this company after May 1st, 1901.
>
> > Yours truly,
> >
> > Robert P. Linderman
> > President

There are very few instances of success in Taylor's personal consulting background. Other individuals were apparently more successful in installing his system. In 1916, C. B. Thompson compiled data on

113 plants that used scientific management.[26] He reported that 59 of them considered their installations completely successful, 20 rated them partly successful, and the remaining 34 viewed the system as a failure. While this is not a spectacular record, it compares favorably with most managerial systems that become popular and are widely tried by organizations. It certainly represents a substantial improvement over Taylor's personal record.

The consultants on these other installations were, for the most part, Taylor's followers. One of the most successful projects was undertaken at the Franklin Auto Company under the direction of Carl Barth. The system was installed between 1911 and 1915, with great care and with strict adherence to Taylor's prescribed approaches. The installation went so well that George Babcock, the Franklin manager who worked with Barth, wrote a book about it and stated: "The Taylor System in Franklin Management has been successful in reaching useful ends, which it would appear could not be attained without it. . . ."[27] Reports such as these implied that Taylor's system could be implemented successfully, though apparently not by Taylor himself.

Issues of Organizational Change

Taylor, perhaps because of his personal failures, seldom underestimated the difficulty of instituting organizational change. In a list of issues to be considered in making changes in the organization of a company,[28] he included, first, the importance of choosing the general type of management best suited to the particular case. Second, he pointed out that in all cases it would be necessary to invest money in the changes and that in many cases a great deal of money would be involved before the changes were completed and costs were lowered. Third, he stated that it took a great deal of time to achieve any organizational change worth aiming for. Finally, he emphasized the importance of making changes in their proper order to avoid deterioration of output and other difficulties.

This list is very similar to those generated by present-day change agents. So, some seventy-five years ago, Taylor demonstrated a sensitivity to the difficulties that are still encountered today.

Taylor also emphasized the importance of top management's commitment to the change being undertaken, the careful introduction of the new ideas to each individual worker, and the importance of talking with workers about the changes and letting them talk as well. He continued to stress "object lessons," believing that workers would best accept new work standards and methods if they saw one of their own people successfully doing the work and then reaping the promised rate. This is a rough application of what would now be called expectancy theory. Expectancy theory states that motivation is a product of the attractiveness of the reward (money) times the worker's expectation that he or she will actually receive it. In his attempt to influence workers' attitudes toward change, Taylor was employing a basic form of psychological thinking that became formulated in a field of study only many years later.

Another point Taylor stressed was the importance of gradual change initially. He wrote:

> Before taking any step toward changing methods, the manager should realize that at no time during the introduction of the new system should any broad sweeping changes be made which seriously affect a large number of the workmen. It would be preposterous for instance in going from day [rates] to piecework to start a large number of men on piecework at the same time. Throughout the early stages of organization each change made should affect one workman only and after the single man affected has become used to the new order of things, then change one man after another from the old system to the new, slowly at first and then as rapidly as public opinion in the shop swings around under the influence of proper object lessons.[29]

Taylor's advice on this issue has rarely been followed. The authors have never seen a contemporary efficiency-improvement system implemented in a gradual fashion. Rather they are implemented in a sweeping manner, across-the-board with everybody starting on the new system as rapidly as possible.

Taylor believed that the introduction of change in organizations was a full-time job and therefore needed to be handled by someone other than the line manager. His experience at the Manufacturing Investment Company, where he had *been* the line manager, had convinced him of that. He felt that because of the line manager's other duties it would take him too long to implement change, and saw as an alternative the kind of staff or consulting role we now call a "change agent."

Though Taylor obviously gave much thought to the ways in which change should be introduced, his personal style was heavy-handed with respect to both workers and owners. His method of gaining worker "cooperation" was heavily authoritarian. For example, Taylor felt that the worst mistake one could make in implementing change was to refer to any part of the new system as being "on trial." Instead, he felt that a change should be implemented "with the understanding that it will go whether anyone around the place likes it or not."[30]

Contemporary change agents may well understand Taylor's point. If changes are seen as trials or experiments, or even as "projects" with a beginning and an end, many persons go along with the change because they expect it to go away. Others, however, have little enthusiasm for the effort because they think it really is not going to last anyway. Taylor was apparently sensitive to this problem and so arrived at his authoritarian "like it or not" attitude. And, perhaps more significantly, Taylor is likely to have expressed his viewpoint in exactly such terms to members of his clients' organizations. Taylor's personal style— more than an ignorance about, or insensitivity to, the need for care in implementing change—caused him to be an unsuccessful change agent.

As we have seen, there was little or no collaboration or mutual decision-making between Taylor and his clients. Taylor stated that he never undertook systematization of a company unless he was positive that the owners strongly wanted scientific management, understood exactly what would be done, and had visited other installations. He would then extract from them a promise that, "Whenever there was a conflict of opinion between themselves and myself as to what details should or should not be used in introducing the new system of management, my decision must be final. . . ."[31] Taylor's handling of the Bethlehem situation illustrates what happened when such conflicts arose.

Taylor's failures as a consultant were predictable on the basis of what we know today about management consulting, but he probably did not realize that his style of implementation (that is, requiring total control as the outside change agent) made success highly improbable. He had some awareness of his own lack of tact, but another of his personality characteristics probably prevented him from seeing the negative impact his style was having. This characteristic was the intensity with which he approached almost everything. It had all the earmarks of religious zeal.

Taylor as an Advocate of Industrial Reform

Taylor had always been intense, a quality illustrated by many incidents in his life. However, after his dismissal from Bethlehem, he reinvested this intensity in a new way. He became a reformer. In 1901 Taylor retired from active consulting to become a proselytizer for scientific management. It was during this last period of his life (1901–1915) that he wrote the major statements of his work, made many of his public addresses, and gained most of the press coverage his ideas were to receive. Taylor's zeal to "sell" scientific management was in full bloom, and this enthusiasm had significant effects on the way he presented his ideas and on how they were received. Kakar suggests that "the industrial world was only an arena for [Taylor's] true calling; and his work in industry was more a vocation in the sense of a summons than an avocation or profession."[32] There is ample evidence that, during these years, Taylor saw himself as pursuing a mission: to promote harmony and cooperation between management and labor, and thereby drastically to increase productivity. He held the following view of the benefits to society of such an accomplishment:

> The general adoption of scientific management would readily in the future double the productivity of the average man engaged in industrial work. Think of what this means to the whole country. Think of the increase, both in the necessities and luxuries, which becomes available for the whole of the country, the possibility of shortening the hours of labor when this is desirable, and of the increased opportunities for education, culture, and recreation which this implies.[33]

Taylor envisioned a society in which there was peace, harmony, and comfort for everyone, and he believed that the efficient management of production systems was the route to such a society. The depth of his feeling on this issue was most clearly demonstrated when someone questioned his motives and goals.

One such instance involved A. J. Portenar, an official of the typographers' union, who had written a book entitled *Problems of Organized Labor*. Pleased with the spirit of the book, Taylor invited Portenar to his home near Philadelphia and then to the plants where scientific management was in operation. The two had a very difficult time getting along, however. Before they parted, Portenar, at Taylor's suggestion, promised to read Taylor's paper "Shop Management."

Later Portenar wrote Taylor a long letter in which he stated that:

> [You desire] the greatest possible production at the lowest possible cost with the greatest possible resulting dividend and the benefits that may flow to the working people are merely incidental. [The working people] are not the object of your management, they are but the means whereby you hope to obtain your object. . . . [I desire] the greatest possible benefit to the people who work and consume and I regard the dividends only as an incident because under the existing industrial system dividends for the owner are the condition precedent to the continuation of the plant. . . . Therefore, to summarize: your object is to me incidental and my object is to you incidental.[34]

Taylor, of course, found this charge very objectionable. In a return letter to Portenar he wrote:

> You are absolutely wrong in your description of what my views regarding management are, nothing could be further from what you state my views to be. . . . As you know, I retired from moneymaking business in 1901 and

have never received a cent of pay for any work that I have done in the interest of Scientific Management. On the contrary, I have devoted nearly all of my time and money to furthering the cause of Scientific Management. This is done entirely with the idea of getting better wages for the workman—of developing the workmen coming under our system so as to make them all higher class men—to better educate them—to help them to live better lives, and, above all, to be more happy and contented. This is a worthy object for a man to devote his life to.

. . . I realize (as you do not seem to realize) that it is utterly impossible to get the maximum prosperity for workmen unless their employers and the owners of the establishments in which they work cooperate in the most hearty way to bring about this end. You seem to think that this result can be brought about by a persistent fight. I am sure that it can be brought about only by friendly, kindly cooperation. Realizing this, it becomes a part of my duty toward the working people (to whose interest I am devoting my life) to induce manufacturers to come into this scheme of hearty cooperation. Therefore, in all of my writings and in everything I say I must emphasize the gain which comes to the manufacturers quite as much as the gain which comes to the workmen otherwise it would be impossible to get the manufacturers to cooperate.[35]

These portions from Taylor's letter illustrate his depth of feeling, his condescending tone, his indignation at being challenged, and his zealousness in pursuing his cause.

One indication of how this zealousness was viewed by others can be obtained from Frank Copley's initial perceptions of Taylor. Copley, later to become Taylor's biographer, first met him in July 1912 while working on a magazine article concerning management systems. As part of his research for the article, Copley interviewed Taylor twice. From those talks he developed two clear and, at first glance, contradictory images of Taylor. The first was that Taylor "did not reveal himself to be the possessor of a nature that ordinarily would be called lovable."[36] At other points in the article, Copley described Taylor as "profane," "pugnacious," "domineering," and "imperious." Having also talked with others about Taylor and his work, Copley reported that "most of the men with whom I talked about Fred Taylor and his work either spoke of him personally with significant reserve or denounced him with a bitterness which sometimes was really remarkable in its intensity." Here again are seen the effects of Taylor's tactlessness in dealing with others.

However, Copley also came away with a second impression, namely, that "this man was no mere tinker of business systems, no unctuous mouther of cant terms like efficiency; . . . that here was not only a great pioneer and discoverer in the world of industry, but a man whose heart was aflame with missionary zeal, a man who was an industrial *revolutionist. . . ."* Copley felt that Taylor was seeking a moral revolution, "demanding that employers experience a change of heart like unto that of a religious conversion."

Taylor, who did view himself as a kind of missionary during these years, doubtless conveyed the impression of missionary zeal to others as well. He presented his ideas more vehemently and with increased fervor, a characteristic that can result in either increased or decreased receptivity, depending on the listener. Copley obviously was positively influenced by Taylor's enthusiasm. Many of his followers were similarly affected. Louis Brandeis, after listening to Taylor talk, commented that Taylor was "a really great man—great not only in mental capacity, but in character."[37] Others were put off by the vehemence of Taylor's presentations.

A reformer with this type of zeal also tends to dramatize and exaggerate the benefits of his program, as well as the data base on which it rests. That Taylor was capable of doing so was recognized by as close an associate as Henry Towne, president of the Yale & Towne Company, where Taylor's system was in use. Testifying before the Labor Committee of the House of Representatives in 1916, Towne said:

> Mr. Taylor was a great friend of mine, and I regard him as having done more as an American engineer in a generation to leave an impress, which will last for all time, in founding a new system than any other man; but he had his faults like the rest of us, and one of them was a very intense temperament, and, as a result of that, a habit of overstatement. He exaggerates, unconsciously but unavoidably, because he is so full of his subject and so intense.[38]

Some of Taylor's exaggerations were undoubtedly unconscious, but Towne was probably being generous in labeling all of them as so. He himself had been involved in a disagreement with Taylor some years before that illustrates Taylor's willingness to exaggerate the positive effects of scientific management with the goal of promoting "reformation."

The Special House Committee to Investigate the Taylor and Other Systems of Shop Management had asked to visit some of the sites where Taylor's system was being used. One such site was the Stamford, Connecticut, plant of the Yale & Towne Company. Henry Towne agreed to the visit and then wrote Taylor asking what "line of investigation" the committee might follow.

This initiated an exchange of letters between Taylor and Towne concerning how best to present data on the wage gains made by workers under scientific management. Taylor wanted to prepare a table showing how much each man had been paid when he joined the company and how much he was now being paid. Another client of Taylor's, the Tabor Company, had prepared a similar table. Towne wrote back that his people had prepared such a table but that the wage increases were "much less striking" than the Tabor data. Towne believed his company's data to be a more accurate reflection of the real benefits to workers of scientific management, pointing out that many other factors, such as promotions and general economic conditions, also contribute to wage increases. Towne correctly stated that the Tabor data did not control for such influences.

Taylor responded that "the most important testimony to bring before the congressional committee is that which proves to them that each workman in your employ is better off now than he was when he came to your company." He added, "Any statement whatever that is prepared is subject to a certain amount of criticism, and it appears to me wise to put the best foot foremost."[39] Towne remained unmoved, writing Taylor that "under any kind of system" a person employed by a company for several years, and receiving promotions, will be receiving more in wages and that these facts "are so obvious as to make it inexpedient, in my judgment, to offer such a statement as that of the Tabor Manufacturing Company as evidence of the results of the new system."[40]

Taylor certainly knew enough about statistics to appreciate the accuracy of Towne's analysis. But Taylor's enthusiasm for his program overrode his desire for a balanced, fair presentation of its benefits.

Taylor's zeal and his flair for the dramatic affected his presentation of the story of "Schmidt," the pig-iron loader. The story was clearly Taylor's favorite illustration of his work, as he included it in almost all his presentations. Taylor must have repeated this story hundreds of times, and a story inevitably changes when it is retold so often. It slowly evolves and takes on new twists. Some features are de-emphasized, some are dropped completely, some are given greater emphasis, and some new elements are added. Sometimes the story even gets combined with other incidents.

These modifications often occur because the storyteller grows tired of repeating the exact same tale and because of memory lapses. But the purpose in telling the story is also a large factor—in this case, to persuade. Taylor intensely wished to accomplish his purpose, and indulged in dramatization and exaggeration to make his points. The ultimate form taken by the Schmidt story was so far from the reality of what actually occurred that Charles Wrege and Amadeo Perroni label it "more fiction than fact."[41]

Wrege and Perroni painstakingly unearthed the facts in the Schmidt case and identified eight types of discrepancies or factors that would have weakened Taylor's argument. These were: (1) the reasons that the pig-iron loading was going on in the first place; (2) the size and composition of the work gang involved; (3) the method of loading that was used (Wrege and Perroni describe a labor-saving device that may have contributed substantially to the productivity improvement but was never mentioned by Taylor); (4) the "scientific" way in which the figure of 47½ tons was arrived at; (5) the "scientific selection" of Schmidt; (6) a new method of loading pig iron that was instituted (one man to a car instead of teams); (7) the real origins of Taylor's "law of heavy laboring" (see Chapter 2); and (8) Taylor's actual non-use of what were described in his story as "rest periods." Wrege and Perroni conclude that the Schmidt story tells us more about Taylor's impudence and imagination than about the facts, and that Taylor seemed to have believed that the end—convincing the public of the rightness of his crusade—justified the means.

Copley defended Taylor but also acknowledged the latter's willingness to stretch the truth:

> He has been called the *beau idéal* of a scientific investigator; no form of charlatanism could find any lodgment in him; yet along with his intensely scientific bent went not only great practicality, but also great amiability and sociability, and this, together with a marked instinct for the dramatic, inclined him to over-popularize his expolisitions or overadapt them to his immediate audience and the passing scene.[42]

The fact that the Schmidt story as reported in "The Principles of Scientific Management," as well as other portions of the paper, were apparently written by Morris Cooke rather than by Taylor himself may have contributed even more to the distortions.[43]

Taylor's other case examples have not been subjected to such close scrutiny, but his instinct for the dramatic probably extended to these as well. Donald Nelson has suggested that Taylor overemphasized scientific management's "least well developed feature—the approach to the worker" because "a partial solution of the labor problem" was the thing in which management was most interested at the time.[44] Thus Taylor's distortions of his work were in part a response to prevailing social conditions. He wished to convert his system into a social program but also had to package his ideas so as to appeal to people in a position to implement them. The result was a considerable, if seemingly uncharacteristic, willingness to distort the presentation of events as they actually happened.

Union Resistance

Union resistance to Taylorism was strong, sustained, and largely based on the perception that the system was aimed at getting more work from fewer people by "speeding up" workers. A particularly strong statement was made by James O'Connell, head of the Machinists Union, who published a paper in the *National Labor Journal* in 1912 asserting that the Taylor system would entirely wipe out trade unions unless it was resisted and destroyed.

Though this was a substantial overestimate of the power of scientific management, Taylor himself had provided the basis for this speculation when he wrote, "The writer has seen several times after the introduction of [scientific management], the members of labor unions who were working under it leave the union in large numbers because they found they could do better under the operation of the system than under the laws of the union."[45] Although there is no evidence to support Taylor's statement, this assertion naturally aroused the antagonism of union leaders.

Largely through union lobbying, bills were introduced in Congress to forbid the use of stopwatches and the payment of bonuses on government work. The debates over these bills indicated that most senators did not understand the Taylor system and voted in accordance with their sympathy or lack of sympathy toward unions. Union lobbyists did succeed in getting riders outlawing stopwatches attached to naval and other appropriation bills. These riders were successfully renewed each year and were extended to all government employees in 1917 and 1918.

These congressional debates contributed greatly to Taylor's controversial public image. Union resistance came to a head in 1911, when the executive council of the American Federation of Labor adopted a resolution denouncing the "premium bonus system" and urged the affiliates of the AFL to resist the spread of what it called the "speeding system." Samuel Gompers held forth sarcastically against Taylorism, stating:

> So there you are wage workers in general, mere machines (considered industrially of course), hence why should you not be standardized and your motion power brought up to the highest possible perfections in all respects including speeds. Not only your length, breadth and thickness as a machine but your grade of hardness, malleability, tractability, and general serviceability can be ascertained, registered and then employed as desirable. Science would thus get the most out of you before you were sent to the junk pile.[46]

During his testimony before a House committee, Gompers denied categorically the existence of the "soldiering" behavior that Taylor described. Then, as now, trade unions had a significant effect on public opinion—and in the case of Taylor this effect was largely negative.

A few years later, in 1915, the government once again examined "Taylorism," when a federal commission on industrial relations established a special committee to investigate scientific management. The chairman of the committee ordered the compilation of two lists: trade union objections to scientific management, and the labor claims of those advocating scientific management. The list of trade union objections, which was approved by a committee of the American Federation of Labor, was widely circulated among labor people and in the press. It included such items as:

1. Scientific Management is opposed to industrial democracy, it is a reversion to industrial autocracy.
2. It forces the workmen to depend upon the employer's conception of fairness and limits the democratic safeguards of the workers.
3. Scientific management greatly increases the number of unproductive workers; that is, those engaged in clerical or supervisory tasks. It tends to destroy individuality and inventive genius.
4. It stimulates and drives the workers up to a limit of nervous and physical exhaustion and overfatigues and overstrains them.
5. It tends to undermine the worker's health and it shortens the worker's period of industrial activity and earning power.
6. It tends to destroy the worker's self-respect and self-restraint and leads to habits of spending and intemperance.
7. It is itself a systematic rate cutting device. It tends to lower the wages of many, immediately and permanently.
8. It means in the long run simply more work for the same or less pay.
9. It tends to lengthen the hours of labor.[47]

The fifth and sixth items on this list arose largely from union complaints concerning the installation of scientific management at the Watertown Arsenal in Massachusetts. In 1913 the unions involved had drawn up a petition which alleged that most men employed at the arsenal were in ill health due to overwork and called for abolition of "the Taylor system." General William Crozier, under the orders of the Secretary of War, investigated these complaints and reported that none of the men were failing in health due to overwork. Nor could he in talking with the workers find any complaint to that effect. Crozier was selected for this task partly because he had had experience with scientific management applications at other War Department facilities and was thus somewhat sympathetic toward the process.

The Watertown Arsenal situation was eventually discussed on the floors of both the House and the Senate. Those discussions were characterized by strong opposition to the Taylor system on the part of the labor union officers but no certain evidence that the rank-and-file members objected to the system. One senator, who lived near the arsenal, apparently received a great deal of mail from his constituents concerning this matter. He reported that the mail—much of it from employees of the arsenal—indicated that the opposition to the Taylor system was trumped up; that many of the 349 signers of the petition did not read it but had just signed it to be agreeable; and that there was no truth to the allegations of overwork and failing health.

It is difficult to draw conclusions about this and other highly publicized instances of union objection. Nevertheless, the public image of scientific management as an inhumane system was reinforced substantially by the publicity surrounding such instances. By the end of the decade, there was some movement toward accommodation between Taylorism and the unions. In 1919, a conference was held involving leaders of the American Federation of Labor and proponents of scientific management. Afterward the AFL somewhat reformulated its program, stating in part:

> Labor is fully conscious that the world needs things for use and that standards of life can improve only as production for use and consumption increases. Labor is anxious to work out better methods for industry and demands it be assured that increased productivity will be used for service and not alone for profits.[48]

One writer commented that this statement marked "the official acceptance by the labor movement of the program of introducing improved and scientific methods into industry."[49]

Eventually even Samuel Gompers took a different attitude. In 1920 he wrote: "The trade union movement welcomes every thought and plan, every device and readjustment that will make expended effort more valuable to humanity. . . . To the idealism and aggressiveness of the labor movement, the technical skill and the inventive genius of the engineer are fitting and needed complements."[50]

So, by the early 1920s the relationship between scientific management and the unions had improved. Nevertheless, the protracted battle had left a substantial impact on the public images of scientific management and of Frederick Taylor.

Taylor's Attitudes Toward Unions

Taylor often stated that he had no basic opposition to unions. He once wrote: "The labor unions—particularly the trade unions of England—have rendered a great service, not only to their members, but to the world, in shortening hours of labor and in modifying the hardships and improving the conditions of wage workers."[51] Taylor refused to prepare an article explaining his system for the journal of the National Association of Manufacturers because its chief purpose was to fight unions.[52]

Taylor felt that unions formed because employers were herding people together in groups or classes and then paying all members of a class the same wage, with no inducements to work harder and no rewards for the superior worker. Under such conditions he felt it was natural for workers to form unions to fend off encroachments by their employers. Yet, Taylor was very often critical of the effects of unions. He felt the typical union situation was unsatisfactory for worker and employer alike, because it led to restriction of output. He wrote: "The most serious of the delusions and fallacies under which workmen, and particularly those in many of the unions, are suffering is that it is for their interest to limit the amount of work which a man should do in a day."[53]

Taylor reasoned that restriction of output was bad for workers because: (1) if the employer's competitive position became affected, the workers might lose their jobs; and (2) ". . . the small day's work which they have accustomed themselves to do demoralizes them, and instead of developing as men do when they use their strength and faculties to the utmost, . . . they grow lazy, spend much of their time pitying themselves, and are less able to compete with other men."[54]

Taylor was firmly convinced that science and not bargaining should be the basis for determining pay, a proper day's output, and the hours to be worked. He believed that an antagonistic, adversarial stance between labor and management worked against the best interests of both the company and the union. In criticizing actions of the unions, he felt he was advocating the best interests of *both* sides. As a result, he was able to answer with complete sincerity a question posed to him by the Special House Committee: "Can you say in one syllable what the relation of labor unions should be to scientific management?" Taylor replied:

> Of all the devices in the world they ought to look upon scientific management as the best friend that they have. It is doing in the most efficient way every solitary good thing that the labor unions have tried to do for the workman and it has corrected the one bad thing that the unions are doing—curtailment of output. That is the one bad thing they are doing.[55]

As suggested by the Watertown Arsenal episode, much of the worker opposition to Taylor's work may have been more apparent than real.

However, any working person would be likely to object to a system that seemed to rob employees of their freedom, and that is precisely how the Taylor system sounded to many people. When the labor aspects of the system are emphasized, it appears that its primary impact is to reduce to a minimum the choices that individuals can exercise in how they perform their work.

In our culture at least, arguments that are perceived as leading to a loss of personal freedom generally receive vigorous resistance. B. F. Skinner's *Beyond Freedom and Dignity* was greeted with the same kind of hostility, though from different sources, as was Taylor's work. Even "small" losses of freedom may appear significant. For example, one of the steps involved in scientific management was the standardization of tools. This was perceived as very threatening by craftsmen whose tools were personal possessions, perhaps ones they had made themselves or at least ones selected to suit their individual tastes. Skilled craftsmen probably also perceived a weakening of their own power because many tasks became systematized.

The perception that freedom of choice was being lost probably also accounts for some of the resistance Taylor's system received from managers and owners. The owners he so often clashed with found that, when Taylor was around, their range of choices was reduced. Managers and supervisors affected by his system found that their opportunities to exercise arbitrary power were reduced. This, of course, was one of Taylor's objectives: the substitution of science for rule-of-thumb management. While Taylor felt the substitution would benefit all parties concerned, the parties themselves often disagreed.

Worker and union resistance was made stronger by the emergence of a large number of "efficiency experts" as Taylor popularized his system. Many of these people knew little of the philosophy of scientific management and focused almost exclusively on the time-study and incentive-wage features of the system. In addition, their methods of implementation typically involved large numbers of workers rather than (as Taylor advised) individual workers one at a time. Thus, when a company employed one of these "efficiency experts" to install "the Taylor system," the worst fears of the workers became reality and scientific management received much undeserved bad publicity.

The Congressional Hearings

The congressional hearings, which resulted in large part from labor's vociferous resistance to scientific management, both clarified and clouded the public picture of Taylor's system. In response to questioning, Taylor made some of his clearest explanations of the underlying principles of his system, providing potential for clearing up misunderstandings. However, much of the publicity and popular discussions about the hearings contributed to, rather than reduced, the amount of distortion of scientific management that existed.

The very fact that the hearings were held at all—and especially the fact that they were held largely to investigate charges against scientific management as an inhumane system based on "speeding up" workers—created a negative image in some people's minds. And much of the questioning was aimed at learning to what extent Taylor's system exploited workers, either by overworking them or by throwing them out of work as part of staff reductions.

The committee members—particularly William B. Wilson, who was later appointed Secretary of Labor—were suspicious that Taylor's system did in fact exploit workers. Wilson's line of questioning was designed to get Taylor to confirm that he was requiring a speedup on the part of employees. Taylor would carefully explain that this was not the case. The discussion would then become contentious. Wilson would generally begin his questions, "Isn't it true that . . . ?" and Taylor would repeat his thinking. Wilson's remarks indicate that he either could not understand Taylor's points or did not think Taylor was really trying to serve the needs of both management and workers. Wilson believed that the needs of workers and the needs of organizations were irrevocably opposed, and since he saw Taylor's system as benefiting the organization, he assumed that this must be at the workers' expense.

Later questioning showed concern for the democracy of Taylorism, dealing with management's absolute power under the system. There was, and there remains today, a perception that scientific management rests on the power of management to coerce workers into any behavior desired. Taylor felt that his system had precisely the opposite effect. He testified, "Under scientific management those men who are in the management, such as, for instance, the superintendent, the foremen, the president of the company, have far, far less arbitrary power than is now possessed by the corresponding men who are occupying those positions in the older types of management."[56]

Taylor believed that under his system, "law" or science governed and that everybody, including management, had to play by the law. Therefore, the workers were much less subject to the *arbitrary* power of management.

The committee also showed concern for the fate of workers considered "not fit" by managers using Taylor's approach. Chairman Wilson asked, "Then you propose that the man who is not in the first class as a workman . . . must be destroyed and removed? Is it not true that a man who is not a good workman and who may not be responsible for the fact that he is not a good workman has to live as well as the man who is a good workman?"[57] Another committee member asked whether it was not an indignity for a worker to submit to time study with a stopwatch, and brought up the charge that this made people nervous and irritable. Still later, Taylor was asked how much money he had made from scientific management and whether it was simply a way to promote the sale of his inventions.

Two members of the committee did, however, appear to be much more sympathetic to Taylor as a witness. For example, they once intervened on Taylor's behalf when Wilson appeared to be badgering him.

The committee eventually concluded that the system had not been in existence long enough to determine its effects on the health and pay of employees. No legislation was recommended. Nevertheless, in many people's minds, the issues raised remained as indictments against Taylor and his system.

The Reporting of Taylor's System by Others

Inspired by the congressional investigations of Taylorism, and the accompanying social climate, hundreds of articles and editorials regarding scientific management were written for newspapers and magazines. Every conceivable point of view was advanced, from sarcastic disbelief concerning Taylor's claims, to firm conviction that he was right, to fears that his system would horribly exploit workers.

The fragmented public image of Taylorism must be understood within the social and political context of the time. Taylor's work is linked in both time and philosophy to the political progressivism era of 1890–1920. Samuel Haber observes that this era gave rise to a pervasive efficiency craze in America, the heart of which was Taylor's scientific management. Haber points out that Taylor's followers, sometimes called the Taylorites, had found a kind of social outlook for the accommodation of business, in which ultimate authority lies at the top, to the environment of political democracy in which ultimate authority lies below. Efficiency provided a standpoint from which those who had declared allegiance to democracy could resist the leveling tendency of the principle of equality."[58]

Contemporary with, and antagonistic to, scientific management was the *industrial betterment movement.* Haber describes this movement as "an uneven mixture of philanthropy, humanitarianism and commercial shrewdness." Some major goals of the movement were to prevent labor trouble and increase employee productivity. Its followers advocated providing lunchrooms, bathhouses, hospital clinics, safety training, recreational facilities, thrift clubs, benefit funds, and profit-sharing plans. Implying that human happiness was a business asset, these people asserted that scientific management neglected the human element and made men into machines. Articles written from this point of view helped sustain the idea that Taylorism was inhumane.

Since Taylor's time, his system has been reported on in many ways by many writers. Not all of them have bothered to read Taylor very carefully; some seem not to have read him at all. The result has been oversimplifications and inaccuracies.

The most persuasive distortion of Taylor's thought has not changed: the tendency to portray him as an anti-humanistic exploiter of workers who wished to reduce employees to mere cogs in the massive American production machine—cogs that should be coerced into speeding up their work. To give just a few examples, B. M. Gross, in a chapter discussing management pioneers, has a section entitled "Taylor: More from Workers" placed next to a section called "Fayol: More from Managers."[59] Cascio says that Taylor's goal was "to obtain more production *from workers*" [italics ours].[60] Siegel and Lane label their entire section on Taylorism "Time Study, 'Speedup,'" and report that "attempts to simply speed up employee activity without regard for the consequent toll in human resources have always been repugnant to workers, psychologists and many managers."[61] The same picture of Taylor's work is suggested by Rensis Likert[62] and by T. A. Ryan and P. C. Smith, who report that "speed was the criterion for the 'best method,' effort being disregarded in Taylor's analyses."[63] All of these authors perpetuate the myth that Taylor's approach was centered on "squeezing" workers for more output.

To read Taylor as advocating coercion of workers to higher levels of productivity is to miss his entire point. Taylor was convinced that this type of management, which he referred to as management by "initiative and incentive," was exactly the root of the problem! As Hugh Aitken has observed, "From start to finish, the Taylor movement represented a fundamental criticism—condemnation is hardly too strong—of the way businesses were actually being managed."[64] Taylor was proposing an *alternative* to simply pushing workers for more speed because he knew that this led to rate-cutting, soldiering, and disputes. He pointed out the deficiencies of many current types of management and wrote that "no system or scheme of management should be considered which does not in the long run give satisfaction to both employer and employee, which does not make it apparent that their best interests are mutual and which does not bring about such thorough and hearty cooperation that they can pull together instead of apart."[65]

Interestingly, the above concept—developing a system of management that simultaneously meets the needs of employers and employees—underlies the thinking of current management theorists with a behavioral science orientation. Taylor's methods for bringing about this rapprochement were crude at best, but he clearly understood the necessity to enlist the active support of workers by offering them something rather than by "driving" them.

The prevalent misrepresentation of Taylor's work has led to the more general assertion that he was unconcerned with the needs and welfare of working people. Cascio, for example, describes Taylor's approach as one in which "almost total attention was focused on the task, and little, if any, focused on the social or personal needs of the individual performing the task. . . ."[66] H. J. Leavitt reports, "Scientific Management was . . . to a great extent a-human, even, it has been argued, inhuman."[67] F. C. Mann and L. R. Hoffman suggest that the psychological fallout of scientific management has been one of "condemning workers to spend their working lives at repetitive, monotonous, and intellectually crushing jobs."[68] J. Ellul tells us that the worker was merely "an object in Taylor's hands" and that Taylor "took nothing into consideration beyond the necessities of production and maximum utilization of the machine, [and] completely ignored the serfdom those factors entail."[69]

Taylorism versus the Hawthorne Studies

Some authors illustrate Taylor's inhumanity by juxtaposing his work with the Hawthorne studies, which they represent as the source of the "human relations" movement in management. For example, Schultz suggests that scientific management's "lack of concern for workers" was replaced by a view that meeting the needs of employees should be a company goal, and identifies this view as emanating from the "Hawthorne and other studies that focused on the workers instead of on production."[70] Terry characteristically presents Taylor as "emphasizing the mechanical and physiological character of management" in contrast to the idea, stemming from the Hawthorne studies, that "people are the important consideration in management."[71]

Taylor's picture of human needs may not have been quite as well developed as ours is today, but he did not ignore the needs he saw and, in fact, tried very hard to take account of them in his system. It is sometimes suggested that the importance of group influences was first discovered in the bank wiring room in the Hawthorne studies and that Taylor was ignorant of the power of groups. In reality, Taylor had considerable insight into group influence. He knew that it was a powerful factor in restriction of production and resistance to change. His efforts to design workers' tasks and set wages on an individual rather than group basis was intended to *overcome* the strength of group influence.

Taylor and the Utilization of Human Talent

Taylor also had a much greater grasp of the importance of effectively using human talent than he is generally given credit for. For example, he saw the folly of using overqualified workers, writing that:

> If the work is of a routine nature in which the same operations are likely to be done over and over again with no great variety and in which there is no apparent prospect of a radical change being made perhaps through a term of years even though the work itself may be complicated in its nature, a man should be selected whose abilities are barely equal to the task. Time and training will fit him for his work.[72]

A criticism frequently leveled at Taylor was that his establishment of a separate planning department robbed workers of the opportunity to think for themselves and be original, independent, and self-reliant. He responded that:

> Those holding this view must take exception to the whole trend of modern industrial development and it appears to the writer that they overlook the real facts in the case. . . . It is true for instance that the planning room and functional foremanship render it possible for an intelligent laborer or helper in time to do much of the work now done by a machinist. Is it not a good thing for the laborer and helper? He is given a higher class of work, which tends to develop him and give him better wages. . . . The demand for men of originality and brains was never so great as it is now and the modern subdivision of labor, instead of dwarfing men, enables them all along the line to rise to a higher plane of efficiency in valuing at the same time more brain work and less monotony.[73]

Taylor apprehended people's need for interesting work and felt that his system addressed that need. However, his approach is characterized in an opposite manner by such authors as Argyris, Bass, and Barrett, who suggest that he advocated rigid, authoritarian organization structures involving the use of such principles as unity of direction, chain of command, span of control, and specialization of tasks.[74] The thrust of such critiques is that Taylor helped construct organizations that conflict with the normal development of the human personality.

Some of the criticisms can easily lead to a considerable confusion about the facts. For example, Edward E. Lawler wrote that "the mechanized assembly line represents the ultimate development of the scientific management approach."[75] Lawler then proceeded to chronicle the problems inherent in such assembly lines, with the implication that Taylor bore ultimate responsibility for those problems. In actuality, Taylor was not responsible for the production-line type of task specialization that Lawler and others ascribe to him. Taylor's work was done almost exclusively in small and medium-size plants manufacturing a variety of items, often to individual order specifications. Never in his career did he apply his system to a production-line situation, nor did he ever advocate installation of a production line. He suggested task specialization only in the sense of separating planning from doing and utilizing functional foremanship.

Taylor *did* advocate standardization and simplification of work methods and, upon observing this aspect of production-line work (for example, at the Ford Motor Company), saw it as consistent with his principles. He was also undoubtedly impressed with the control over work flow and routing of work that the production line offered. However, Taylor often designed varied daily tasks for workers, and he saw no need for specialization as long as it was possible to delineate clearly the dimensions of a complete task.

As for the other three principles attributed to him—span of control, chain of command, and unity of direction—Taylor not only did not advocate these but actually argued against them, especially at the lower levels of supervision. He pointed out that most managerial jobs that developed in accordance with these ideas violated all four of his basic principles concerning the design of work—namely, a large daily task, standard conditions, high pay for success, and clear loss (of job or of pay) in the case of failure. He stated that managers' jobs were not clearly circumscribed and could not be accomplished in a day because standards were unclear; therefore, clear identification of success or failure was impossible.[76] The detailed remedy that he proposed makes clear his opposition to the traditional unity-of-command type of organization structure.

Finally, Taylor has been accused of demonstrating a constricted view of the needs of workers by focusing exclusively on economic returns. A typical comment is: "Taylor represents those who believe that the average workman is dull and has no interests except earning more money."[77] Some writers give Taylor indirect credit for considering employees' other needs but still emphasize his belief that economic needs override all others. For example, Dowling and Sayles say, "Taylor's view of the working man—and for that matter the executive too—as a purely economic animal was always a partial view. His belief that the increased wages made possible by the division of labor would more than offset any loss caused by a shrinkage of the intrinsic inter-est of the job was never as generally palatable as Taylor assumed."[78]

To describe Taylor's view of the working man as a *purely* economic animal is to grossly oversimplify his thinking. Taylor did believe that money played a major role in motivation, but he also was concerned with the nature of the *task* involved. For example, in his testimony during the congressional hearings, Taylor explained his perception of his system of piece-rate pay:

> . . . there is no implied bargain under scientific management that the pay of the man shall be proportional to the number of pieces turned out. There is a new type of bargain, however, and that is this: Under scientific manage-ment we propose at all times to give the workman a perfectly fair and just task. . . . But that the moment we find a new and improved or a better way of doing the work everyone will fall into line and work at once according to the new method.[79]

As Boddewyn points out, "The reward was not for *producing more* —in a spirit of the more you produce the more you earn—but for *car-rying out orders.*"[80] Taylor most often referred to his wage system as the "task and bonus" plan, and his preferred label for scientific man-agement was "task management."

Taylor felt that an "accurate study of the motives which influence men" was needed and suggested that one of the most important areas to investigate was the role played by clearly defined tasks. Being given such a task to perform, he said, "furnishes the workman with a clear-cut standard, by which he can, throughout the day measure his own progress, and the accomplishment of which affords him the greatest satisfaction."[81]

Taylor was emphatic that without the "task idea," his proposed wage system was ineffective. He even wrote: "Perhaps the most prom-inent single element in modern scientific management is the task idea. . . . Scientific management consists very largely in preparing for and carrying out these tasks."[82]

A Continuing Game of Telephone

A more careful reading of Taylor by many of those who have re-ported on his work would have produced a more accurate picture of his system, one more easily integratable with other schools of thought. As a closing note, we offer an example of a particularly sloppy repre-sentation of Taylor that reminds us of the child's game of telephone, in which a message is whispered in the ear of a succession of participants and then announced aloud by the last person in the circle to see just how distorted it has become. In 1960, Daniel Bell wrote the following brief description of the Schmidt story:

> . . . But it was in 1899 that Taylor achieved fame when he taught a Dutchman named Schmidt to shovel forty-seven tons instead of twelve-and-a-half tons of pig iron a day. Every detail of the man's job was specified: the size of the shovel, the bite into the pile, the weight of the scoop, the distance to walk, the arc of the swing and the rest periods that Schmidt should take. By systematically varying each factor, Taylor got the optimum amount of barrow load. By exact calculation, he got the correct response.[83]

Bell apparently confused pig-iron loading, which was performed by picking up pigs (each weighing in excess of ninety pounds) in one's hands, with the *shoveling* of iron ore, with which Taylor also experimented. It is clearly impossible for most of us to raise a shovel loaded with a ninety-pound pig over and over, day after day. Apart from this obvious error, Bell includes in his report a variety of other misunderstandings concerning the incident. Nearly twenty years later, Bell's apocryphal account was repeated, with a few additional inaccuracies, in a textbook on applied psychology by Cascio.[84]

Certainly Taylor has also had his defenders, such as Viteles, Filipetti, and Drucker[85] (although these individuals have not always presented accurate pictures either). However, the critics have been in the majority and have profoundly influenced the prevailing view of Taylor and scientific management as being a hard, engineering, antihumanistic approach that detractors attack and sympathizers feel compelled to defend.

NOTES

1. Frederick W. Taylor, "Principles of Scientific Management." In *Scientific Management* (New York: Harper & Row, 1947), pp. 44–46.
2. Ibid., p. 46.
3. Ibid., p. 48.
4. For example, M. Blum and J. C. Naylor, *Industrial Psychology* (New York: Harper & Row, 1968), pp. 576–577; and R. A. Ryan and P. C. Smith, *Principles of Industrial Psychology* (New York, Ronald Press, 1954), pp. 324–326.
5. H. H. Farquhar, "Positive Contributions of Scientific Management." In E. E. Hunt, *Scientific Management Since Taylor* (New York: McGraw-Hill, 1924), p. 49.
6. Frederick W. Taylor, Testimony before the Special House Committee of the U.S. House of Representatives in 1912, p. 173. Cited in Frederick W. Taylor, *Scientific Management* (New York: Harper & Row, 1947).
7. Frederick W. Taylor to Frank B. Copley, August 19, 1912. Taylor Collection at Stevens Institute of Technology, Hoboken, N. J.

8. Peter F. Drucker, *The Practice of Management* (New York: Harper & Row, 1954), p. 279.
9. Taylor, Testimony, p. 174.
10. Ibid.
11. Ibid., p. 172.
12. R. Bendix, *Work and Authority in Industry* (New York: Wiley, 1956), pp. 286–287.
13. Taylor, Testimony, p. 31.
14. D. Nelson, "Scientific Management, Systematic Management, and Labor, 1880–1915," *Business History Review,* Winter 1974, p. 479.
15. Ibid., p. 486.
16. Ibid.
17. R. F. Hoxie, *Scientific Management and Labor* (New York: Appleton, 1920).
18. H. K. Hathaway, "Logical Steps in Installing the Taylor System of Management," *Industrial Management,* October 1920, p. 95.
19. Frank B. Copley, *Frederick W. Taylor,* Vol. 2 (New York: Harper, 1923), p. 149.
20. Ibid.
21. Taylor, "Principles," p. 88.
22. Frederick W. Taylor, "Shop Management." In *Scientific Management* (New York: Harper & Row, 1947), p. 176.
23. Transcript of an informal talk given at Boxley on June 4, 1907. Taylor Collection.
24. Ibid.
25. Robert Linderman to Frederick W. Taylor, April 17, 1901. Taylor Collection.
26. C. B. Thompson, "Relation of Scientific Management to Labor," *Quarterly Journal of Economics,* February 1916, pp. 311–351.
27. George D. Babcock, *The Taylor System in Franklin Management* (New York: Engineering Magazine Company, 1917), p. 146.
28. Taylor, "Shop Management," pp. 60–61.
29. Ibid., pp. 134–135.
30. Ibid., p. 136.
31. S. Kakar, *Frederick Taylor: A Study in Personality and Innovation* (Cambridge, Mass.: M.I.T. Press, 1970), p. 180.
32. Ibid., p. 40.
33. Taylor, "Principles," p. 142.
34. Quoted in Copley, *Frederick W. Taylor,* Vol. 2, p. 237.
35. Ibid., pp. 237–238.
36. Frank B. Copley, "Frederick W. Taylor: Revolutionist," *The Outlook,* September 1, 1915, p. 1.
37. Kakar, *Frederick Taylor,* p. 2.
38. Quoted in Copley, *Frederick W. Taylor,* Vol. 2, p. 78.
39. Frederick W. Taylor to Henry Towne, November 9, 1911. Taylor Collection.
40. Henry Towne to Frederick W. Taylor, November 10, 1911. Taylor Collection.

41. C. Wrege and A. Perroni, "Taylor's Pig-Tale: An Historical Analysis of Taylor's Pig Iron Experiments," *Academy of Management Journal,* March 1974, p. 6.
42. Copley, *Frederick W. Taylor,* Vol. 1, p. xxv.
43. C. Wrege and A. Stotka, "Cooke Creates a Classic," *Academy of Management Journal,* October 1978, pp. 736–749.
44. Nelson, "Scientific Management, Systematic Management."
45. Taylor, "Shop Management," p. 69.
46. M. Notvony, *Scientific Management and the Unions* (Cambridge, Mass.: Harvard University Press, 1955), p. 51.
47. Hoxie, *Scientific Management and Labor,* appendixes.
48. H. B. Drury, *Scientific Management: A History and Criticism* (New York: Columbia University Press, 1922), p. 27.
49. Ibid.
50. Ibid., p. 29.
51. Taylor, "Shop Management," p. 194.
52. Samuel Haber, *Efficiency and Uplift* (Chicago: University of Chicago Press, 1964), p. 70.
53. Taylor, "Shop Management," p. 188.
54. Ibid.
55. Taylor, Testimony, p. 287.
56. Ibid., p. 166.
57. Ibid., p. 168.
58. Haber, *Efficiency and Uplift,* pp. xi–xii.
59. B. M. Gross, *The Managing of Organizations* (Glencoe, Ill.: Free Press, 1964), pp. 121–136.
60. W. Cascio, *Applied Psychology in Personnel Management* (Reston, Va.: Reston Publishing, 1978), p. 348.
61. L. Siegel and I. Lane, *Psychology in Industrial Organizations* (Homewood, Ill.: Irwin, 1974), p. 265.
62. Rensis Likert, "Motivation and Increased Productivity," *Management Record,* July 1952, Vol. 18, No. 4, pp. 128–131.
63. T. A. Ryan and P. C. Smith, *Principles of Industrial Psychology* (New York: Ronald Press, 1954), p. 327.
64. Hugh Aitken, *Taylorism at the Watertown Arsenal* (Cambridge, Mass.: Harvard University Press, 1970), p. 103.
65. Taylor, "Shop Management," p. 2.
66. Cascio, *Applied Psychology,* p. 348.
67. H. J. Leavitt, "Applied Organizational Change in Industry." In J. G. March, ed., *Handbook of Organizations* (Chicago: Rand-McNally, 1965), p. 1149.
68. F. C. Mann and L. R. Hoffman, *Automation and the Worker* (New York: Holt, 1960), p. 68.
69. J. Ellul, *The Technological Society* (New York: Vantage, 1964), pp. 264, 350.
70. D. Schultz, *Psychology and Industry Today* (New York: Macmillan, 1978), p. 231.
71. G. Terry, *Principles of Management* (Homewood, Ill.: Irwin, 1968), p. 9.
72. Taylor, "Shop Management," p. 141.

73. Ibid., pp. 146–147.
74. Chris Argyris, "Organizational Leadership and Participative Management," *Journal of Business,* January 1955, pp. 1–7; B. Bass and G. Barrett, *Man, Work, and Organizations* (Boston: Allyn & Bacon, 1974), p. 112.
75. E. E. Lawler, *Motivation in Work Organizations* (Monterey, Calif.: Brooks/ Cole, 1973), p. 148.
76. Taylor, "Shop Management," pp. 94–109.
77. M. Blum and J. C. Naylor, *Industrial Psychology* (New York: Harper & Row, 1968), p. 578.
78. W. Dowling and L. Sayles, *How Managers Motivate* (New York: McGraw-Hill, 1971), p. 19.
79. Taylor, Testimony, pp. 232–233.
80. J. Boddewyn, "F. W. Taylor Revisited," *Academy of Management Journal,* August 1961, p. 105.
81. Taylor, "Principles," pp. 120–121.
82. Ibid., p. 39.
83. Daniel Bell, *The End of Ideology* (Glencoe, Ill.: Free Press, 1960), p. 232.
84. Cascio, *Applied Psychology,* p. 347.
85. M. Viteles, *The Science of Work* (New York: Norton, 1934), p. 49; G. Filipetti, *Industrial Management in Transition* (Chicago: Irwin, 1946); Peter F. Drucker, "The Coming Rediscovery of Scientific Management," *Conference Board Record,* June 1976, pp. 23–27.

4

The Legacy of Scientific Management

Few people would dispute the lasting impact of Taylor's ideas. His work strongly contributed to a rich and continuing tradition in management thinking, and his techniques became widely utilized in organizations. Much folklore, and many beliefs about how to manage organizations, were produced. His followers founded the Taylor Society, which today is known as the Society for the Advancement of Management. The society's Taylor Key Award is one of the most distinguished honors a management theorist can receive.

The legacy has, of course, been filtered through the distortions described in the preceding chapter. Some of the myths generated have become translated into rituals and have taken on a reality of their own. Some have even given rise to cults, a problem that has haunted many other management theorists.

The Work of Taylor's Close Associates

Taylor's legacy has naturally been influenced by the subsequent work of his close associates, who were reported to be "very faithful to his teachings" when acting as consultants.[1] However, after Taylor's death, some of them began to write and speak about scientific management in ways that altered the original concepts. Over time, Taylor himself had shifted his emphasis in some respects, but he had always seen scientific management as (1) a method of business improvement, (2) a science, and (3) a social program. In the years following Taylor's death, some of his disciples separated and went their own directions, often emphasizing just one dimension instead of all three.

Of his major disciples, Carl Barth and H. K. Hathaway strayed from Taylor's thinking the least. Henry Gantt and Frank Gilbreth both introduced additions and revisions, and were eventually cast out by the more orthodox members of the Taylor Society. Barth was especially rigid in his devotion to Taylor, and his position contributed to the split among Taylor's followers.

Barth and Hathaway—as well as Cooke—kept Taylorism alive as an applied business service. Gilbreth became the representative of the science of Taylorism, and Gantt took up the task of emphasizing its social implications. Whereas Gantt and Gilbreth went beyond the mechanics of Taylorism, Barth did not. Barth's focus may partially explain why, in some current industrial engineering circles, the mechanics rather than the underlying philosophy of scientific management are emphasized.

Gilbreth's work must also have contributed to this emphasis. Gilbreth had a strong interest in eliminating unnecessary motions and selecting the best work methods. He became convinced that Taylor was a great man, and Taylor, in turn, often praised Gilbreth's work in the bricklaying trade. Taylor, however, later became very upset with the emphasis that Gilbreth gave to motion study. Taylor regarded motion study as only a minor extension of time study. Gilbreth was disappointed with this attitude, and each man felt the other did not understand his work. The break finally came when, in response to a complaint from a Gilbreth client, Taylor sent "a more dependable follower" (Cooke) to take over Gilbreth's job. Gilbreth went on to develop highly sophisticated methods for breaking down jobs into fixed time components, and he emphasized to a much greater extent than Taylor the "one best way" concept of doing work.

Gantt, as already noted, developed the social reform implications of Taylor's system. As early as 1908 he had shown a strong interest in issues of human welfare, when he presented a paper to the American Society of Mechanical Engineers emphasizing that "workers were first of all human beings and not machines . . . and that they should be led, not driven, by management."[2] Gantt later became fascinated with the idea of substituting facts for opinions, and concluded that the engineer, a man of facts, should be the architect of social reform.

Gantt came to believe that the best place to strike at inefficiency was not in the work methods of the laborer but in those of management. Thus he developed what we know as Gantt production charts, cost systems, and related techniques. All were attempts to set standards for management's work analogous to the stopwatch standards for the worker.

Later Gantt attacked the profit system itself and showed admiration for the Soviet Union's economic system. In the late 1920s Walter Polakor, one of Gantt's followers, went to Russia to help map Stalin's first five-year plan on Gantt charts.

In their own ways, then, several of Taylor's followers altered his original concepts and created different impressions of the nature of scientific management. In considering the contemporary legacy and impact of Taylor's work, we will first discuss the methodological implications and then the broader social impact of his ideas.

Methodological Implications

The most obvious methodological descendants of Taylor's work are the functions performed by industrial engineers and other specialists in the area of work measurement and time study. Taylor's work gave great impetus to the establishment of industrial engineering as a profession. George Soule wrote: "As a separate movement [scientific management] virtually disappeared in the Great Depression of the 1930s, but by that time knowledge of it had become widespread in industry and its methods and philosophy were commonplaces in many schools of engineering and business management."[3] Certainly the founding of the American Institute of Industrial Engineers in 1948 owes much to Taylor's work. His techniques formed the basis for the principles and methods of time study and other work-measurement techniques involved in industrial engineering.

Today many management groups sponsor training programs that teach these same techniques. Labor unions train their representatives in the same kinds of methods and work-analysis skills. The Industrial Management Society presents time-and-motion-study clinics in which government, labor, and industry review current developments in methods of analyzing work and wage payments. The Society for the Advancement of Management, formed in 1936 through a merger of the Society of Industrial Engineers and the Taylor Society, has presented its highest award, the Taylor Key, to such illustrious people as Peter Drucker and the late Fritz Roethlisberger. American Management Associations offers its annual Gantt Memorial Medal to the most distinguished contributor in industrial management.

Scientific management also became influential in the thinking of noncapitalists. Lenin had an active interest in the application of such techniques. In a 1918 article in *Pravda,* he wrote:

> We should try out every scientific and progressive suggestion of the Taylor System. . . . To learn how to work—this problem the Soviet authority should present to the people in all its comprehensiveness. The last word of capitalism in this respect, the Taylor System, as well as all progressive measures of

capitalism, combine the refined cruelty of bourgeois exploitation and a number of most valuable scientific attainments in the analysis of mechanical motions during work, in dismissing superfluous and useless motions, in determining the most correct methods of work, the best systems of accounting and control, etc. The Soviet Republic must adopt valuable and scientific technical advance in this field. The possibility of socialism will be determined by our success in combining the Soviet rule and the Soviet organization of management with the latest progressive measures of capitalism. We must introduce in Russia the study and teaching of the new Taylor System in its systematic trial and adaptation.[4]

The literature on work measurement and on work-methods analysis is vast. In a 1919 book on the subject, *Fatigue Study,* Frank Gilbreth gave Taylor the following tribute: "It is the great work of Dr. Taylor to divide an operation, that is, a piece of work to be measured, into units for timing with a stopwatch and to separate rest units from work units. From its beginning scientific management has recognized the importance of the part played by fatigue."[5] About twenty years later, W. T. Holmes published *Applied Time and Motion Study,* a book that grew out of Taylor's influence and offers a clear, step-by-step approach to the use of motion study.[6] Almost thirty years later, in 1965, Karger and Bayha published *Engineered Work Measurement* and acknowledged their Taylor heritage. The authors advocate methods of time measurement which, they report, are actively used in the United States, Canada, France, Holland, England, Sweden, Switzerland, Japan, and many other countries. These authors express the opinion that "much of what Taylor said is as valid today as it was when it was originally penned."[7]

This literature is, of course, matched by widespread utilization of Taylor's principles by management engineers and industrial engineers. In almost any firm with a substantial manufacturing capability, trained industrial engineers establish standards and work methods. Most large clerical organizations, such as banks and insurance companies, also have work-measurement groups. Some consulting firms engage in this type of work, either implementing work measurement directly or training client personnel to do so.

Work Simplification

In the early 1930s the concept of work simplification was introduced by industrial engineer Allen Morgenson.[8] (First use of the term "work simplification" itself is generally attributed to Professor Erwin Schill.) Work simplification emphasizes that the Taylor/Gilbreth techniques of motion and time study should be utilized within the framework of worker participation. The purpose is to inspire members of an organization's work force to make a concerted attack on costs by examining the way they have been working and then, using work charting and analysis techniques, coming up with suggestions for improvement.*

Work Improvement

The term "work improvement" has been used in different ways. Industrial engineer Guy Close writes that a variety of activities— including operations improvement, job enlargement, work simplification, and methods work of all kinds—should come under this heading. He defines work improvement as "an organized approach for solving work problems and reducing costs through the use of systematic analysis and higher common sense."[11] Close lists ten specific objectives of work improvement, all relating to efficiency and none to worker satisfaction or interest. He suggests that the broad objective of work improvement is "to make the operation pay."

Close makes elaborate use of flowcharts, operations charts, right- and left-hand motion charts, process diagrams, work-sampling approaches, work-distribution studies, and time balancing. His approach illustrates how Taylorism suggested further methods of gathering and organizing information for the purpose of improving costs. It is also symbolic of the extent to which Taylor's concern for meeting the needs of employees has been subsequently segregated from the utilization of his analysis techniques.

Records Management

An example of the far-reaching implications of Taylor's approach is found in a 1972 article by Brickford entitled "The Relationship of Records Management Activities to the Field of Business History." Brickford notes: "The intellectual basis of records management as well as the administrative problems it seeks to solve owes much to the application of F. W. Taylor's principles of scientific management to the office."[12]

Brickford's article explains how records management can help people who are interested in business history to organize and utilize their material. Taylor's legacy apparently includes contributions to methods of organizing information of many kinds, including archives and historical material.

---

* Detailed descriptions of the procedures involved can be found in *American Management Association Management Handbook*[9] and in Reynolds's *Work Simplification for Everyone.*[10]

Mass Production

There has been disagreement about whether Taylor was influential in the development of mass production. Burlingame, writing in 1949, credited scientific management and Taylor with providing the tools necessary for Henry Ford's foray into mass production.[13] He argued that both Taylor's time-study techniques and Gilbreth's motion studies were absolutely essential to Ford's process—time study to determine how to divide up tasks so that the line could move continuously, and motion study because this approach had shown a need (through the bricklaying studies of Gilbreth) to bring work "waist high," eliminating bending and stooping that would have made mass production speed impossible.

The other side of the issue has been most clearly expressed by Charles Sorenson, a long-time executive at Ford, who stated, "One of the hardest-to-down myths about the evolution of mass production at Ford is one which credits much of the accomplishment to scientific management. No one at Ford, not Mr. Ford, not Flanders, not Wills, not Pete Morton, not I was acquainted with the theories of the 'father of scientific management'—Fredrick W. Taylor."[14]

Taylor's biographer, Frank Copley, reports that Taylor visited Ford's Highland Park plant for the first time in 1914 and expressed surprise to find that Detroit industrialists "had undertaken to install the principles of scientific management without the aid of experts." This, combined with Sorenson's assertion that none of the top executives at Ford were acquainted with Taylor's theories, indicates that the rise of the assembly line occurred independently of scientific management.

In reality the key insights involved in establishing the assembly line were different from, though compatible with, those of Taylor. Taylor's studies dealt with work that involved producing pieces one at a time. The assembly line involves a concept that seems superficially related: interchangeable parts. The transfer of parts from one piece to another, without a need for further adjustment, makes an assembly line feasible. However, neither the concept of assembly lines nor that of interchangeable parts is found in any of Taylor's writings.

Though scientific management and mass production are often confused, each embodies different insights into the production process. When combined, they have an additive influence. Peter Drucker asserts that the legacy of Taylor includes, ultimately, automation. He suggests that automation is a logical extension of Taylor's scientific management, stating that "once operations have been analyzed as if they were machine operations and organized as such (and scientific management did this successfully), they should be capable of being performed by machines rather than by hand."[15] Drucker occasionally sounds a bit euphoric about Taylor and overstates the case. A more reasonable assessment is that scientific management, coupled with the logic of mass production, may have contributed to the development of automation.

Organization Design

Taylor's concept of separating the planning of work from its execution has had significant methodological implications. Such separation is prominent in industry today, with the existence of production planning departments. If Taylorism is credited with this general innovation, then the methodological fallout of Taylorism is extremely broad. The idea of separating the planning and doing of work leads not only to the installation of separate production planning departments but to the widespread practice of placing most decision-making at management levels.

Industrial Psychology, Human Relations, and Personnel Management

A direct link exists between Taylor's work and the fields of industrial psychology and personnel management. Hugo Munsterberg's *Psychology and Industrial Efficiency,* generally regarded as the first textbook on industrial psychology, presents scientific management as integral to, and a foundation of, this field. Munsterberg wrote that the purpose of industrial psychology is to discover "how to find the best possible man, how to produce the best possible work, and how to secure the best possible effects."[16] As examples of such efforts he cited Taylor's work with pig-iron loading, shoveling, and bicycle ball inspecting, as well as Gilbreth's bricklaying studies. The link between scientific management and industrial psychology is thus direct and acknowledged.

Similarly, Loren Baritz asserts that Taylor and his followers first demonstrated that management could expect a definite return from the investigation and analysis of human behavior, and that this demonstration led a few bold managers to allow the earliest industrial psychologists to investigate ways of increasing human effectiveness in industry. Baritz states, "For this the industrial psychologist should be eternally in debt to Taylor's movement."[17]

Baritz suggests that scientific management not only conditioned the industrial climate for the psychologists but significantly determined the direction, scope, and nature of the research done in that field. He points out that engineers had raised most of the problems with which the industrial psychologists later grappled. Further, scientific management gave to industrial psychology its purpose: assisting industry to achieve the ends it defined for itself in the most efficient way. This objective became characteristic not only of industrial psychology but of the later forms of human relations approaches and applied management sciences.

Taylor was in great part responsible for the very existence of the field of personnel management. Milton discusses Taylorism's contribution to the development of personnel management extensively.[18] Taylor proposed that a disciplinarian handle cases of lateness, absence, and adjustment of wages, and suggested that this person also handle the employment function. He wrote: "The knowledge and character of the qualities needed for various positions acquired in disciplining the men should be useful in selecting them for employment—this man should of course consult constantly with the various foremen both in his function as disciplinarian and in the employment of men."[19] Milton suggests that this particular idea of Taylor's was the precursor of the personnel manager, who did not appear until the 1920s.

Milton also emphasizes that Taylor's system replaced a kind of *laissez-faire* rationale of personnel administration that had been prevalent before the advent of scientific management. Traditionally, a worker who was unable to perform a task had simply been discharged, the assumption being it was the worker's problem. Scientific management maintained that *management* was responsible for selecting the right people, figuring out the best ways to do the various jobs, and teaching employees to do them. These responsibilities, of course, are also precursors of contemporary personnel functions. As Gardner and Moore put it, examination of a standard textbook in the personnel field "will show how personnel management developed out of the Taylor model. . . . Personnel management is typically concerned with job analysis, selection, training, wage and salary administration and supervision. The close relationship of these interests to the Taylor model is immediately apparent."[20]

Assessments of Scientific Management's Social Impact and Implications

As we have seen, Taylor had a pervasive impact on the techniques of work analysis and on management systems. Indeed, some critics have charged that Taylor's work is best characterized as a collection of techniques that are devoid of any meaningful social philosophy apart from lip service to the economic climate of the day. However, it can be argued that Taylor's influence has gone far beyond managerial techniques, affecting the nature of relationships within organizations and even the character of our society.

Peter Drucker has for years been one of the staunchest advocates of Taylor's contributions. He maintains, "Indeed scientific management is all but a systematic philosophy of worker and work. Altogether, it may well be the most powerful as well as the most lasting contribution America has made to Western thought since the Federalist papers."[21]

In Drucker's eyes, Taylor deserves credit for making a large contribution to the control of costs and inflation. "Taylor solved, in essence, the problem of production; as long as we cannot produce we need not spend time or thought on distribution let alone on human relations." Taylor "produced a revolutionary cut in the cost of manufactured goods, often to one-tenth or even one-twentieth of what they had been before." Drucker states that Taylor thereby "made possible sharp increases in wages while at the same time lowering the total cost of the product."[22] Drucker argues strongly for the humanism of Taylor's system, writing that: "Hitherto lower costs of a finished product had always meant lower wages to the worker producing it, but scientific management preached the contrary: that lower costs should mean higher wages and higher income for the worker; to bring this about was indeed Taylor's main intent and that of his disciples. Unlike many earlier technologists they were motivated as much by social as by technical considerations."[23]

This reading of Taylor—that it was he who first suggested a mutually beneficial synergy between the needs of individuals and the needs of organizations—is one that was recognized as early as 1915, the year in which Taylor died. Edward Jones presented an eloquent discussion of the importance of a person's passion for the work itself as a source of motivation and efficiency. He concluded that the scientific management people understood this idea and were trying to promote it in their work.[24]

Any detailed examination of Taylor's work shows that Taylor did, in fact, intend for scientific management to meet both the needs of individuals and the needs of organizations. He is thus a forerunner of such current management theorists as Chris Argyris, Peter Drucker, Douglas McGregor, Abraham Maslow, Rensis Likert, and Frederick Herzberg, who all espouse the concept that well-managed, well-designed organizations can simultaneously meet individuals' needs for growth and companies' needs for productive efficiency.

Another assessment of Taylor's contribution comes from labor expert William Gomberg.[25] Gomberg points out that two Taylor followers, Robert Valentine and Morris Cooke, tried, with some success, to involve workers more in decision-making. Gomberg believes that these and other Taylor followers indicated ways in which work-measurement techniques could be converted from substitutes for and threats to collective bargaining into tools for collective bargaining. Thus Gomberg suggests that the heritage of the scientific management movement includes the sophistication of modern collective bargaining. Such an argument is of particular interest given the historical view that Taylor's work was a threat to unionism and the process of collective bargaining. Drucker further embellishes Gomberg's point:

> To have made the manual worker productive is indeed the greatest achievement of management to date. Frederick Winslow Taylor's scientific management is often attacked these days (though mostly by people who have not read Taylor). But it was his insistence on studying work that underlies the affluence of today's developed countries: it raised the productivity of manual work to the point where yesterday's laborer, a proletarian condemned to an income at the margin of subsistence by the iron law of wages into complete uncertainty of employment from day to day, has become the semi-skilled worker of today's mass production industries with a middle-class standard of living with a guaranteed job or income security. Taylor thereby found the way out of the apparently hopeless impasse of 19th century class war between the capitalist exploitation of the laboring man and the proletarian dictatorship.[26]

Drucker is obviously less than reserved in his admiration of Taylor. At one point, he writes, "Taylor made obsolete both 'isms' of the 19th century, capitalism and communism. In fact, he solved what the 19th century considered *the* social question: he showed that the basic problem is not who should get the immutable pie but how to make the pie larger. . . . I do not think it extravagant to consider Frederick Taylor as the one relevant social philosopher of this, our industrial civilization."[27] Drucker's enthusiasm pushes the case for Taylor's social contributions as far as the limits of credibility will allow.

Drucker's enthusiasm aside, there is convincing evidence that Taylor has had a broad intellectual influence on the social philosophy of industrial society. The fact that the methods of Taylorism were utilized by Western industrialists and Lenin alike testifies to the scope of his thinking on the problems of production. He truly was, as Copley stated, "no mere tinker of business systems."

Taylor's view of himself in his later years—as a man with the social mission of resolving the conflicting economic interests of labor and management—had come a long way from his efforts as a young gang boss to eliminate soldiering. His initial motivation had not been humanistic but to increase production. His experiences had convinced him that high performance was not attained through fear and coercion. He sought a system that would increase production and could be implemented in an atmosphere of cooperation rather than conflict. Even as a young man, he realized that achieving this would require integration of the needs of workers with those of the organization. Throughout his life he staunchly believed that if a system was properly managed, most workers would be cooperative.

Taylor was not an anti-humanist. He did, however, believe that conventional management approaches reinforced a natural tendency toward laziness in most people. He held this opinion about managers as well as workers. Consequently, he intentionally developed a system that removed most of the self-control and freedom of choice from work. He believed this would free workers from the arbitrary authority of management and improve their economic situation.

Taylor saw the heart of his system as the mental revolution that had to take place among both managers and workers. In today's language, Taylor sought nothing less than a cultural change within organizations. However, he remained baffled as to how it could be achieved. Taylor was no more successful in achieving his "mental revolution" than today's specialists in organizational change have been. Nor did he succeed in creating an atmosphere of trust and cooperation between management and workers. The legacy, profound as it is, has not corresponded with the intentions of the man.

Scientific management has undergone significant development and revision over the years. Of all the misinterpretations and distortions we have cited, the trend to which Taylor would have probably most strongly objected is the separation of technique from theory. Taylor's work often appears to have been a collection of techniques because that aspect of his work received widest application while his theory and motives were obscured or misrepresented. His name has taken on the authoritarian mystique of the "engineering view" in management. Yet it is abundantly clear that Taylor's position was much more complex. As a theorist and practitioner he was a systematizer of organizations. As a person he was a compulsive elitist, with little tolerance for others. However, he laid much of the blame for "the labor problem" at the feet of arbitrary, authoritarian management practices. Having looked at the complexities of Taylor and Taylorism, we will next consider another development in the line of management thought.

NOTES

1. D. Nelson, "Scientific Management, Systematic Management, and Labor, 1880-1915," *Business History Review,* Winter 1974, p. 490.

2. "Henry L. Gantt: Management Pioneer," by the editors of *Systems and Procedures Journal,* July-August 1963, pp. 19–21.
3. George Soule, *Economic Forces in American History* (New York: Harper & Row, 1952), p. 241.
4. N. Lenin, "The Urgent Problems of the Soviet Rule," *Pravda,* April 20, 1918, pp. 41–42.
5. Frank Gilbreth, *Fatigue Study* (New York: Macmillan, 1919), p. 10.
6. W. T. Holmes, *Applied Time and Motion Study* (New York: Ronald Press, 1938).
7. D. W. Karger and F. H. Bayha, *Engineered Work Measurement* (New York: Industrial Press, 1965).
8. Allen H. Morgenson, *Common Sense Applied to Motion and Time Study* (New York: McGraw-Hill, 1932).
9. R. Moore, ed., *American Management Association Management Handbook* (New York: American Management Association, 1970), pp. 33–50.
10. C. Reynolds, *Work Simplification for Everyone* (Coatesville, Pa.: Pyramid Publishing, 1962).
11. Guy Close, *Work Improvement* (New York: Wiley, 1960), p. 11.
12. M. Brickford, "The Relationship of Records Management Activities to the Field of Business History," *Business History Review,* Summer 1972, p. 221.
13. R. Burlingame, *Backgrounds of Power* (New York: Scribner's, 1949).
14. Charles Sorenson, *My Forty Years with Ford* (New York: Wiley, 1956), p. 41.
15. Peter F. Drucker, *Technology, Management and Society* (New York: Harper & Row, 1970), p. 81.
16. Hugo Munsterberg, *Psychology and Industrial Efficiency* (Boston: Houghton Mifflin, 1913), p. 24.
17. Loren Baritz, *The Servants of Power* (Middletown, Conn.: Wesleyan University Press, 1960).
18. C. R. Milton, *Ethics and Expediency in Personnel Management* (Columbia: University of South Carolina Press, 1970).
19. Frederick W. Taylor, "Shop Management." In Frederick W. Taylor, *Scientific Management* (New York: Harper & Row, 1947), p. 119.
20. B. Gardner and D. G. Moore, *Human Relations in Industry* (Homewood, Ill.: Irwin, 1964), p. 86.
21. Peter F. Drucker, *The Practice of Management* (New York: Harper & Row, 1954), p. 280.
22. Peter F. Drucker, "Frederick Taylor: The Professional Management Pioneer," *Advanced Management Journal,* October, 1967, p. 8.
23. Drucker, *Technology, Management and Society,* pp. 79–80.
24. Edward D. Jones, "The Relations of Education to Industrial Efficiency," *American Economic Review,* March 1915.
25. William Gomberg, "The Impact on Labor of More 'Science' in Management," *Conference Board Record,* June 1976, pp. 28–31.
26. Drucker, "Frederick Taylor," p. 10.
27. Ibid., p. 9.

Suggested Readings for Part One

Aitken, H. *Taylorism at the Watertown Arsenal.* Cambridge, Mass.: Harvard University Press, 1970.

Bendix, R. *Work and Authority in Industry.* New York: Wiley, 1956.

Copley, F. B. *Frederick W. Taylor* (two volumes). New York: Harper, 1923.

Haber, S. *Efficiency and Uplift.* Chicago: University of Chicago Press, 1964.

Hunt, E. E. *Scientific Management Since Taylor.* New York: McGraw-Hill, 1924.

Kakar, S. *Frederick Taylor: A Study in Personality and Innovation.* Cambridge, Mass.: M.I.T. Press, 1970.

Nadworny, M. *Scientific Management and the Unions.* Cambridge, Mass.: Harvard University Press, 1955.

Nelson, D. "Scientific Management, Systematic Management, and Labor, 1880–1915." *Business History Review,* Winter 1974, pp. 479–500.

————. *Managers and Workers: Origins of the New Factory System in the United States, 1880–1920.* Madison: University of Wisconsin Press, 1975.

Wrege, C., and A. Perroni. "Taylor's Pig Tale: An Historical Analysis of Taylor's Pig-Iron Experiments." *Academy of Management Journal,* March 1974, pp. 6–27.

PART TWO

Hawthorne and the
Human Relations Movement

5

Hawthorne and the Emergence of Human Relations

Textbooks on organization theory generally agree that the Hawthorne studies represent the foundation stone of the human relations movement in industry. Few workplace experiments have had such an impact on theory and practice.

In *Management and the Worker,* the most widely read report of the research, Fritz Roethlisberger and William Dickson concluded that none of the data from various Hawthorne experiments "gave the slightest substantiation to the theory that the worker is primarily motivated by economic interest."[1] For many readers that observation was the opening volley of what was to become behavioral science's continually escalating attack on the concept of "economic man."

The conceptual guidance in interpreting the Hawthorne studies came primarily from Elton Mayo. In Roethlisberger's words:

Mayo was an adventurer in the realm of ideas. The Hawthorne researches provided him with unusual opportunity to test his ideas in the industrial arena. Executives of the company came to him because they could not interpret their findings. He gave them an interpretation which later achieved recognition by having not his name, but the company's name—the Hawthorne effect—given to it.

Again and again Mayo performed this function of interpretation. The data were not his; the results were not his; the original hypotheses and questions were not his; but as the researches continued, the interpretations of what the results meant and the new questions and hypotheses that emerged from them were his. Also, the way of thinking which he brought to the researches and which finally gave them a sense of direction and purpose was his.[2]

A principal theme in Mayo's theoretical work was the importance of social skills in an industrial society, especially skill in recognizing and alleviating the mental preoccupations of individuals and the false perceptions that result from such preoccupations. For Mayo, an ability to do this was closely linked to what was perhaps his most strongly felt intellectual concern: the need to elicit collaborative effort in society and thus maintain social cohesiveness.

Mayo's influence has extended over a wide range of research. Some studies that supplement or extend the conclusions arrived at in the Hawthorne research are William F. Whyte's studies of human relations in the hotel and restaurant industries and of the impact of money on motivation,[3] W. Lloyd Warner's research into the social system of the community and factory,[4] and Donald Roy's studies on worker restriction of output.[5]

The development of these various researches was certainly not linear. Sometimes the perspectives underlying different research studies were even antagonistic to one another. The common denominator of all the early research was an emphasis on firsthand personal observation—what Mayo repeatedly referred to as painstaking, firsthand acquaintance with the subject matter. What emerges from the research is a picture of social, as opposed to economic, man. The popularization of the Hawthorne studies created an interested and enthusiastic audience for the new human relations orientation.*

Mayo's line of research stemmed from his psychoanalytical orientation, started with a focus on compulsive "overthinking" of situations by individuals, and branched into an anthropological concern with the social setting of the workplace.

The impact on managerial practices was significant. Although management initially resisted the recommended emphasis on "people skills," gradually company after company began to introduce human relations training as a part of management development and personnel programs. A new industry was born as human relations consultants found a growing market for their services. Industrial psychologists were no longer retained only for job analysis and employment screening. Instead, they provided methods designed to help supervisors deal with a wide range of job-related people problems. Human relations became more than a school of thought: it developed into a profitable industry.

Thus, the Hawthorne studies occupy a prominent niche in the land-

---

*The theories of Kurt Lewin, developed independently of Mayo's theories, led to the subsequent "group dynamics" approach and also made important contributions to the acceptance of a human relations orientation in industry.

scape of management theories. They are discussed in nearly all basic management courses and included in almost every standard management text. A host of disciplines ranging from industrial engineering to sociology take the Hawthorne research into account. The Hawthorne studies represent a striking event: a research effort that seemingly pulled together a number of intellectual currents and established a school of thought that itself became divided into many subschools. The studies were, perhaps, previously equaled only by Taylorism in their impact on industrial relations.

Criticisms of the Hawthorne Studies

The Hawthorne studies were not without critics. They have been attacked frequently—most intensively during the late 1940s and 1950s—with much of the criticism being theoretical in nature and directed at the philosophy of Elton Mayo.

A major source of contention between Mayo and his critics was his emphasis on cooperation as the central problem confronting industrial society. In Mayo's view, industrial society was characterized by increasing technological means for producing economic goods and a decreasing capability for eliciting collaboration. Mayo often quoted extensively from Brooks Adams's *Theory of Social Revolutions,* noting Adams's argument that industrialism has stimulated considerable progress in technological and specialized research but has produced no similar development of administrative or executive capacity. Mayo agreed with Adams's conclusion that "the relative overstimulation of the scientific mind has now become an actual menace to order because of the inferiority of the administrative intelligence."[6] Mayo maintained that only through skill in diagnosing the social aspects of working situations could managers elicit the cooperation necessary for effective organization.

Some critics, such as Clark Kerr, argued that "accommodated conflict" is characteristic of a healthy, free society. To Kerr, Mayo's emphasis on the need for universal collaboration was a move away from liberty and toward totalitarianism. Kerr summed up the feelings of many of Mayo's critics when he wrote: "Mr. Mayo assumes what he has yet to prove: That there is a natural community between worker and manager."[7] Other critics directly charged Mayo with a pro-management bias. They felt his objective was a situation in which workers were placated and manipulated into conforming to management's goals and objectives.

Mayo was also attacked for failing to consider the larger institutional framework that shapes the basic nature of conflict within the factory.[8] The problems Mayo grappled with, it was charged, reflect the social dynamics of the ecomomic system and generally cannot be satisfactorily resolved between worker and supervisor. Some critics, in seeking to illustrate Mayo's blindness as a social theorist, cited his failure to recognize that the significant issues in industrial relations were being taken out of the plant and placed on the bargaining table. They noted that the crucial interface was not so much between supervisor and employee as between the complex institutions of corporation and union. Mayo was also criticized for his tendency to examine the individual solely within the context of the workplace.

In fact, Mayo's writings tended to generate as many negative interpretations as they did positive ones. Mayo wrote with a broad brush, describing what in his mind were the significant forces shaping industrial civilization. His work, in which he drew selectively from empirical research to illustrate his themes, provided the initial social philosophy of human relations. Since the philosophy was broad, it drew broad criticisms. It continues to do so with the objections occasionally having a strong Marxist overtone.

More specific criticism has been directed toward the Hawthorne research itself—criticism that challenges both the data and the way the data were interpreted by Roethlisberger and Dickson. Some of these challenges of the research are convincing and damage the credibility of the studies, yet they have received relatively little attention in textbooks discussing the Hawthorne work. The criticisms, scattered sparsely in different journals, have been overshadowed by the persuasive conclusions advanced by advocates of the studies—conclusions that have become part of the conventional wisdom on management. Only very recently have textbooks begun to shift their interpretations, in some instances noting that the data might be seen as somewhat supportive of the "economic man" perspective of the worker.[9] Defenders of Mayo's interpretation argue that viewing the research in this way misses the original insight the studies provided.[10]

What actually did take place at Hawthorne? To what extent were the positions adopted by later human relations theorists supported by the data from Hawthorne? How reliable, and how accurate, were the popular interpretations of the research? Answers to these questions must begin with a description of the studies themselves.

Introduction to the Hawthorne Studies: The Illumination Experiments

Many managers associate the term "Hawthorne" with a series of lighting experiments. In actuality, the lighting studies were only a part of the research undertaken at the Western Electric Company, and did not figure substantially in the subsequent analysis and reporting of data by the Harvard group. However, they received most of the subsequent publicity.

The initial impetus for the studies came from a controversy following the development of the tungsten lamp.* This lamp provided more light per watt, and its widespread deployment posed a threat to the revenues of electrical companies. In 1909 the companies began campaigns for increased lighting levels in the workplace, the effect of which would, of course, be to sustain levels of electric consumption.

In 1918 the electrical companies began sponsoring tests, the results of which supported their contention that increased lighting leads to higher productivity. However, industrial executives remained skeptical of the findings, and in 1923 the General Electric Company funded a series of studies to be conducted by the Committee on Industrial Lighting (CIL). The CIL selected Charles Snow to conduct the illumination experiments at the Hawthorne plant of Western Electric in Chicago. Wrege reports that committee memoranda record that Hawthorne was selected for the tests in part because of the plant superintendent's interest along with that of his assistant in the effect of illumination both on employees and on productivity.

Between 1924 and 1927, Snow conducted three major sets of studies, utilizing both control and test groups. The results were inconclusive, showing no consistent, direct relationship between intensity of illumination and output rate. However, during the experiments there was an *overall* increase in production, whether a particular test involved an increase or decrease in illumination. Even more bewildering was the fact that output increased in the control groups—groups in which no change at all had been made—as well as in the test groups.

Snow's close observation of the initial test groups led him to conclude that factors other than illumination were affecting production. He cited "(1) social pressures used by foremen to increase production; (2) physiological and psychological factors; and (3) influence of home environment."[12] After Snow communicated these observations to the plant superintendent, Western Electric undertook studies of the impact of supervision upon worker efficiency. These studies were conducted during the summer of 1925 with the cooperation of Snow and with the active involvement of his assistant, Homer Hibarger. Hibarger, who was regarded as having a friendly, outgoing personality, supervised the workers in the test. During the period of the studies a gradual increase in productivity was reported.

---

*The account that follows is based on an article by C. D. Wrege,[11] who painstakingly located and analyzed the original documents pertaining to the illumination studies.

In the second CIL series of tests, conducted during 1926, the illumination levels were increased for two groups of women operators. Another group served as a control group; for this group, no conditions at all were changed when the tests began. A fourth group was tested for the psychological effects of being in the experiment. The women in this group were given the impression that they were in a test group, but the illumination level (unknown to them) actually remained unchanged. A comparison of results between the two test groups and the psychological group showed no evidence that illumination level had an independent influence on production. These tests led Snow to conclude that "psychological factors attached to the test conditions completely masked any effect of illumination on production."[13]

Hibarger then conducted his own special illumination test—one resting on the premise that some work could be done with almost no light, as long as the workers had a cooperative attitude. Two willing operators were provided with working facilities in a room that could be made completely dark. The illumination was gradually reduced to 0.06 of a foot candle (approximately moonlight). During the reduction, production generally *increased* until the 0.102 level, when a slight decrease occurred, and at the 0.06 level there was a drastic decline in output.

Hibarger's results influenced the general CIL tests, which were then conducted with less illumination. The operators protested vigorously, but output declined only slightly. Convinced that a critical point of illumination was impossible to determine, the researchers began to focus more directly on how supervision affected output.

At the conclusion of all these tests, the chairman of the CIL was ready to let the project, with its inconclusive results, wind down into obscurity. But Hibarger had arrived at two conclusions: first, that illumination had only a minor impact on productivity; second, that supervision definitely did affect productivity but the nature of the effect was as yet unknown. He convinced the assistant superintendent at Hawthorne that if a small group of workers were placed in a carefully controlled environment and their work habits were carefully examined, the reasons for increased and decreased production could be determined. This study was to include the potentially significant influence of fatigue. A basic question to be addressed was the reason for output dropping in the afternoon. Thus in 1927 the relay assembly test room studies, which will be discussed later, were gotten underway.

These, then, were the widely reported lighting experiments which managers most often view as the major thrust of the Hawthorne studies, and which did, in fact, shape much of the research that was to come. These studies created a sympathetic atmosphere for the interpretations Mayo would give to the later work. Certainly, Pennock was already sympathetic to the supervisory style hypothesis to which Roethlisberger and Dickson attributed the results in the relay assembly test room.

The illumination studies preceded the active involvement of Elton Mayo, Fritz Roethlisberger, and the other members of the research group from the Harvard Business School. Indeed, Mayo was not aware of the research until after the subsequent relay assembly test room had already been in place for close to a year. The Harvard group did not draw substantially on the lighting experiments in their analyses, and seem to have had little detailed knowledge of them.

Mayo's involvement began in 1928. On March 15th of that year, T. K. Stevenson, an executive of the Western Electric Company, whom Mayo had met previously, sent him copies of the results to date of the "study on rest periods" in the relay assembly test room. In his letter, Stevenson makes reference to a speech Mayo had delivered earlier that winter at the Harvard Club, when apparently the two men had a brief conversation. Stevenson invited Mayo to critique the data, and added that he hoped Mayo would find them interesting.[14] Mayo responded that he indeed found the data interesting and said he would make "extended comment when we are sufficiently acquainted with its details." His extended comments followed, and over the next few months the two men established a regular correspondence which, if nothing else, attests to the reliability of the mail service at that time.

Mayo's first visit to the plant was not until April 24, 1928, during the tenth experimental period of the relay assembly test room. His second visit was six months later in October of that year, during the twelfth research period. Mayo's role in the relay assembly test room was thus interpretative, the design of the study having preceded his involvement.

The Relay Assembly Test Room

The relay assembly test room was the experimental research effort at Hawthorne on which many of the popularly reported conclusions were based. The discussion that follows relies chiefly on the account by Fritz Roethlisberger and William Dickson, with Thomas North Whitehead's presentation also considered. We will here describe the studies as they were presented by the Harvard group and as they are traditionally reported. Dissenting and alternative interpretations will be considered in later chapters.

Essentially, the relay test room involved six young female employees (five assemblers and a layout operator) who were asked to perform their jobs in a separate room in which they would be somewhat removed from the regular work force. The purpose of selecting a small group of employees was to reduce the number of variables that might intervene in a large group situtation. This was one lesson the researchers believed they had learned from the illumination studies.

The work consisted of assembling approximately 35 parts and securing them together into a fixture using four machine screws. The complete operation required about one minute. As each operator assembled around 500 relays a day, the job was highly repetitive. It is, however, described as highly skilled in both *Management and the Worker* and *The Industrial Worker.* Each operator had to select parts from small bins in front of her, pick them up, place them in a "pill up" in front of her, and complete the assembly with a high degree of efficiency. On average, a relay assembler might have to assemble many different types of relays over the course of weeks.

Organization of the Experiment

In order to control for the element of learning during the test, the researchers chose operators who were all thoroughly experienced in relay assembly. The investigators also felt it important that the women selected be willing and cooperative. Two assemblers who were friendly with each other were invited to participate in the test, and were then asked to select the remaining four members of the group. Five of the women were assemblers (called operators), and one was a layout operator. The latter individual procured and stocked parts for the other five, assigned work, and when necessary instructed the others in the assembly of new types of relays.

An observer was also in the test room. His principal responsibilities were to keep accurate records of everything that happened and to create and maintain a friendly atmosphere in the test room. The latter responsibility reflected the researchers' belief that to attain true experimental control, variables such as the operators' feelings toward the experiment had to be held relatively constant. This, they believed, was another of the lessons of the illumination studies.

The observer kept a log sheet on which he entered for each operator the type of relay worked on, the exact time work was started on it, the time when the operator changed to another type, and all intervals of nonproductive time. The observer also kept a daily record of remarks made by the operators, concerns expressed by the investigators, observations of behavior, and anything else that might have bearing on the interpretaton of the operators' output curves.

Each operator's output was recorded by an automatic device that had been developed to facilitate data collection during the experiment. An operator would drop a completed relay down a chute. The device would record this by punching a hole in a moving paper tape and would also advance a numerical register counter. Each hole represented a relay, and the space between holes the time it took to complete the relay. Readings from this record were taken every half hour. The layout operator also kept a record of the operators' performances. This record, containing information similar to that in the observer's log sheet, was a regular department form used for payroll purposes.

All told, the experimental design resulted in the following differences between the test room and the conditions in the regular department. As the study progressed, these differences acquired unintended but increasing significance with regard to the interpretation of the results.

1. The room was smaller.
2. There were better lighting fixtures, resulting in a slightly more uniform distribution of light.
3. The test room was equipped with fans, which were used only on summer days.
4. In the test room one layout operator serviced five operators, as compared to six or seven in the regular department.
5. The chute mechanism for counting output was new and involved a procedure for handling relays that made the work slightly easier.
6. With the exception of one operator, the women now assembled fewer types of relays.
7. The pay rates were altered. The group incentive was now based on a group of 5 as opposed to a group of 100.
8. The procedure for handling repairs was altered.
9. A new method for calling out defects and interruptions was instituted (but was then discontinued).
10. The women were members of a small group, rather than a large one.
11. The test observer took over some of the supervisory functions.
12. The women were given periodic physical examinations, invited to the office of the superintendent, and in other ways made the object of considerable attention.
13. The women were permitted to talk more freely in the test room.

Items 10, 11, 12, and 13 were eventually to figure prominently in the investigators' interpretations of the results. Some critics of the "Harvard human relations school" were to argue that items 5, 6, 7, and 8 represented key changes that the researchers had too cavalierly rejected as explanations for the experiment's favorable results.

The test room investigation was organized into periods. During each period, a specific set of working conditions was in force. The thrust of the experiment was the impact of rest periods and of shortened workdays and workweeks on employee performance. Although the relay assembly test room existed for five years (1927–1932), Roethlisberger and Dickson reported on only the first thirteen periods (1927–1929). The researchers' experiences up to that point significantly changed the direction of their inquiry, and their interest in the experiment declined.

The First Thirteen Test Periods

Below we summarize Roethlisberger and Dickson's discussion of the first thirteen test periods.

Periods 1–3. The first three periods were not experimental ones but represented a sequential phasing of the women into the test room situation. During this time, the researchers attempted to establish experimental control over the operators.

During period 1, which lasted two weeks, the operators tentatively selected for the test remained in the regular department while their output was measured from regular department records. This was an attempt at collecting baseline measurements. The women under consideration were invited to a meeting with the superintendent of the Inspection Branch, who was personally overseeing the experiment. Among the points covered were:

1. The illumination studies and how the findings had revealed that many employees were hesitant to answer questions frankly.
2. The questions the study hoped to answer (such as the impact of rest periods and shorter working days) and the fact that any changes of this would be discussed with the women in advance to get their thoughts and ideas.
3. The fact that the women would be informed of results as the experiment progressed.
4. That the test was not designed to determine maximum output, and they should work at a comfortable pace.
5. The company had no idea how long the test would run—possibly six months or longer depending on the results.
6. That they could opt not to join the test group if they had any hesitation about it.

All of the women agreed to participate in the study. Toward the end of the two weeks, the women underwent physical examinations to ensure that none of the operators had any physical condition that might affect their performance during the test.

Period 2 began when the women moved into the test room. The purpose of this period, which lasted about a month, was to allow the women to adjust to the new environment.

Period 3 lasted for almost eight weeks. The women were now made a separate group for payment purposes. Essentially, the relay assemblers were paid on a group incentive piecework system. Where previously each woman had been paid as part of a group of approximately 100 operators, now the women in the test room were to be paid as members of a group of 5. The primary objective was for each woman to receive the same amount of work proportionate to the group. Nevertheless, the reduction in group size meant that the total amount of compensation received would be more closely related to each woman's production. It was hoped that any resulting effect on output would reflect itself during period 3, before the experimental changes were introduced.

Two changes in the work procedures were also introduced during this period. Where previously an inspector would return defective relays during the afternoon and repairs would be made at once, in the test room repairs were to be made on Wednesday and Friday afternoons. This was done to avoid a daily break in output records.

The other change was for each operator to call out whenever she encountered a difficulty in the assembly operation, naming the kind of difficulty. The test room observer would mark these interruptions on the output record. Personal interruptions were also recorded. This procedure of calling out difficulties was discontinued five weeks later, however, because the operators disliked it.

Periods 4–7. With period 4 came the first experimental changes. The researchers began testing the effects of rest periods. Periods 4, 5, 6, and 7 involved two five-minute breaks, two ten-minute breaks, six five-minute breaks, and a fifteen-minute and a ten-minute break, respectively. During period 7 a hot mid-morning lunch was provided by the company during the morning break. The table on page 102 summarizes the key characteristics of each period, including the results.

There were individual variations, but overall, the average hourly output of the operators was higher through this phase than it had been during periods 1 through 3. Two of the operators showed a relatively consistent pattern of rising output. One operator maintained essentially a constant output rate. Two increased their output rates during periods 4 and 5, but their rates began to decline during periods 6 and 7.

Table 1. Summary of periods 4 through 7.

Experimental Period	Length of Time	Nature of Experimental Change	Results in Hourly Output	Other Events During Period
4	About a month	Two 5-minute breaks at 10 A.M. and 2 P.M.	Increase in average hourly output over period 3 for four of the five operators.	Overall positive reaction from the operators.
5	About a month	Two 10-minute breaks at 10 A.M. and 2 P.M.	Increase in average hourly output over the preceding period.	Overall positive reaction from the operators.
6	Four weeks	Six 5-minute breaks at 8:45, 10:00, 11:20, 2:00, 3:15, and 4:30.	Decrease in average hourly output over the preceding period for two of the operators. No meaningful change for one of the others. Two showed a slight increase.	The operators had expressed opinions favoring the 15 minutes, and clearly disagreed with the concept of six 5-minute breaks.
7	Eleven Weeks	15-minute break at 9:30 A.M.; 10-minute break at 2:30 P.M. Food served during morning break.	Increase in average hourly output for two of the operators. One operator exhibited no change in hourly output. Two operators had a decrease in average hourly output.	A personnel problem involved two of the operators, who had tended to be antagonistic toward the test room authorities for some time. They engaged in excessive talking. By the end of the period it was decided to replace these two operators in the test room.

In keeping with the effort to maintain positive attitudes toward the experiment, the operators were allowed to select the timing for the breaks. In period 7 they had input into the menu for the lunch served during the morning break. The operators were apparently in favor of the gradual lengthening of the breaks from one period to the next.

Only once did the researchers go against the expressed wishes of the operators. For period 6, the operators unanimously favored two fifteen-minute rest breaks over six five-minute rest breaks, but the researchers opted for the latter. Throughout period 6 the operators expressed their dislike of the break schedule, and none achieved an increase in output.

Two other incidents merit mention. First, during period 5, the investigators decided to pay the test room operators the same incentive earnings that operators in the regular department received. Once a month the test room operators would be paid the difference between the departmental earnings and their actual earnings (which, because of their increased production levels, were now higher) as a bonus. The investigators thought this would better demonstrate to the women the differences in their earnings from the regular department.

However, the women in the test room responded negatively, voicing the belief that the intent of the new system was to confuse them and perhaps cheat them out of some of the money. Because of the extent of the reacton, the investigators abandoned the planned system and maintained the one preferred by the operators: getting the total amount of earnings each week.

Another problem involved the disciplinary action that was taken against the two operators whose rates declined during periods 6 and 7. For some time, the investigators had felt that these women were not displaying the desired degree of cooperation. The major problem was considerable talking between the two. Excessive talking became a general problem in the test room, but the researchers saw the two operators in question as the instigators. These women had also made comments exhibiting some degree of antagonism toward the investigators. Afraid that a decrease in cooperation might jeopardize the controlled nature of the experiment, the investigators made efforts to correct the situation, including discussions of the problem with the two operators. Their output continued to drop, however.

As the test room authorities stepped up their efforts toward remedying this lack of cooperation, the other operators began to isolate themselves from the two and otherwise express resentment toward the problem operators. Finally, it was decided to replace them, a change that was made during the first week of period 8.

Periods 8 through 13. Period 8 represented the beginning of a new phase in the studies: experimentation with the effects of shortening the workday and workweek. This phase was to include three experimental periods (8, 9, and 11) interspersed with three check periods (10, 12, and 13). During the check periods, conditions similar to those of earlier periods were reinstated.

Prior to the start of period 8, the women were given two options for reduction of the workday. They unanimously decided to stop work one half hour earlier in the afternoon, at 4:30 instead of 5:00 P.M. The fifteen-minute morning break with lunch and the ten-minute afternoon break were continued (these breaks became standard for all the remaining periods except the thirteenth). The combined breaks and shorter work-day represented a 10 percent reduction in weekly hours from the original forty-eight-hour week. The average hourly output increased for all five operators. Total output, in comparison to output in previous periods, also increased.

During period 9 the workday was, with the approval of the operators, reduced an additional half hour. This proved to be too drastic a cut. Although the operators favored the shorter hours and worked harder (four operators had increased average hourly outputs, and one had the same output), total weekly output was lowered. Consequently, the women's earnings were affected.

Period 10 marked a return to a full forty-eight-hour week, although the break schedule remained the same. The women often complained of fatigue and expressed a decided preference for the shorter day. Roeth-lisberger and Dickson interpreted these comments as showing resentment against the return to "reality." The average hourly output was lower than for the preceding period, although total output increased.

Period 11 was a nine-week experiment with a five-day week, with Saturday mornings off. Breaks were continued as previously. Two of the nine weeks during this period were vacation weeks for the entire group. Although the women had Saturday mornings off, they were paid their basic hourly rate for the time. Roethlisberger and Dickson suggest that the investigators made this financial arrangement because they did not want the operators to suffer a loss in earnings because of the experiment. There is no record of the operators' reactions during this period. Average hourly output was higher than during period 10 for four of the five women, with the other operator working at about the same rate. As would be expected given the time off each week, total output decreased.

The twelfth period was to become critical in the lore of Hawthorne: Elton Mayo was to emphasize it again and again in his writings. This period, lasting twelve weeks, was a return to the forty-eight-hour week with no rest pauses. The operators were told that this was just another phase of the experiment and more variations would follow. Nevertheless, the period was unpopular with the operators.

While total weekly output increased, average hourly output declined for four of the operators. Mayo was later to attach great importance to the increase in total weekly output, attributing it to the social cohesiveness of the work group, including the relationship between the supervisor (the test room observer) and the operators.

During period 13, the fifteen-minute morning and ten-minute afternoon rest breaks were reinstated. However, the women had to provide their own mid-morning lunches. The company continued to provide hot tea.

The operators clearly welcomed the return to the rest periods, stating "we never want to work without rest periods again." The average hourly output for all five operators reached the highest point yet, although total weekly output increased in only three instances. The table on the next two pages summarizes periods 8 through 13.

Mention should be made of two occurrences that Roethlisberger and Dickson report during periods 8 through 13. First, the two new operators were both experienced relay assemblers, and were desirous of participating in the test, and had output levels comparable to those of the women they were replacing.

Second, an attitude of cooperation emerged among the operators, coupled with a certain casualness toward supervision in the test room. By period 13 the operators were making increased efforts to assist one another on the job. For example, the women showed willingness to work at an increased pace to offset periodic "off days" of their co-workers. In a questionnaire administered to the group during period 10, the women showed a distinct preference for the test room over the regular department. Key factors cited by Roethlisberger and Dickson as underlying this preference were "smaller group," "no bosses," "less supervision," "freedom," and "the way we are treated." In addition, the operators increasingly included the test room authorities in their good-humored joking and conversation.

Roethlisberger and Dickson were to interpret the above as illustrative of the development of a cohesive work group that was unique to the test room. They felt that the cohesiveness stemmed from the supervisory climate that was created.

Interpretation of the Relay Assembly Test Room Results

One point that stood out in the minds of the investigators, when they analyzed the above results, was that no simple correlations existed between the actual experimental conditions and the rate of work. With the exception of periods 10 and 12, the average output curves

Table 2. Summary of periods 8 through 13.

Experimental Period	Length of Time	Nature of Experimental Change	Results in Hourly Output	Other Events During Period
8	About a month and a half	Workday was shortened a half-hour by ending work at 4:30 instead of 5:00. Rest breaks were the same as in period 7, with mid-morning lunch served.	Average hourly output rate increased for all five operators. Total output also increased.	Two new operators joined the test room, replacing the two problem operators. All but one of the operators enjoyed the shorter day.
9	Almost a month	Workday was shortened an additional half-hour. Rest breaks were the same as in period 8.	Average hourly output rate increased for four of the operators. One remained the same. Total output dropped.	Some antagonism emerged between operators as they tried to speed up to maintain earnings during the now drastically reduced workday. One of the new operators began to assert herself as the leader of the group, roles previously played by two of the remaining original women. She eventually succeeded in emerging as the new leader.
10	Twelve weeks	Full workweek with 15-minute rest in the morning and 10-minute rest in the afternoon. The lunch was still served during the morning break.	Average hourly output rate decreased for all five operators. Total output increased.	Operators expressed obvious preference for the shorter day. A questionnaire given the operators revealed that they preferred the test room over the regular department because there were no bosses and they had more freedom and were treated better.

11	Nine weeks	Five-day week with Saturday morning off; operators were paid basic hourly rate for Saturday morning. Rest periods were the same as in period 7.	Average hourly output rate increased for four of the operators and stayed the same for one. Total output decreased.	No comments recorded.
12	Twelve weeks	Return to the original hours of work; 48 hours per week with no rest breaks.	Average hourly output rate decreased for four of the operators. It increased slightly for the fifth operator. At the end of the period the hourly output rate was clearly trending downward for two of the operators and possibly a third. Total output increased.	Operators disliked working conditions and began to take "informal" rests at their benches.
13	Seven months	Rest periods reinstated (15 minutes in the morning and 10 minutes in the afternoon). The women were asked to provide their own mid-morning lunch. The company provided the hot tea.	Average hourly output increased for all five operators. Total output increased for three of the operators (one only slightly) and remained the same for two of the operators.	Operators clearly welcomed the return of the rest periods.

for the women showed a steady rise from period 2 onward. (Exceptions were the two women replaced at the beginning of period 8 and one operator who, from one period to the next, had much more modest increases or remained consistent in output.) Additionally, it is notable that periods 7, 10, and 13 had identical experimental conditions. While hourly output rates declined during period 10, in comparison to period 9, the average for period 10 remained well above that for period 7. Period 13 had a sharp increase in the hourly rate, much above that in periods 7 or 10. Finally, the output rate during period 12—when the women returned to the forty-eight-hour week without rests—declined but never reached the level of period 3 when similar working conditions prevailed. Thus, overall, the hourly output rate had shown an upward trend, with the rate for the last period, 13, being substantially higher than that at the beginning of the test. Indeed, in period 13 one of the women had increased her output rate by approximately 40 percent over period 1.

The test room history record also revealed changes in the women's attitudes toward the investigators. As the test progressed they became more relaxed with the researchers and began to express their liking of the test room situation. In the words of Roethlisberger and Dickson, "their first line supervisor [the observer] ceased to be one who 'bawled them out' in case things went wrong; instead he came to be regarded as a friendly representative of management."[15]

The investigators found the general upward trend in output and the improvement in worker attitudes—both of which occurred independently of specific work conditions—to be somewhat puzzling. They believed that the phenomena of increased output and improved outlook were related but were not sure of the exact nature of the relationship. Five interpretations were advanced, each of which is discussed below.

The improved work methods hypothesis. One proposed explanation was that improved material conditions and work methods had been present in the test room. This possibility was rejected on several grounds. The previous illumination experiments suggested that the slightly more uniform light distribution in the test room would not explain the data. The fans were in use for only a small part of the year. Further, the test room was small and allowed less free circulation of air than did the regular department. The alterations in the assembly operation itself seemed insignificant to the investigators.

Only the reduction in the number of types of relays assembled struck the researchers as being of any importance. For example, one test room operator had more different types of relays to assemble than the others, and her output rate showed the least improvement. Roethlisberger and

Dickson do not pursue this last point any further, possibly because the investigators eventually opted for one of the other explanations.

The wage-incentive hypothesis. This interpretation involved the increased wage incentive that had been created in period 3. According to this hypothesis, by receiving payment as part of a small group, the women were motivated to work harder because their earnings were more directly in proportion to individual effort expended. Proponents of this view argued that the improvement in output began with this change.

The researchers' efforts to test this explanation are of particular interest. The resulting data led Roethlisberger and Dickson to reject the wage-incentive hypothesis. However, one present-day expert on compensation, Edward Lawler III, interprets the data as indicating that a considerable amount of the increased productivity in the test room was due to the change in the pay system.[16]

This difference in interpretation on the part of the Hawthorne researchers and writers such as Lawler strikes at the heart of one of the crucial issues in the popular understanding of what happened at Hawthorne. Most managers and students think of Hawthorne as providing evidence that incentives do not result in increased productivity, which was the Roethlisberger and Dickson interpretation. However, some investigators have concluded just the opposite—that careful analysis of the data tends to support the wage-incentive hypothesis. Here we will simply describe the conclusions of the researchers, leaving until later a more detailed discussion of this discrepancy of opinions.

In order to test the wage-incentive explanation, two additional experiments were conducted: the second relay assembly group and the mica-splitting test room. In the second relay assembly group, five experienced assemblers were formed into a special group for pay purposes. They were to be paid on the same basis as the women in the original relay test room. However, they remained in the regular department. With the exception of their being moved to adjacent positions for purposes of record-keeping, no other changes were made.

The actual experiment ran for nine weeks. Additionally, the outputs of these women were studied for a base period of five weeks prior to the experiment and for a post-experimental period of seven weeks following their return to the standard method of payment.

Every operator had a higher output rate during the experimental period, than during the base period. The increases during the experiment ranged from 8.3 to 17.4 percent, with the group average being 12.6 percent above the base period. After the experimental period, the output rates of all the operators dropped, in two cases to below the base period figures.

Roethlisberger and Dickson did conclude that the system of a smaller payment group had an important influence on performance. However, they also noted that the second group had exhibited a rapid initial increase without any subsequent rising trend, and felt that the wage-incentive factor could not explain the continuing increase in performance in the original test room. They further suggested that if the second experiment had run for a longer time period, the increase might not have appeared so dramatic and performance might have tailed off.

The second experiment designed to test the wage-incentive hypothesis was the mica-splitting test room. The objective was to re-create a situation similar to that of the relay assembly test room without changing the wage-incentive method. Mica splitting was already compensated on an individual piecework basis. Should this second test room also exhibit a steady upward trend in output, it would suggest that the change in wage incentive had not been a dominant factor in the original experiment.

The job of mica splitting was highly repetitive but, as with relay assembly, was considered to require considerable skill. Essentially, an operator took a small block of mica (which was used as insulation in telephone apparatus) and, using a sharp needle-like instrument and a knife blade, split off thin layers that were just a few thousandths of an inch in diameter. Each operator tested her work with an indicating gauge. The operation was not physically taxing, but it required precise movements.

Initially, five operators were selected at random. Only two of five agreed to participate, however. These two selected three others for the test room. Meetings were then held in the superintendent's office, and the plans for the experiment were discussed in detail.

The physical environment of the mica test room resembled that of the relay test room in most ways. The records kept were similar to those in the relay assembly test room. Output was not, however, recorded mechanically. Also, the women were paid on an individual piecework basis, just as they had been in their regular department. This latter difference was, of course, the main point of the experiment.

The mica test room experiment continued for two years and was divided into five experimental periods. Period 1 was an eight-week base period while the women were still in the regular department. During this time, the women were asked whether they wished to continue to work the same amount of overtime when the experiment commenced; they unanimously favored doing so. At the time, production demands on the department were strong.

During period 2, which lasted five weeks, the operators were in the test room but no experimental changes were made. Early in this period, the group expressed a preference for the test room.

During period 3, two ten-minute rest breaks were introduced, one at 10:00 A.M. and the other at 2:30 P.M. The daily history record indicates that the women immediately responded positively to the breaks. Throughout the period, overtime hours were continued, and on seven occasions Sunday work was added. Sunday work paid double time, while overtime was paid at time and a half.

In Period 4, overtime was eliminated, for business rather than experimental reasons. Period 5 involved shortening the workday by forty-five minutes and cutting out all Saturday work, with the change again being part of a general retrenchment program carried on throughout the plant. Eventually in 1930, as the Great Depression worsened, the work schedules for mica dropped so low that the test room was discontinued.

From period 3 through the first four months of period 4, the test room showed a moderate but steady increase in the output rate. However, there were wide individual variations. Only two of the mica-splitting operators came close to the rate of increase that had been typical of all the people in the relay assembly test room. During the second year of the test, the output rate declined steadily. Roethlisberger and Dickson attribute this to concern over the rumors that the mica work was going to be transferred to a plant in another city. As the second year wore on the women's concern over the worsening economic depression deepened. Because of this, the investigators chose to ignore data from the last year of the experiment.

Roethlisberger and Dickson decided to reject the wage-incentive hypothesis. In the case of the second relay assembly group, they pointed to the average increase in output rate of 12.6 percent versus 30 percent in the first relay assembly test room. They noted that the second test group did not demonstrate a sustained increasing trend. Finally, they suggested that other factors, such as a desire to top the results in the first test room, contributed to the 12.6 percent increase.

In the mica-splitting room, output had risen an average of 15 percent in fourteen months. Roethlisberger and Dickson interpreted this figure as the minimum that would be caused by changes other than wage-incentive alterations in a test room environment. They therefore concluded that no more than half of the 30 percent increase in the first relay assembly test room was attributable to the wage-incentive factor. They also pointed to differing conditions in the mica-splitting room and the first relay assembly test room: the changes that occurred in the mica room had been dictated by general economic conditions and did not represent special privileges, and the individual wage incentive did not promote group solidarity. Roethlisberger and Dickson further argue that since the operators had been on strict piecework in the regular department, they probably had been already working nearer to their maximum capabilities before entering the mica-splitting test room.

It is suggested in *Management and the Worker* that all these factors tended to operate against increases in the rate of output in the mica-splitting room. Therefore, Roethlisberger and Dickson concluded that the percentage of output in the relay assembly test room attributable to wage incentive was probably less than 50 percent.

On the basis of the above interpretation of the second relay assembly group and the mica-splitting test room results, the wage-incentive hypothesis was rejected by Roethlisberger and Dickson.

The fatigue hypothesis. Another interpretation was the possibility that, although output was not related to a particular work schedule, the rest pauses and shorter working hours during the experiment had provided relief from cumulative fatigue. According to this line of reasoning, the volume of production did not drop during period 12 because of the women's improved physical health. Actually, the rate of output for the women was lower during this period than during the preceding one. And the assumption of fatigue reduction was clearly speculative, since the various physical examinations given during the experiments showed no evidence of improved health.

To test this hypothesis, the investigators utilized what they called the fatigue curve. H. M. Vernon described this curve as follows:

> As the worker warms up to his task, his output rate rises. It continues to rise in the morning, until the cumulative effects of fatigue from work done balance with any gains due to practice. From that point on the output rate goes progressively downward. Following lunch, the worker has had some opportunity to recuperate but at the same time, has lost some of his gains due to practice. The curve starts at a point lower than in the morning, reaches a maximum more quickly and again drops off, this time more rapidly.[17]

The investigators had expected that changes in work patterns, such as rest pauses, would lead to certain predictable variations in the women's production curves. During certain periods the curves of the test room operators moved slightly in the predicted direction. During other periods the curves moved in manners contradictory to expectations. The investigators concluded that relief from fatigue did not account for output changes during the periods in which they would be most expected to occur. The fatigue hypothesis was rejected.

The monotony hypothesis. A fourth interpretation was that the introduction of rest pauses and shorter working hours had reduced the monotony of the work. The investigators believed the relay assembly job required sufficient attention to prevent the mind from wandering, but did not require complete mental absorption. Other writers had suggested that this was the kind of task most likely to generate boredom.

The monotony hypothesis was tested in a manner similar to the one regarding fatigue. A theoretical monotony work curve was described, being characterized by: (1) a drop in the work rate in the middle of a work period; (2) an increased variability in the work rate; and (3) an increase in the work rate (end spurt) at the end of the work period. If relief from monotony explained the data, the operators' production curves would be expected to vary from the description of the monotony curve in a predictable direction. However, the work curve of only one operator resembled the expected behavior of a monotony curve. Therefore, this explanation was also dropped.

The supervisory style hypothesis. The fifth interpretation of the relay test room results was the one accepted by the researchers: "The increased output and improved attitude in the test room could best be associated with the changes in the method of supervision that had gradually taken place."[18] A major reason for the changes in supervisory methods was the attempt to maintain a controlled test. To regular supervisory personnel, control meant upholding department rules and regulations. To the test room observer, control meant maintaining cooperative attitudes among the test room operators and thus holding the psychological variable constant.

In efforts to achieve this experimental control, virtually all the usual personnel practices were altered. The women were given a voice in what experimental changes would be introduced in the test room, their opinions were eagerly sought and their reactions recorded by the observer, and they had the privilege of talking on the job (within broadly defined limits). Gradually, the observer came to identify with the women and take a sympathetic interest in their problems. In short, by attempting to create a controlled test environment, the investigators created a social situation drastically different from what existed in the regular department. The daily history record showed the women's gradually changing perception of the observer.

The researchers' major conclusion about the relay test room results was that considerable latent energy and cooperative effort could be released by a supervisor who created the proper social conditions. Understanding employee attitudes seemed to be the key to creating these kinds of conditions. In arriving at this conclusion, Roethlisberger and Dickson provided the initial justification for what was to become known as participative management. They wrote:

> The chief result of the first two years of experimentation in the Relay
> Assembly Test Room, then, had been to demonstrate the importance of
> employee attitudes and preoccupations. All attempts to eliminate such
> considerations had been unsuccessful. The importance of employee atti-
> tudes had been apparent in the "apprehension of authority" which had
> been common to all the operators, although in different degrees, in the
> early stages of the test room and which could be "lit up" at the slightest
> provocation. It had been evident in the effects of the experimentally intro-
> duced changes in working conditions, which had proved to be carriers of
> social meaning, rather than mere changes in physical circumstances. It had
> shown itself in the output variations of certain operators, which could be
> related to their personal preoccupations, and which continued as long as
> these preoccupations persisted.[19]

The Hawthorne researchers increasingly directed their interest toward the study of worker attitudes and the factors that influenced
these attitudes. They embarked on a new research strategy: an extensive interviewing program which, from 1928 to 1930, was sponsored
in the Hawthorne plant. During this time, 21,126 people were interviewed. The program generated volumes of data on supervisory practices, employees' attitudes toward their work, and the kinds of problems people experienced on and off the job. These data were used to
support many of the conceptual conclusions arrived at by Roethlisberger and Dickson.

The interviewing began in the inspection branch, with supervisors
being given explanations of the program. Three men and two women,
each with a thorough knowledge of the shop, were selected to do the
interviewing. A set procedure was followed, which involved:

1. Financially compensating employees for time spent away from
   the job during interviews
2. Keeping all discussions confidential and stressing this confi-
   dentiality to employees
3. Explaining that the interviewer was interested in the positive
   as well as the negative factors in the work environment
4. Taking almost verbatim notes
5. Neither agreeing nor disagreeing with employees' comments
   and opinions
6. Never giving advice to employees

Generally, both employees and supervisors reacted positively to
the program in the inspection branch, and plans were made for expanding the effort. In February 1929 the Industrial Research Division
was formed at Hawthorne. This division was responsible for both the

expanding interviewing program and continuation of the test room studies. The interviewing program was largely discontinued in 1931 because of the decline in business conditions.

During the course of the program, a significant change in interviewing method occurred. Initially, the interviewers had attempted to follow a specific outline. They soon discovered, however, that employees tended to divert from the interview questions to topics that seemed of primary importance to themselves. Several interviewers commented on their inability to prevent interviewees from continually returning to such topics.

The result was a switch to an interviewing format that emphasized nondirective listening. Whenever an employee talked spontaneously, the interviewer was to listen and not interrupt or change the topic. Above all, any question the interviewer asked should not suggest a simple yes-or-no answer. Thus, emphasis during the interviews shifted from topics that interested the interviewer to topics that interested the interviewee. The current applications of basic listening skills, popularized by human-relations-oriented psychologists, are traceable to the nondirective interviewing technique that emerged during this phase of the Hawthorne studies.

The new approach certainly made the Hawthorne interviewers more sensitive to the preoccupations of workers—especially obsessive and morbid thinking, where a worker might brood over some event for years. Some of the interview data suggest that employees will often project all their troubles, including personal ones, onto one single object in the work situation. They may feel that a supervisor is "out to get them," for example. An employee's complaint might reflect a series of problems, many relating to family or other personal situations.

Roethlisberger and Dickson observed that when a supervisor responded to an obstinate employee by taking the person's actions at face value instead of listening and attempting to learn the true source of the problem, the result was likely to be unsatisfactory. Generally the supervisor would deliver futile ultimatums, whereas making certain allowances or expressing sympathy might result in the employee becoming a more responsive worker. In listening, a supervisor must be concerned not only with the manifest content of employee complaints but with any latent content.

In developing this line of analysis, Roethlisberger and Dickson made conceptual distinctions between "Class A," "Class B," and "Class C" comments. Class A comments refer to objects and conditions that can be seen, touched, or concretely defined. In short, they are capable of being verified. Class B comments refer primarily to sensory experiences other than those of sight and touch. They "include terms for which no physical or logical operations exist which can be agreed upon as defining them. They are terms whose meanings are biologically or socially determined and hence vary with time, place, age, nationality, personality, social status, and temperaments. Examples of such statements are: 'The work is dirty,' 'The lockers are unsanitary,' 'The job is dangerous,' 'The work is hard,' and 'The room is hot.'"[20] Such comments are generally less subject to objective verification.

Although Class B comments often can be reliably correlated to a given set of physical circumstances, this is not the case with Class C comments. These comments, Roethlisberger and Dickson maintained, are expressions of sentiment: beliefs and attitudes that grow out of the social situation of the work group and the personal characteristics of its members. Such sentiments are subject to a logic of their own, a logic rooted in the values of the group. Roethlisberger and Dickson gave the following example, in which Worker A feels he is doing a similar job to that of Worker B but thinks B is earning more money than he is. Worker A might complain in the following different ways:

Relation of Worker A to Worker B	*Worker A's Complaint*
A has less seniority than B	Earnings are not commensurate with the job being performed.
A has more seniority than B	Seniority is not being rewarded.
A is single; B is married	Married employees are being given preference over single employees.
A is married; B is single	Home responsibilities should be taken into account by the company.

Roethlisberger and Dickson wrote that such complaints are illustrations of sentiment; they are neither facts nor errors, but nonfacts. "They are complaints in which fact and sentiment are inextricably mixed so that verification in most cases is impossible."[21]

The interviewing program had turned toward the preoccupations of individual workers, and then toward the influence of group values and experiences. What had begun in the relay assembly test room as an inquiry into rest periods developed into an almost psychoanalytical investigation into the nature of worker attitudes. As Roethlisberger and Dickson put it, "Certain complaints were no longer treated as facts in themselves but as symptoms or indicators of personal or social situations which needed to be explored."[22] Still later, a social-anthropological concern with group norms emerged from the interviewing program. This was a gradual shift from issues of personal equilibrium toward questions of social equilibrium.

The Bank Wiring Observation Room

During the interviewing program, while the investigators were becoming increasingly interested in social equilibrium of the work group, they also realized that the data being generated revealed only how employees *said* they acted. The relationship between what employees reported and what they actually did was problematic. To gain a better idea of this, the bank wiring observation room was created. In this phase of the studies, direct observation was to be the primary method of research.

The study in the bank wiring observation room was conducted from November 1931 to May 1932. It involved fourteen male operators who worked under standard shop conditions. The only differences were that they were segregated from the rest of the department and that they were aware of being studied.

Nine wiremen, three soldermen, and two inspectors were selected for the study. The wiremen wired banks into what was referred to as an equipment. Each solderman soldered the work of three wiremen. Each completed equipment was checked by an inspector.

The test room observer adhered to the following rules:

1. Not giving orders or answering questions in any way that suggested supervisory authority.
2. Not entering into any arguments.
3. Not forcing himself into a conversation or appearing over interested in the group's behavior.
4. Never violating confidences.
5. Not using language or behaving in ways that would set him off from the group.

This last rule placed the observer in a significantly different posture than had been the case in the relay assembly test rooms. Whereas in the earlier situations the observer had actively attempted to keep the attitudes of the women constant, in the bank wiring room he was to be as unobtrusive as possible. In short, the observer's job was to describe what happened in the observation room while attempting not to influence the workers' behavior and attitudes.

The observer was expected to record any procedures or occurrences that differed from what the formal organization prescribed. He was also to describe the manner in which each individual participated in the social life of the group. In addition to the observer, an interviewer periodically spoke with the workers in the wireroom. This individual remained quite remote, entering the wireroom ony to request an interview or for some other necessary reason.

For eighteen weeks prior to the study, base period data were collected. The production records of the proposed group members were measured. Interviews were conducted with thirty-two members of the wiring room to obtain their attitudes as well. Additionally, an observer watched the work habits and behavior of the men in the group for ten days prior to their being informed of the studies.

The men were first told of the study by the foreman. Then, the research director explained the purpose of the study in detail. It was emphasized that no one from the research department had supervisory authority over them and that the information obtained would not be used by regular department officials.

When first placed in the observation room, the men avoided talking in the presence of the observer. By the second week, however, their behavior was notably less restrained. In the third week, the men voluntarily included the observer in their conversations, which indicated he had gradually become accepted by the group.

Worker Behavior and Output

The observers' notes contained a range of comments on the manner in which the workers managed their output—a matter closely associated with pay. In bank wiring, workers were compensated through a group piecework system under which the entire department was considered to be a unit for payment purposes. Each employee was also assigned an hourly wage rate that largely reflected his level of efficiency. This rate was guaranteed to the worker should the department's output prove insufficient to cover his minimum wage. The hourly rate was multiplied by the hours worked each day. Excess earnings, based on the actual amount of output by the department, were distributed among the workers on a percentage basis, thus providing the incentive.

Within the confines of this incentive system, the investigators were struck by the workers' concept of a fair day's work. The men generally agreed that a fair day's work was either 6,000 or 6,600 connections (depending on the type of equipment involved), which amounted to two completed equipments. This did not correspond to any official standard of performance; company standards were higher. Nevertheless, operators frequently stopped work once they had met this unofficial quota, even when it was not yet quitting time. Some of the employees who wished to turn out more work were reluctant to do so because of prevailing group attitudes. In short, it appeared that group production norms were undermining one of the basic purposes of the incentive plan—to encouraging maximum production.

Additionally, the workers generally tried to maintain a high degree of consistency in their individual levels of production. An individual's reported output rate would tend to remain consistent from week to week, although they did not strive for identical levels of output. This behavior seemed rooted in the belief that if a person's output showed much change either from day to day or week to week, something bad would happen.

In their efforts to maintain consistency in output, employees had developed two practices. First, a wireman would usually report that he had produced either more or less than he actually had. Second, a wireman would claim time credit for work stoppages that were beyond his control. Many of these situations were difficult for the company to verify, and the amounts of time claimed were greater than actual events would justify. This practice obviously lessened the amount of output needed to maintain a given level of production. However, it did not financially benefit the worker; its sole function was to enable him to maintain a reasonably uniform output rate.

The major motivation for the above behaviors seemed to be the workers' concern that if more output was produced, management might raise the standard, cut their rates, or make some other alteration to their detriment. The investigators reported that they could find no basis for this belief in the past experiences of the employees. Nevertheless, the belief was strong and greatly influenced employee behavior. On the other hand, the workers also tried not to let output fall too low, so as to head off criticism from management.

Worker Attitudes Toward Supervisors and One Another

Another area documented in the observers' notes was attitudes toward the supervisors. The men seemed less inclined to submit to the authority of lower-level supervisors (group chief and section chief) than higher-level supervisors (assistant foreman and foreman). The operators would argue with the group chief and section chief about some order with which they disagreed. In the presence of the group chief, the men would behave in ways counter to company rules and regulations, but would adhere to procedures when the foreman came into the room. His authority was never challenged.

In effect, the lower-level supervisors were caught between pressures created by subordinates—on whose cooperation they depended—and the need to enforce company rules. The higher-level supervisors would pressure the group and section chiefs to elicit better operator performance, but the chiefs had to deal directly with the men on a regular basis. To resolve this situation a chief was likely to side with the men and not provide the foreman with an objective account of what was happening in the bank wiring room. Largely because he wanted the good will of his men, the group chief tended to acquiesce to their preferences. As a result, the information flowing to management tended to become distorted.

One of the most widely reported outcomes of the bank wiring observation room was the description of informal employee organization. There was a wide range of group norms regarding who had what privileges. Usually privileges, or informal authority, were related to a man's job. For example, company regulations stated that wiremen were to wire and soldermen were to solder. No job trading was permitted—yet it occurred. When it did, it was almost always a wireman who requested the trade and a solderman who obeyed. Similarly, it was a solderman who went to the lunch counter to get the group's lunch. A wireman never did this chore.

The two inspectors performed a job that tended to place them in a superordinate position to the rest of the group. Additionally, they reported to a different supervisor than the other men in the wireroom and typically wore coats and vests similar to those of the higher-level supervisors.

However, inspectors were considered outsiders and lacked certain powers. For example, an inspector would not attempt to close a window because the room was cold. Control over the windows and heat belonged to the wiremen and soldermen; the inspector would just complain and hope one of the wiremen or soldermen would close it. Should an inspector attempt to overstep this informal boundary, he would meet with resistance from the group.

Within the bank wiring observation room, two cliques of workers became noticeable. The observer was able to represent these cliques diagrammatically. Further, one clique tended to regard itself as superior to the other. Among other things, these cliques usually organized the informal activities in which the men engaged as respite from work.

The informal organization of the bank wiring room generated the informal rules (such as restricting output) that so successfully undermined the company's control systems (such as the incentive plan). A man could not violate the group's rules without becoming isolated from his peers.

To Roethlisberger and Dickson, these findings represented one of the most significant outcomes of the Hawthorne researches: the discovery that management systems based on the rational logic of cost and efficiency clashed with the logic of sentiment that was an important characteristic of employee informal organization. For the researchers, the implications were clear. Management, if it attempts to understand the "nonrational" nature of employee sentiment, can often elicit cooperation from the informal organization. Indeed, if such understanding is present, the informal organization will strive to achieve the same goals as management.

The researchers now interpreted occurrences in the relay assembly test room as having resulted from the observers' behavior. They pointed out how management's failure to recognize an informal organization and the logic of sentiment underlying it can result in the informal organization subverting the formal one, as exemplified in the bank wiring observation room. They noted that the interviewing program had also provided illustrations of how employee attitudes and "nonrational" sentiments affect their behavior at work.

Thus, Roethlisberger was later to write that "workers are social animals and should be treated as such." He said it was the meaning that a worker attaches to an event, not the objective event itself, that largely shapes job behavior. And an employee's perception of meaning is greatly influenced by his or her place in the social structure of the work group. These became significant points in the theoretical perspective of the human relations school. Roethlisberger also emphasized two tools that supervisors need in order to elicit cooperation from a group: interviewing (or listening) skills and observation skills. This point was to become a principal thrust of the human relations approach to supervising people—the legacy of Hawthorne for the practice of management.

NOTES

1. Fritz J. Roethlisberger and William J. Dickson, *Management and the Worker* (Cambridge, Mass.: Harvard University Press, 1933), pp. 575–576.
2. Fritz J. Roethlisberger, *The Elusive Phenomena* (Cambridge, Mass.: Harvard University Press, 1977), p. 50.
3. William F. Whyte and E. L. Hamilton, *Action Research for Management* (Homewood, Ill.: Irwin, 1965). Also Whyte, *Money and Motivation* (New York: Harper, 1955).
4. W. Lloyd Warner and J. W. Low, *The Social System of the Modern Factory* (New Haven, Conn.: Yale University Press, 1947).
5. Donald Roy, "Quota Restriction and Goldbricking in a Machine Shop," *American Journal of Sociology,* Vol. 57 (1952), pp. 427–442.
6. Quoted in Elton Mayo, *The Human Problems of an Industrial Civilization,* 2nd ed. (Boston: Graduate School of Business Administration, Harvard University, 1946), p. 168.
7. Clark Kerr, "What Became of the Independent Spirit?" *Fortune,* Vol. 48, July 1953, p. 110.
8. Examples of criticism along these lines are Kerr, "What Became?"; R. Bendix and L. N. Fisher, "The Perspectives of Elton Mayo," *Review of Economics and Statistics,* Vol. 31, 1949, pp. 312–321; and Daniel Bell, "Adjusting Men to Machines," *Commentary,* Vol. 3, 1974, pp. 79–88.

9. An example is Edward Lawler III, *Motivation in Work Organizations* (Monterey, Calif.: Brooks/Cole, 1973).

10. See W. I. Wardwell, "Critique of a Recent Professional 'Put-Down' of the Hawthorne Research," *American Sociological Review,* Vol. 44, 1979, pp. 858–861.

11. C. D. Wrege, "Solving Mayo's Mystery: The First Complete Account of the Origin of the Hawthorne Studies—The Forgotten Contributions of C. E. Snow and H. Hibarger," *Academy of Management Proceedings,* 1976.

12. Ibid.

13. Ibid.

14. Correspondence in the Mayo file, archives of Baker Library, Harvard Business School.

15. Roethlisberger and Dickson, *Management and the Worker,* p. 86.

16. Lawler, *Motivation.*

17. H. M. Vernon, *Industrial Fatigue and Efficiency* (London: George Routledge and Sons, 1921).

18. Roethlisberger and Dickson, *Management and the Worker,* p. 88.

19. Ibid., p. 184.

20. Ibid., p. 259.

21. Ibid., p. 265.

22. Ibid., p. 496.

6

Hawthorne Critics and Revisionists:
A Story of Interpretations

One writer has observed that there seem to be as many different opinions about the significance of Hawthorne as there are commentators on the studies.[1] A review of the literature reveals this to be not much of an overstatement. The data reported by Roethlisberger and Dickson and by Whitehead lend themselves to a number of possible interpretations, many quite contradictory. Indeed, as some have said of the Bible, there seem to be various aspects of the Hawthorne data that give support to almost everyone's position.

Responses to Hawthorne range from highly critical to highly supportive. Some writers see the research as lending support to rather traditional approaches and explanations; they maintain that hypotheses rejected by the Harvard group are actually supported by the data. In this view, wage incentives, changes in work methods, the reassertion of authoritarian management, and the like explain a large portion of the results in the first relay assembly test room. Other writers, usually from the behavioral science tradition, have reinterpreted the studies in a fashion more supportive of Roethlisberger and Dickson. These authors agree with the popular assessment that the answer to what happened in the relay assembly test room is traceable to supervisory style, the social environment, or both. Recently a comprehensive empirical analysis of the data from the relay assembly test room has provided strong evidence in support of the former view.

This chapter examines both the critics and the revisionists. Our emphasis is on the data themselves and on the events associated with them. First we will look at some of the early critics of how the studies were originally interpreted. Next we will review the work of the revisionists, and finally we will examine the most recent empirical evidence. This approach is intended to show how the debate has unfolded over time. We find that such a review reveals several surprising factors with implications for the practice of management.

Critical Interpretations

Any series of studies that succeeds in establishing a major new school of thought is likely also to generate a considerable amount of antagonism. The Hawthorne studies have proved no exception. From the time of the first published reports and interpretations, a flow of papers critical of the conclusions derived from Hawthorne has been generated.

Criticism of the Hawthorne studies tends to fall into two broad categories. The first centers around Elton Mayo, who is generally afforded the status of "high priest" of the human relations school. Although some of these critics refer to Roethlisberger, Dickson, and Whitehead, the target is the philosophy of "Mayoism." The principal criticisms were outlined in the preceding chapter. Those who have found Mayo's positions objectionable have generally cited the research reports on the Hawthorne studies as illustrative of his misconceptions.

A second stream of critics has focused more on the research itself. Here the target is not the perspective of Mayosim but the purported mishandling of data by the researchers. These critics charge that the data suggest conclusions other than those reached by the principal reporters of the research. This line of criticism ultimately challenges the basic operating principles of human relations, as popularized by Mayo and his associates.

Hawthorne and the Effectiveness of Economic Incentives

One can make a convincing case that the Hawthorne investigators sought to discredit the idea that people were primarily economically motivated. Certainly Roethlisberger felt that social man was not to be placed on a parity with economic man in one's attempt to understand the behavior of the industrial worker. Rather, he argued that the concept of social man was becoming the relevant theoretical perspective.

Roethlisberger was not interested in refining the existing paradigms, meaning scientific management.* He felt what was needed was

---

* This view was reinforced by a conversation one of the authors had with George F. F. Lombard, a close associate of Mayo and Roethlisberger.

a major reformulation of the problem, one that adequately expressed the distinct human characteristics of organizations. Economic motivation was to be recognized, but placed in a substantially different perspective.

Following their discussion of the relay assembly and mica test room experiments, Roethlisberger and Dickson stated:

> At least two conclusions seemed to be warranted from the test room experiments so far: (1) there was absolutely no evidence in favor of the hypothesis that the continuous increase in output in the Relay Assembly Test Room during the first two years could be attributed to the wage incentive factor alone; (2) efficacy of a wage incentive was so dependent on its relation to other factors that it was impossible to consider it as a thing in itself having an independent effect on the individual. Only in connection with the interpersonal relations at work and the personal situations outside of work, to mention two important variables, could its effect on output be determined.[2]

Later, when discussing the bank wiring observation room, they again concluded that the operators, who were restricting their output, were not acting in their own economic interests. The causes for such worker behavior, Roethlisberger and Dickson stated, lay more in social variables than in economic ones. In summing up the entire series of studies, they wrote:

> The results from the different inquiries provided considerable material for the study of financial incentive. None of the results, however, gave the slightest substantiation to the theory that the worker is primarily motivated by economic interest. The evidence indicated that the efficacy of a wage incentive is so dependent on its relation to other factors that it is impossible to separate it out as a thing in itself having an independent effect.[3]

Thus, Roethlisberger and Dickson concluded that economic incentives were not an effective means of increasing production. Rather, sociopsychological factors were the primary variables influencing worker performance. The Roethlisberger-Dickson conclusion established a theme that came to be understood by managers as a basic postulate of most theories in industrial psychology: money is not a motivator.

Several writers have challenged this interpretation. These critics have reevaluated the Hawthorne results and concluded that Roethlisberger and Dickson had gone to considerable lengths to minimize the importance of data unfavorable to their point of view. An example can be found in Alex Carey's close examination of the findings pertaining to the second relay assembly test group and the mica-splitting room.[4] Carey notes that Roethlisberger and Dickson's conclusion that wage incentives did not have an independent effect on the worker was contradicted by their previous observation that "in general, the findings from the Second Relay Assembly Group tended to substantiate the hypothesis that the formation of a small group for the purpose of determining piecework earnings was an important factor in the Relay Assembly Test Room performance."[5] Output in the second relay assembly group had increased by an average of 12.6 percent, an increase most researchers would regard as providing some substantiation that financial incentives influence employee behavior.

Roethlisberger and Dickson tempered this figure by first noting that group output remained constant throughout the experiment. After the initial increase in output, the group did not exhibit the subsequent increases observed in the original test room. Roethlisberger and Dickson went on to speculate that the apparent positive impact of the wage-incentive change might have worn off had the experiment continued longer, but they themselves admit this was conjecture.

The experiment was ended after nine weeks, when the foreman reported that the group's existence in the midst of the regular department was creating problems with the other operators. They, too, wished to be paid on a similar basis. In order to maintain the department's morale, the second test group of assemblers was returned to the regular method of payment. Unhappily, Roethlisberger and Dickson do not elaborate on this event. Their report gives the impression, however, that many of the operators in the regular department preferred the payment method used with the test group. Roethlisberger and Dickson still expressed doubts that the wage-incentive change explained the test group's increase in output, instead suggesting that a competitive spirit had emerged between the second relay assembly group and the original group. Members of the second group, they said, may have been trying to prove that they could produce as much output as the original test room operators.

Carey challenges the data used to support this observation, which is a single one-sentence entry in the history record stating that one of the test room operators reported that members of the second group had a "lively interest" in the output of the test room. Carey notes that the observation is interesting and even plausible but can hardly be considered of sufficient weight to merit rejection of the economic interest hypothesis.

As Carey points out, Roethlisberger and Dickson also placed considerable weight on a similar comment made by the layout operator in the original relay assembly test room.[6] Curiously, Roethlisberger and Dickson did not speculate about how this competition—to whatever extent it actually existed—may have influenced the relay assembly test room operators. The competition factor might suggest another possible hypothesis for future testing.* But Roethlisberger and Dickson instead used the few worker comments as data supporting their rejection of the wage-incentive hypothesis.

The pattern that emerges is a series of conjectures on the part of Roethlisberger and Dickson that either serve to cloud data favorable to the wage-incentive hypothesis or promote the authors' thesis. Their argument moves from an initial comment that the data at least partially support the wage-incentive hypothesis to the eventual, and much publicized, conclusion that there was no evidence of wage incentives having an independent impact on output rates.

This pattern is clearly evident in the case of the mica-splitting test room. This test was to duplicate the original relay assembly test, with the exception of the wage-incentive factor. The job involved was already on individual incentive, so no change in payment method was required when the operators moved into the test room.

In retrospect, the conditions created did not duplicate those of the relay assembly test room. For one thing, the changes in working hours were dictated more by external economic factors than by the experimenters. Only one change in rest breaks—introduction of a ten-minute break—was introduced. There was also overtime during this period, due to production demands. Despite these differences, Roethlisberger and Dickson equated the two situations in arriving at their conclusion that the difference in the two output increases—roughly 30 percent in the first relay assembly test room and 15 percent in the mica-splitting room—was the maximum that could be attributed to the change in wage incentive.

At times Roethlisberger and Dickson appeared determined to deny that the wage-incentive factor was of any importance at all, in the face of their own data to the contrary. When attempting to explain why the mica-splitting room did not achieve more dramatic results, they advanced the following argument:

> The fact that mica splitters were on individual piecework was another important factor. They did not have a vital interest in one another's output around which to organize a social group. It seemed fair to assume, besides, that under straight piecework the operators would tend to work closer to their maximum capacity than they would under group piecework. In other words, the mica splitters probably did not have the same reserves of skill and energy to call upon at the beginning of the test as the relay assemblers had; consequently, the increase in output which occurred in the mica

---

*Snow observed a competitive atmosphere between test groups during the illumination studies, suggesting that such feelings did exist to some extent.[7]

group was probably less than it would have been had the operators been on group piecework.[8]

The reader is being given the convoluted message that if the mica-splitting operators had not already been working so hard because of the individual wage incentive, perhaps they would have had more energy reserves to demonstrate that wage incentive is not an important influence on output rates! A manager reading this paragraph might well flirt with the idea of installing an individual wage-incentive system. Yet, two paragraphs later the authors end their chapter with a conclusion that wage incentive in and of itself is not a relevant factor.

If we accept the methodology employed by the Hawthorne researchers, recognizing the difficulties in conducting applied research in industrial settings, the data reported by Roethlisberger and Dickson would seem to merit the following conclusions. It might be argued that a wage-incentive factor can account for a 12–15 percent increase in output rate. This increase does not appear to be a steady one over a period of time but rather an abrupt increase that levels off. Thus, one must consider the possibility that the change in wage incentive partially influenced the output rates in the relay assembly test room. A further hypothesis is that the nature of a wage-incentive system can help shape the personal relationship patterns that emerge in a work group.

Such conclusions would have placed the Roethlisberger and Dickson findings in line with the later experiences of many non-human-relations-oriented researchers in installing incentive systems. For example, Edward Lawler has reviewed the literature on individual wage-incentive plans and concludes that even the most conservative results from such studies suggest they can increase productivity by 10–20 percent.[9] Ironically, Lawler cites the Hawthorne studies as tending to demonstrate the positive influence of incentives on productivity.

However, instead of confronting the data and attempting to integrate the wage-incentive influence into their theories, Roethlisberger and Dickson denied that influence. As a result, a strong element of fiction became part of the human relations lore stemming from Hawthorne. The belief that these studies demonstrated the unimportance of wage incentives remains strong.

Sykes makes points similar to Carey's when he concludes that in their discussions of the bank wiring room, Roethlisberger and Dickson went to considerable lengths in arguing that their data contradicted the idea of economic man.[10] The data collected by the observer in the bank wiring room indicated that the men were not producing up to their full capacity. In other words, the group-incentive system was not functioning properly since the operators were not producing at a level that would maximize their personal incomes. The men justified this restriction of output on the grounds that something harmful (such as a cut in the piece rates) would happen should they produce too much.

This behavior has, of course, been observed elsewhere.[11] The common interpretation of output restriction is that workers are motivated by perceived economic self-interest: maximum production will result in reduced rates for the job, the firing of some workers, or some other negative economic consequence. Roethlisberger and Dickson wrote that such an interpretation of the Hawthorne data was wrong.[12] They based their position on six basic arguments. Sykes considers each of the six in some detail.

First, Roethlisberger and Dickson argued that the workers were confused and unclear about what would happen should they maximize production. The men talked about the rates being cut but used the term "rate" differently. Some used it interchangeably with "bogey," which was a production target that management gave the men to shoot for. A change in this rate would by itself have no direct effect on earnings. Other men were confused about whether the term "rate" referred to piece, hourly, or other rates. Thus, the authors concluded that the men's reactions were not based on a logical appraisal of their work situation.

Sykes observes that this is at best a curious line of reasoning for Roethlisberger and Dickson to pursue. However inarticulate the men may have been in expressing themselves, it is evident from the research reports that, to the operators, "cutting the rate" clearly meant a management action whereby they would have to do more work in order to sustain their incomes. In short, while the men may not have understood the incentive system, they apparently believed that by restricting output they were forwarding their economic interests. It is interesting that Roethlisberger and Dickson exhaustively discussed employee attitudes and sentiments yet, in this situation, offered an extensive logical rebuttal to a belief that was obviously strongly felt by the workers.

Second, Roethlisberger and Dickson argued that none of the operators in the bank wiring room had experienced any of the things (such as cuts in piece rates) against which they were guarding. The implication is that the real objective of output restriction could not be the one cited by the men, simply because they had never experienced the occurrence that they said they feared.

The notion that people cannot fear conditions they have not directly experienced is nonsense. Besides, as Sykes notes, the workers at

Hawthorne might indeed have experienced rate-cutting. His source is John Mills, who wrote:

> Reward is supposed to be in direct proportion to production. Well, I remember the first time I ever got behind that fiction. I was visiting the Western Electric Company, which had a reputation of never cutting a piece rate. It never did; if some manufacturing process was found to pay more than seemed right for the class of labor employed on it—if in other words, the rate setters had misjudged—that particular part was referred back to the engineers for redesign and then a new rate was set on the new part.[13]

However, whether rates had ever been cut at Hawthorne is a moot point, since behavioral and social science findings show that people frequently take action on the basis of beliefs rather than experience.

The third argument advanced by Roethlisberger and Dickson was that the workers, if they had been economically motivated, would have wanted flexible rates of pay. This line of reasoning maintained that operators should have wanted the rates raised or lowered to reflect changes in an individual's efficiency since such flexibility was the only way earnings could be made to correspond with output. Under the group piecework plan in the bank wiring room, the earnings of any one individual were affected by the output of the other operators. To control for individual differences in working speeds, a worker was assigned an hourly rate based on his own average hourly output. This hourly rate was the basis for dividing the piecework earnings among the men. Roethlisberger and Dickson argued that under this system, a person motivated by economics would have wanted the rates to be flexible: such a system would have increased the hourly rates of those who worked hardest while reducing the hourly rates of the low producers. In fact, the high producers, who would have benefited from flexible rates as well as low producers, did not want them.

Sykes observes, and we concur, that in developing this line of argument Roethlisberger and Dickson were defining economic interest in a very particular and narrow fashion. In so doing, they had to overlook some basic realities of industrial relations. While flexible rates might be in the short-term economic interests of the high producers, such an arrangement might not be in their best interest over the long term. The arrangement would establish management's right to freely alter the hourly rates. Labor leaders have since expended much effort in opposing the establishment of such a precedent in companies.

Some of the workers were not acting in their immediate economic interest but they certainly may have been acting in accordance with other economic interests. In the absence of evidence to the contrary, it is most reasonable to assume that the men were primarily concerned about rate reduction, especially as it might occur in the future. They may have been willing to sacrifice short-term economic gain for what they perceived to be their long-term interests.

In defending their line of reasoning, Roethlisberger and Dickson introduced another argument. They asked the reader to assume for the moment that the piece rate was somehow in danger of being cut should output exceed the workers' concept of "a fair day's work." Why would not every worker push his output up to 6,600 connections per day and then hold it at that point? This would secure the maximum earnings possible without endangering the piece rate. Yet, several operators were far below this level, and were not working at their top capacity.

In his rebuttal of this argument, Sykes again states that economic interest was being defined in the narrowest of terms. No study of industrial workers has ever found employees sticking rigidly to the maximum limit. Typically, a worker's output curve will tend to approximate a given level over time, but individuals are careful not to show the same output daily. To produce a perfectly even level of output day in and day out would call attention to the fact that workers were restricting or controlling their output.[14] Such behavior is far from illogical: when workers believe that management will change the rates if they show they can work faster, their refusal to maintain a constant level of production makes perfect sense. Again Sykes concludes that just because the workers were not acting in accordance with one definition of their economic interest, this does not mean they were unconcerned with their economic interest at all.

The fifth argument advanced by Roethlisberger and Dickson was that the operators, if they had been economically motivated, would have wanted flexible rates because these would rise with the cost of living. Here the authors implied an optimistic definition of rate flexibility: namely, the idea that rate would go up. Certainly Roethlisberger and Dickson provided no data indicating that the operators opposed a *rise* in their rates. The other side of "flexibility" was probably on their minds. When, throughout the history of labor relations, workers have argued for fixed rates, they have meant that rates must not be lowered.

In arguing that the bank wiring room operators were against rates being lowered or raised, Roethlisberger and Dickson appear to have completely misunderstood how the workers generally used the term "fixed rate." This is a notable departure from their usual emphasis on understanding exactly what meaning workers attach to events and terminology.

Finally, Roethlisberger and Dickson asserted that the workers could not effectively control the actions of management regardless of how they behaved. In reality, the reasons for changing the rates often lay outside the control not only of the workers but of management. Besides, the company policy was to change rates when a manufacturing process changed, and engineers made such changes whenever significant savings appeared likely. In fact, however, the workers' restriction of output might even precipitate a rate change, since this behavior tended to increase unit costs.

This argument involves two questionable assumptions. One is that workers know they cannot influence the rates and so would have no reason to restrict output because it will be economically beneficial. The other assumption is that management will act logically and not try to cut rates because they know that increased production means cheaper labor costs.

Roethlisberger and Dickson offered no evidence in support of these assumptions. Other studies have produced evidence that workers *do* believe they can influence a piece-rate wage structure by controlling their output, and comments of the bank wiring room operators gave some indication that they believed likewise. Roethlisberger and Dickson's argument again seems to contradict a central theme in their work: the idea that the beliefs and sentiments of workers must be investigated thoroughly if their behavior is to be understood.

Further, there is no evidence to support the assumption that management would act logically and not cut rates because it might lead to higher labor costs. John Mills's observation about how changes in manufacturing processes are used to reduce piece rates certainly adds an element of realism to the workers' fears in this regard.

To summarize, Roethlisberger and Dickson's discussion of the bank wiring observation follows the same pattern that is evident in their presentation of the relay assembly test room: they go to great lengths to reject a hypothesis of economic incentive, avoiding many plausible interpretations that might grant at least partial explanation of the results to financial self-interest. We have concluded, through a critical reading of Roethlisberger and Dickson's discussion of the bank wiring room test, that Sykes's analysis is valid. Roethlisberger and Dickson expend considerable intellectual energy developing positions that rest on the narrowest possible definition of economic interest and that fail to explain the data as comfortably as other interpretations. Further, one of their conclusions rests on a striking internal inconsistency. Roethlisberger and Dickson argue that a major source of industrial unrest is management's insistence on using formal logic to predict employee behavior. In one breath, the reader is told that rational management control systems (such as incentives) fail because management assumes workers will respond in accordance with the logical criteria utilized in developing their systems. Then the reader is told that the idea of workers being economically motivated is disproved by their failure to respond to just such a system—a system that has been described as irrelevant to worker behavior.

Thus, rather than taking the seemingly obvious path of exploring how workers interpreted their economic interest, the authors seemed bent on establishing the unimportance of economic interest in industrial human relations. Although they produced no evidence to disprove the commonly accepted view that workers restricted output out of financial self-interest, their conclusion to the contrary became part of the lore of management, accepted by many as fact and still believed credible in many quarters.

The Impact of Changes in the Task and in Rest Periods

It will be recalled that, in addition to the possibility that a change in the incentive system might explain the increased output in the first relay assembly test room, three additional hypotheses were advanced and rejected. One was that changes in the nature of the work task itself might account for part of the output increase. The other two hypotheses related to a reduction of either fatigue or monotony because of the introduction of rest periods and a reduced number of working hours.

Roethlisberger and Dickson never gave the first hypothesis close scrutiny. They noted that the only change in work methods which seemed important was that the test room operators had to assemble fewer types of relays than in the regular department. This, they admitted, could not be entirely ignored. They pointed out that Operator 5, who had the most different types of relays to assemble, had shown the least improvement in output. Whitehead reported that later in the experiment, when this operator's working conditions were more in line with the others', her performance definitely improved.[15] However, like Roethlisberger and Dickson, Whitehead rejected the work-methods explanation. He stated that during the experiment all the operators experienced a fair number of changes in relay type, so the situation was not so dissimilar from that in the regular department. Whitehead also noted that Operator 5 had obtained the lowest score on an intelligence test that was given, and suggested this as an "obviously possible" alternative explanation.

Roethlisberger and Dickson's conclusion with regard to the work-methods hypothesis reflects a recurring trend throughout their writings: the rejection of nonpreferred hypotheses on the ground that there is no conclusive evidence or no evidence that the hypothesis can alone account for all of the results. Yet, Roethlisberger and Dickson applied neither of these criteria to the conclusions they advanced themselves. Rather, their arguments appear highly speculative.

It is this characteristic of the Roethlisberger and Dickson arguments that critics repeatedly focus on. It is unlikely that the change in work methods accounted for all the occurrences in the relay assembly test room. However, Roethlisberger and Dickson (and Whitehead as well) appeared to deny that the change had *any* affect. This is the same position they adopted in discussing the impact of incentives, despite suggestive evidence to the contrary.

Other changes were also created by the experimental design of the relay assembly test room. Roethlisberger and Dickson stated that the new chute mechanism made the work slightly easier. There was one layout operator for five women instead of one for six or seven operators as in the regular department. This probably was not influential; Whitehead commented that, to his knowledge, the operators in the regular department were not having problems being serviced by layout operators. No information is available on whether the layout operator in the test room helped the operators in any special way. Finally, the test room operators experienced longer runs of a given relay type than was true in the regular department.

Any conclusion regarding the cumulative effect of these changes on the output rate would necessarily be speculative. Roethlisberger and Dickson take the position of completely rejecting the work-methods hypothesis.

Michael Argyle, having reviewed the data from the relay assembly test room, is less eager to reject this explanation.[16] Argyle points out that the changed work methods, combined with other physical variables in the test room, could have significantly contributed to the increased output rate. Unfortunately, the design of the studies and the available data do not permit adequate testing of this explanation.

Although Roethlisberger and Dickson likewise rejected hypotheses regarding the contribution of rest periods to relief of fatigue or monotony, the data tend to raise questions about such a conclusion. The authors admitted that the evidence was contradictory. Their argument is based on the notion of a fatigue curve in which morning output should be higher than in the afternoon. They reasoned that if fatigue were a factor, there should be less difference between morning and afternoon output rates during the experimental periods with rest breaks. During periods 2 and 3, when the women worked without any rest breaks, the difference between the morning and afternoon rates averaged 3.3 percent. In periods 8 and 9 (marked by both rest periods and a shorter workweek), the difference dropped to an average of 0.3 percent. During period 11, when the researchers described the working conditions as relatively adverse, the average difference mounted to 2.9 percent. Roethlisberger and Dickson admitted that the changes during these periods were "strictly in accordance with the fatigue hypothesis."[17]

However, the average difference between morning and afternoon was 3.9 percent in periods 4 and 5 (when rests were first introduced), which contradicts the fatigue hypothesis. Also, in period 13 the average afternoon rate exceeded the morning rate. The authors concluded that "although there is considerable evidence in the morning and afternoon output data to support the case for relief from accumulation of fatigue within the working day, there are several important observations which cannot be reconciled with this interpretation."[18]

In examining composite daily work curves for individual operators, Roethlisberger and Dickson failed to find conclusive evidence in favor of either the fatigue or monotony hypotheses. The authors noted that "caution should be exercised in reasoning about fatigue from production curves, since output curves are not pure fatigue curves."[19] As these curves represent the principal basis on which the fatigue and monotony hypotheses were rejected, one again wonders how they could be so confident in rejecting these explanations.

In period 11, when the original conditions were imposed, the rate of production gradually declined. Roethlisberger and Dickson conceded that this was rather convincing evidence in favor of the fatigue hypothesis. Morris Viteles, in a critical review of the Hawthorne studies, pointed out that such results "are exactly the same used by other investigators in illustrating the effectiveness of rest pauses by reason of reduced fatigue."[20]

In sum, the Hawthorne data left open the possibility that the rest breaks and shorter hours during the experimental periods partly or largely contributed to the increased output because of reduced fatigue and possibly monotony. Although at times the results were equivocal, suggesting other influences as well, many of the data tended to support this hypothesis.

Supervisory Style in the Relay Assembly Test Room

Taken in their entirety, the data reviewed so far indicated that changes in wage incentives may have contributed significantly to the results in the relay assembly test room. The possibility also existed that changes in work methods were contributing factors. Though the data regarding the fatigue and monotony hypotheses were mixed and the variables complex, these hypotheses could not be rejected out of hand.

No single one of these hypotheses was adequate to explain all the data, but all the above data could have had partial or interactive effects.

Roethlisberger and Dickson rejected all these explanations in favor of the one that was to become the underlying theme of the human relations movement: the hypothesis that the increased output in the relay assembly test room was a result of the changes in supervisory methods that had occurred. The authors emphasized that the operators in the test room were not apprehensive about authority and cited other social changes that had accompanied the alterations in supervisory approach. Roethlisberger and Dickson did not apply the same severe critical analysis to the testing of this hypothesis as they did with regard to the other explanations. Alex Carey has done so, however, making some telling points in the process.[21]

Carey views the relay assembly test room experiment as consisting of three phases. During the first phase, lasting three and a half months, supervisors were consistently friendly. The test room investigators were most anxious for the women to maintain a cooperative attitude because, as noted earlier, they wished to establish experimental control over this important variable.

During this time, the investigators were also confronted with a dilemma. The operators talked to one another so much that, as Roethlisberger and Dickson reported, they were paying insufficient attention to work. Records show that twelve weeks into the test, four of the women were reprimanded by the foreman for talking too much. The problem continued, but the experimenters made no real attempts to control it because they were not sure how to intervene without jeopardizing the "experimental control" they hoped to achieve. Any reprimand tended to be met with a comment such as, "We thought you wanted us to work as we feel."

This led to a second phase, during which supervision became more stern. Two of the operators became less and less cooperative, further threatening desired experimental control. A company executive suggested that the supervisor hint to the women that the free lunches would be discontinued if things did not improve.[22] Whether this idea was followed through is unclear. Finally, one of the uncooperative women was told in a conference with the test room authorities that she was "moody, inattentive and not cooperative."[23] By this time, the split had emerged between the two problem operators and the others, and the investigators returned the two operators to the regular department.

The third phase, according to Carey's analysis, began when two new women replaced the operators. Roethlisberger and Dickson, as well as Whitehead, clearly indicated that one of these new operators had unusual character and motivation.[24] Her family largely depended on her for support, and shortly after she entered the test room her father became unemployed and she was under still more economic pressure. In addition, she was described as being ambitious beyond her current station and as being deeply convinced of the experiment's importance. She held all the records in speed and output tests, and scored highest in dexterity and intelligence.

Immediately, this operator established leadership over the group. She both exhorted them to increase production and influenced the group to maintain internal discipline. With her arrival, the supervisory atmosphere again became more relaxed.

The output figures for the group during each of these phases are interesting. In the first phase there was no "appreciable change in output" followed by a "downward tendency" over the course of the first five weeks. At the end of five weeks, the new wage-incentive system was implemented, in which the women were treated as a separate group of five for payment purposes (as opposed to part of a group of one hundred in the regular department). Although a direct comparison with their prior production levels was impossible because the piece rates were also changed at this time, the investigators did measure a 4–5 percent increase in output after the five women became a separate payment group. (The change in piece rates was made because the women were assembling fewer types of relays. The new rates enabled them to earn the same amount of money for an amount of work equivalent to what they had done before the experiment began.)

Throughout this first fifteen-week phase of the study, supervisors were making every effort to be open, friendly, and nonauthoritarian with the women. The principal result during this period, the 4–5 percent increase in output, appears to have been associated with implementation of the new incentive system.

The next phase was marked by introduction of the rest pauses. At first the supervisors remained open and nonauthoritarian. Output remained essentially consistent, but the talking problem grew worse and the supervisors became more disciplinarian, eventually removing the two women who appeared to be instigators. It was with the introduction of the highly motivated operator with leadership qualities that output began its impressive, steady climb. The supervisory climate again became relaxed.

This sequence of events raises several questions not specifically dealt with by Roethlisberger and Dickson. Was the increase in output later in the experiment a function of the personality skills and somewhat unique motivations of one of the replacement operators? If so, how frequently does this combination of characteristics occur in the work force in general? To what extent were the supervisory style changes *caused* by the favorable output in the test room, instead of supervisory style changing output?

It seems clear that the "open" supervisory style in the test room did not have an immediate positive effect. Nor was it able to resolve the talking problem. The extent to which the subsequent disciplinary measures influenced the other operators was not explored by the investigators.

When the supervisory style approach was initiated in the mica-splitting test room, results did not match those of the relay assembly test room. Roethlisberger and Dickson suggested that the fact that the mica operators were on individual wage incentive may have had something to do with this outcome. As we have said, this comment certainly contains an implication that certain forms of wage incentive may be just as influential as supervisory methods in sustaining high productivity.

In sum, the events at Hawthorne raised many issues relative to the supervisory style hypothesis that remained unexplored by Roethlisberger and Dickson. Despite the finality in tone of some of their assertions, the case supporting their conclusions is surprisingly weak. Carey sums up his feelings as follows.

> The results of these studies, far from supporting the various components of the "human relations approach," are surprisingly consistent with a rather old-world view about the value of monetary incentives, driving leadership, and discipline. It is only by massive and relentless reinterpretation that the evidence is made to yield contrary conclusions. To make these points is not to claim that the Hawthorne studies can provide serious support for any such old-world view. The limitations of the Hawthorne studies clearly render them incapable of yielding serious support for any sort of generalization whatever.[25]

Carey's conclusion may be somewhat extreme, but at minimum the data suggest that factors other than supervisory style were influential in generating some of the results obtained in the relay assembly test room. At best, given the data-analysis techniques employed by the investigators, the supervisory style hypothesis could be considered a partial but not necessarily critical explanation for what occurred. Our reference to the data-analysis techniques that were used is significant. All of the criticisms discussed above deal with the logic used in interpreting the studies and do not rely on analytical tools unavailable to the Hawthorne-Harvard researchers. As we will see shortly, contemporary statistical analysis of the data has yielded findings even more damaging to the supervisory style hypothesis.

Subsequent human-relations-oriented research has overwhelmingly established that the link between job satisfaction and productivity, while positive, is very weak. In other words, satisfied workers are not always productive. The apparent inconsistency between the majority of research results and the conclusions drawn from the Hawthorne studies largely evaporates once one realizes the nature of the data on which the Hawthorne conclusions were based. In retrospect, the link between supervisory style, satisfaction, and productivity described by Roethlisberger and Dickson was not very convincing.

The Revisionist Perspective

Writers like Sykes, Carey, and Argyle challenge Roethlisberger and Dickson's handling and interpretation of their data and believe that strong arguments can be made in support of more traditional conclusions. Other theorists have reinterpreted the data in a more conciliatory manner. Essentially, these writers argue that the original reports of the studies were erroneous not because the researchers chose to ignore the obvious, but because subsequent behavioral research into management problems has provided new perspectives not available to the Hawthorne investigators. Instead of arguing for a more traditional interpretation of what happened at Hawthorne, these revisionists believe that the data support more contemporary behavioral theories.

Parsons and the Operant Conditioning Theory

One representative of this position is H. M. Parsons, who argues that the results in the relay assembly test room can be largely explained by operant reinforcement contingencies.[26] Parsons notes that in the test room, counters that measured the output of each operator were visible and accessible to the women. Readings from these counters, which had been specially installed for data-collection purposes, were taken every half hour. All told, Parsons argues, the women had available to them a massive amount of information on their production that operators in the regular department did not receive. How this information was shared with the test room operators is not systematically discussed in the investigators' original accounts. Parsons attributes this oversight to the fact that in the early 1930s there were virtually no theories suggesting that feedback could be a crucial variable influencing work behavior.

Parsons notes, however, that comments recorded in the history sheets reveal that the operators knew how their current production compared to that of the preceding day. Further, in a letter to Parsons, the test room observer stated that the half-hourly cumulative totals from the counters were kept in a place where any of the operators could see them. Each woman did periodically check the data, especially if she believed her production to be significantly above or below her standard. The observer also said that each woman's daily output was reported to her at the end of every day or the following morning.

Thus, operators in the relay assembly test room apparently received knowledge of results frequently and systematically. This did not seem to be true in either the second relay assembly group experiment or the mica-splitting test room experiment. In the former case, five operators were grouped together for payment purposes. Their work stations had no counters or other devices to record completed relays. Nor is there any evidence that they had the type of access to their own production information as was true of their counterparts in the first test room. It will be remembered that the second group's production rose an average of 12 percent with the change in payment method, but did not show the continuous increase observed in the test room.

In the mica-splitting test room, output had to be counted by hand. Parsons notes that the data from this experiment tend to support the wage-incentive, fatigue, or monotony hypotheses as explaining part of the results. No detailed information is available on the feedback aspects of the experiments, but Parsons argues that payment based on individual incentives is an important form of personal feedback.

In making such points, Parsons is pursuing a line of criticism similar to that of Carey and others: he suggests that the investigators ignored variables that may have had a demonstrable effect on results. Parsons goes on, however, to suggest that the continuous rise in output observed in the first relay assembly test room can be explained by operant conditioning theory. He concludes:

> But even if the other demand characteristics of the experiment had not implied instructions to work faster, the frequent feedback of information about output rate would have done so. The girls kept setting higher goals of productivity because of knowledge of results. Their own remarks tell us they were setting goals. . . . This conclusion ties the Hawthorne research into a large and growing body of applied research in behavior modification; and couples the reward system (small group piecework pay) and the information system (feedback from the recording of performance data) nicely together to explain why the output rate in the principal Hawthorne experiment kept going up.[27]

Parsons finds this interpretation superior to those which attribute the increased output to vaguely defined variables such as attitude or morale.

In summarizing Parsons's position, it is important to note that:

1. He acknowledges that part of the results obtained in the relay assembly test room may be attributable to traditional work-method concerns such as rest periods and shorter hours.
2. In his operant conditioning explanation, he explicitly states that the piecework system itself was a factor in the increased output.
3. He attributes the continuous rise in output to the *total* feedback system, involving not only rewards but frequent information on results.

Parsons advances this explanation as an alternative to the hypothesis of supervisory style, though he takes into account most of the other factors that may have influenced the Hawthorne results.

Hawthorne and the Quality of Work Life

Another revisionist look at the Hawthorne data has been taken by writers closely identified with the quality-of-work-life, or human-resources-utilization, approach to management. Generally, these writers see themselves as part of a research tradition that began with Hawthorne and has since undergone considerable refinement and development. For them, reinterpreting Hawthorne is largely a matter of emphasis: redefining which of the data now appear significant in light of more advanced research.

A key variable in this new interpretation is participation. Robert Kahn states the issue succinctly:

> My own answer . . . involved the hypothesized effect of participation itself; not participation in an experiment but participation in shaping the conditions and expectations of a major life role. I have become convinced that the young women in the relay assembly test room were offered and increasingly took the opportunity to alter their work roles in content, duration, pace, rewards and relationship to conventional authority. There was, in short, a genuine transfer of power, in significant degree and for no trivial period of time.[28]

Under this view, the Hawthorne studies unwittingly provide support for the experimental quality-of-work-life practices that were implemented in the Topeka pet food plant, various Swedish car manufacturing plants, and other sites.

The Hawthorne reports do provide descriptive material that appears supportive of such a view. It is impossible to evaluate the impact of the variables involved but the following points are suggestive.

1. The investigators invited two experienced operators who were known to be friendly with each other to participate in the test and asked them to select the remaining members of the group. Thus, these two women must certainly have felt a sense of participation in shaping the work environment.
2. In most instances the women were more than merely informed about the experimental changes to be implemented: they had a certain amount of control over them. For example, the operators set the timing of the rest breaks and often had a choice about the frequency of breaks as well. This was also true of the work hour changes.
3. The physical examinations that the women were requested to take were initially unpopular. Their reactions led the investigators to suggest that ice cream be served following the examinations. When the women were enthusiastic about this, the idea was implemented. The women furnished cake, and a party was held after each examination.
4. When the investigators said they planned to defer payment of part of the bonus money earned until the end of the month, the women objected and the plan was quickly dropped.
5. The investigators stated their intention of returning to a test period under the original forty-eight-hour workweek, but postponed this action because they had earlier promised the operators that a five-day workweek would be tried during the summer months.

Whitehead further supported such arguments when he noted that not only were the operators promised an "effective voice" in the design of the experimental conditions, but their suggestions regarding the layout of the work area were given consideration and, where practicable, acted upon.[29] For example, footrests were installed at the request of the operators.

Within the job itself, workers were allowed individual freedom in how they completed the assembly operation, receiving no systematic training in a previously determined "best way" of performing the process. According to Whitehead's report, one difference between the test room and the regular department was that in the test room each operator had to repair her own defective relays. In the regular department this practice was not always followed. Each assembler was also responsible for inspecting and rejecting any unsuitable parts. This enlarged job description, combined with the feedback mechanism discussed previously in connection with Parsons's arguments, corresponds remarkably to recent job-redesign experiments.

Additional illustrations of the operators' control over their tasks and their work environment abound in the Whitehead report. For example, the plant custom was for summer vacations to be taken at different times by operators in a department. When the test room operators expressed a desire to take their summer vacations at the same time, this was permitted. The group also exerted influence over members' time off. When an operator wished to be absent for a half day or full day, she would state her reasons to the group. The group would discuss her reasons and either approve or reject the absence, although it had no formal authority to enforce its decision. This custom emerged because even when a substitute was obtained for a day, the absences tended to reduce the weekly output since the substitutes were not as fast as the regular operator.

The extent to which the operators' ideas influenced the experimental conditions is illustrated by Whitehead's description of a luncheon that was held to commemorate the second anniversary of the test room. "During the course of the lunch [the superintendent] asked the operators what they thought the next experimental change should be, and they were all in favor of having Saturday mornings off. This accordingly was agreed upon for the next experimental period."[30]

The above incidents indicate that the women in the test room experienced personal and group responsibility for many aspects of their working environment. Although much of this responsibility evolved informally, it can reasonably be stated that these operators had significantly more control over their work lives than operators in the regular department. Roethlisberger and Dickson attributed the test room results to friendly supervision along with the sociable interpersonal relationships that evolved. A close reading of their report, however, suggests that more fundamental changes occurred in the job content, roles, and responsibilities of the test room operators—changes similar to those implemented during many job-redesign and quality-of-work-life experiments.

This provides a different perspective for assessing Carey's arguments that friendly supervision did not achieve the results reported. There certainly is reason to question Roethlisberger and Dickson's hypothesis that friendly supervision was a powerful explanation for the results obtained. Yet, what Carey describes as incidents of authoritarian management style during certain critical points of the experiment *can* be viewed as examples of role negotiation between supervisors and operators, with the latter trying to learn the boundaries of the responsibilities in a new work structure. Such conflicts are often observed during quality-of-work-life experiments.

One possible illustration of role negotiation is found in the sixth experimental period of the relay assembly test room. This was the period during which the women were asked whether they thought two fifteen-minute rest pauses (one in the morning and one in the afternoon) should be tried. Roethlisberger and Dickson reported: "In spite of the unanimity of opinion among the girls in favor of the single period of fifteen minutes, the investigators decided to try the six five-minute rests first and explained to the girls their reasons for doing so."[31] Throughout this period, the women expressed hostility to the break schedule, often returning from breaks late and interrupting their work to laugh and talk. In short, after the investigators overruled the operators' previously established prerogative to decide the break schedule, they encountered continued resistance despite their careful explanations of the reasons behind the decision.

In the mica-splitting test room, the various changes in rest periods and working hours were basically determined by economic conditions outside the plant. The shorter working hours, for example, corresponded to a general cutback in the regular department. There is little evidence that the women involved achieved anywhere near the levels of autonomy and personal control over the work environment that had been experienced by the operators in the relay assembly test room.

Thus, the mica-splitting experiment never came close to duplicating the relay assembly experiment. One could speculate that this lack of control and decision-making power better explains the mediocre results achieved in the mica-splitting test room than do the reasons advanced by Roethlisberger and Dickson. The mica-splitting test room might be viewed as a poor imitation of the relay assembly test room, much as a company's later quality-of-work-life efforts are often pale imitations of their predecessors in terms of spirit and control. In any event, the mica-splitting test room scarcely resembled the relay test room, in terms of either experimental conditions or the operators' roles and responsibilities.

From the perspective of humanistic psychology, this is a far more satisfying explanation for what happened in the mica-splitting test than Roethlisberger and Dickson's argument that, because of the individual wage-incentive system, the women had already been producing close to capacity before entering the test room. However, given the available data, it is impossible to determine which is the better explanation or to determine (if we assume a combination) the extent to which each factor influenced the outcome.

Clearly, there are important differences between the relay assembly test and the kinds of work-redesign and quality-of-work-life experiments currently being attempted by researchers and managers who are striving to create innovative work environments. Yet, the role content of operators in the principal Hawthorne test room experiment resembled some of the characteristics of contemporary work-redesign efforts. To the revisionists, it is not human relations but the restructuring of roles and responsibilities that accounted for the continuing upward trend in output.

In considering this conclusion, we should note another similarity between the relay assembly test room and many of the current experimental efforts at work restructuring. The investigators who selected the women for the test room considered it important that they be willing and cooperative. This selectivity was later reinforced when two of the operators were removed from the group because of lack of cooperation and replaced with two other carefully chosen operators. This is similar to the approach taken during the highly publicized work-restructuring experiment at the Topeka pet food plant, where employees were carefully selected from a large number of applicants. As at Hawthorne, the Topeka researchers were looking for highly motivated and cooperative workers. Any traditionalist will be quick to point out that neither experiment particularly demonstrates the effectiveness of job restructuring, participation, or any similar change on the less than cooperative employee.

A Recent Statistical Interpretation: Support for the Critics

Recently, Richard Franke and James Kaul conducted an extensive statistical analysis of the Hawthorne data.[32] Using time-series regression procedures, Franke and Kaul reanalyzed the data from the relay assembly test room by quantitatively expressing three performance variables (output quantity per worker per hour and per week, and a negative measure of output quality based on repair time per worker per day) and twelve independent variables embedded in the working environment. These latter variables included such factors as managerial discipline and economic depression. The analysis covers all twenty-three of the experimental periods that occurred from 1927 to 1933, not just the first thirteen.

Franke and Kaul concluded that "three variables—managerial discipline, the economic adversity of the depression, and time set aside for rest—explain most of the variance in quantity of output for the group and generally for individual workers."

Franke and Kaul provided direct support for the arguments of Carey and Argyle:

> This exercise of managerial discipline seems to have been the major factor
> in increased rates of output for the now altered group including increased

production by the three individuals remaining. It may be speculated that improvement resulted from the positive example of the two new workers, as well as from the aversive effects of management's disposal of two of the original workers. Clear support is given to the suggestion by Carey . . . that this intervention was a key part of the first relay experiment. As pointed out by Argyle . . . , the Hawthorne researchers had provided "no quantitative evidence for the conclusion for which this experiment is famous—that the increase of output was due to a changed relation with supervision." Quantitative evaluation now does provide such evidence. However, it is not "release from oppressive supervision," . . . but its reassertion that explains higher rates of production.[33]

Using contemporary statistical techniques, Franke and Kaul developed a line of reasoning that was possible from the original reports but was rejected by the Harvard researchers. Franke and Kaul's conclusions imply rejection of the revisionist interpretations of the studies. But they were careful not to overstep the data, observing that "on the other hand, such activities as participative management, industrial democracy, and sensitivity or consideration training may have benefits transcending the criteria considered here."

It is important to bear in mind that the Franke and Kaul data deal with the relationship between certain traditional management variables and the output rate in the relay assembly test room. However, there remains the fact that changes in the quality of the relationship between the experimenters and the women could have had a facilitating impact on how the reassertion of discipline, for example, was received. Also, one of the replacement operators had some intangible leadership qualities that may have affected the results of the experiment.

An Overview of Hawthorne

The Hawthorne studies, especially the relay assembly test room experiment, clearly are open to different interpretations, many in seemingly direct opposition to one another. Perhaps the most ironic observation is that much of the impressive amount of information reported by Roethlisberger, Dickson, and Whitehead is damaging to the position they were hoping to advance.

However, close readings of the original research reports do establish two points, both of which run counter to widely held beliefs about the studies. First, the studies did *not* demonstrate that the workers involved were unmotivated by economic considerations. If anything, the data tend to support the opposite conclusion. The results seem to indicate that, at least under certain conditions, incentives can generate an increase in production.

Second, the experimental conditions (rest pauses and shorter hours) may well have generated some of the increased output in the relay assembly test room. The original data suggested that this explanation was plausible and recent statistical reevaluations support this view. Additionally, there is some evidence that the changes in work methods involved in the experiment (such as the reduction in different types of relays assembled) might have contributed to the outcome.

Therefore, contrary to popular belief, the Hawthorne data are not especially damaging to traditional viewpoints on management. In fact, the studies produced results that might quite easily be seen as supporting the theories popularly associated with scientific management.

The question of how changes in the operator's roles affected results is a speculative one. But it certainly is worthy of note that the operators participated in staffing the test room, contributed to the layout of the work area, made decisions regarding rest periods and work hours, received direct feedback on their job performance, corrected their own mistakes, and informally approved one anothers' absences.

Perhaps the real contribution of the Hawthorne studies is one that has gone largely unnoticed, even by some of the strongest contemporary critics. In many respects, Hawthorne is an inadvertent example of an action research experiment that combined factors generally associated with traditional management approaches (incentives, rest pauses, greater product specialization) with work-restructuring and quality-of-work-life concerns (employee input regarding working conditions, more complete jobs, some autonomy of action). Over the years, those who have discussed the Hawthorne data have tended to look for *the* single variable, or set of related variables, that can be advanced as the final explanation. Many of the variables involved are associated with management philosophies that are traditionally viewed as being diametrically opposed. This perceived polarity has reinforced the tendency of some writers to reject certain variables.

The existing data suggest that a significant portion of the output gains in the relay assembly test room was associated with traditional management variables and economic conditions. On the other hand, additional factors may also have been at work. For example, the assemblers did not generally exhibit the adversarial attitudes that often arise when traditional management methods are used. It seems possible that a large number of factors, including the restructuring of the operators' roles, contributed to a qualitatively altered work situation. This may in part have facilitated the continuing improvement in the output rate without the hostility often found in industrial settings. This, of course, admittedly involved only a small, select group of workers.

The practical result of Hawthorne was to tend to divide students of management into two adversarial camps: the human relationists versus the scientific management technocrats. Might this division have evolved largely out of misinterpretation of the studies—that is, out of myth rather than reality?

NOTES

1. W. Dowling, *Effective Management and the Behavioral Sciences* (New York: AMACOM, 1978), p. 203.
2. Fritz J. Roethlisberger and William J. Dickson, *Management and the Worker* (Cambridge, Mass.: Harvard University Press, 1939), p. 160.
3. Ibid., pp. 575–576.
4. The following discussion benefits from observations made by Alex Carey in "The Hawthorne Studies: A Radical Criticism," *American Sociological Review,* Vol. 32 (1967), pp. 403–416.
5. Roethlisberger and Dickson, *Management and the Worker,* p. 133.
6. Ibid., p. 134.
7. See C. D. Wrege, "Solving Mayo's Mystery: The First Complete Account of the Origin of the Hawthorne Studies—The Forgotten Contributions of C. E. Snow and H. Hibarger," *Academy of Management Proceedings,* 1976, p. 14.
8. Roethlisberger and Dickson, *Management and the Worker,* p. 159.
9. Edward Lawler III, *Motivation in Work Organizations* (Monterey, Calif.: Brooks/Cole, 1973).
10. A. J. M. Sykes, "Economic Interest and the Hawthorne Researches: A Comment," *Human Relations,* Vol. 18 (1965), pp. 253–263.
11. For a classic study conducted at the time of the Hawthorne researches, see Stanley B. Mathewsen, *Restriction of Output Among Unorganized Workers* (New York: Viking Press, 1931).
12. Roethlisberger and Dickson, *Management and the Worker,* pp. 531–535.
13. John Mills, *The Engineer in Society* (New York: Van Nostrand, 1946), p. 93.
14. See, for example, B. B. Gardner and D. G. Moore, *Human Relations in Industry* (Homewood, Ill.: Irwin, 1952), p. 186.
15. T. N. Whitehead, *The Industrial Worker* (Cambridge, Mass.: Harvard University Press, 1938), p. 65.
16. Michael Argyle, "The Relay Assembly Test Room in Retrospect," *Occupational Psychology,* Vol. 27 (1953), pp. 98–103.
17. Roethlisberger and Dickson, *Management and the Worker,* p. 107.
18. Ibid., p. 108.
19. Ibid., p. 91.
20. Morris Viteles, *Industrial Psychology* (New York: Norton, 1932), p. 476.
21. Carey, "The Hawthorne Studies."
22. Whitehead, *The Industrial Worker,* p. 116.
23. Roethlisberger and Dickson, *Management and the Worker,* p. 55.
24. Roethlisberger and Dickson, *Management and the Worker,* pp. 167, 171–172; Whitehead, *The Industrial Worker,* p. 120.

25. Carey, "The Hawthorne Studies."
26. H. M. Parsons, "What Happened at Hawthorne?" *Science,* Vol. 183, March 8, 1974.
27. Ibid.
28. Robert L. Kahn, "In Search of the Hawthorne Effect." In Eugene Louis Cass and Frederick G. Zimmer, eds., *Man and Work in Society* (New York: Van Nostrand Reinhold, 1975).
29. Whitehead, *The Industrial Worker,* pp. 27, 108.
30. Ibid., p. 136.
31. Roethlisberger and Dickson, *Management and the Worker,* p. 49.
32. Richard Herbert Franke and James D. Kaul, "The Hawthorne Experiments: First Statistical Interpretation," *American Sociological Review,* Vol. 43, No. 5, October 1978, pp. 623–643.
33. Ibid., p. 636.

7

The Harvard Group:
How the Studies Were Reported

As we have seen, there has been ample disagreement about what accounted for the events at Hawthorne. A case can be made that the principal authors of the research reports strove mightily to minimize the importance of data that lent support to traditional hypotheses in order to advance an alternative and preferred explanation. As was shown in the preceding chapter, the traditional hypotheses merited more consideration than was forthcoming from Whitehead, Roethlisberger, and Dickson. The proponents of new human resources strategies have a different perspective on the studies. They argue that the Hawthorne investigators overlooked the true sociopsychological explanations of what was happening. These revisionists basically accept the behavioral science perspective on management that gained prominence through the studies, but feel that the perspective has been refined through further investigations of employee behavior.

In this respect the Hawthorne experiments met one criterion of a successful case study: they provided sufficient richness of detail to suggest a range of hypotheses, many of them contradictory. The experiments also have a common limitation of case studies: they do not provide conclusive evidence for any particular theoretical perspective. Whatever may have happened at Hawthorne, there is no dodging the fact that the relay assembly test room involved a very small, select group of young, female assemblers drawn from a single industrial setting.

Certainly the studies present an interesting puzzle to students of the history of management thought. The revisionists reinterpret the studies in light of contemporary behavioral science insights that Mayo, Roethlisberger, and their associates could hardly be expected to have anticipated. Critics of the researches accuse Roethlisberger and Dickson of taking an almost cavalier attitude in rejecting certain hypotheses. And indeed, the Harvard group underplayed a significant amount of variance in the data with which they were working. The question of why they did so may be the only truly significant issue concerning the Hawthorne studies.

For the Harvard group the studies were an opportunity to illustrate a phenomenon that they believed they had encountered elsewhere and suspected was occurring at Hawthorne as well. Indeed, prior to the reporting of the research, both Mayo and Roethlisberger were conversant with many of the ideas that would later appear in their conclusions about the studies. Instead of providing a startling new insight, the Hawthorne data represented to Mayo and Roethlisberger a class of phenomena with which they were already deeply involved.

The Mayo–Roethlisberger Relationship

Roethlisberger stated that his youth was marked by a striving for knowledge and certainty: he found reassurance in the concrete achievements of science and technology. Many of the ways in which people expressed emotion left him feeling less assured; social ritual often left him uncomfortable, for reasons of which he was not yet aware. In his seventies, in reflecting on his teenage years, he remarked, "Even at that time I could distinguish slightly between words that produced useful things and words that seemed to produce mostly hurts, fights, and paroxysms. . . . Exactly what constituted the difference it took me many years to learn."[1] Roethlisberger's recollections present a picture of a youth expending considerable energies to deny certain aspects of the human condition, yet also being troubled by them. These concerns later became the center of his career.

In 1921 Roethlisberger received an A.B. degree from Columbia University, after transferring to M.I.T. for a period. At M.I.T. he had studied engineering administration, a combination of economics and engineering. The economics portion of his studies turned out to be "scientific management" and "Frederick Taylorism." Roethlisberger had the following vehement reaction:

> In one of my classes the professor advocated keeping the toilets hot in the summer and cold in the winter, so that employees would not congregate there. He also asserted that a shower bath was more efficient than a bath in a tub, because one could wash his hair at the same time. I was infuriated with these examples of efficient practice. This was not the

kind of knowledge for which I had come to M.I.T. Behind these practices I saw no theory of the kind I found in physics and chemistry. To me they were pure, unadulterated nonsense. I am using strong language because it expresses the strong feelings I had at the time. For many years thereafter, I took great delight in collecting such "horror stories" about Course XV. By telling them with embellishments in certain quarters, I was able to become the life of the party. Had anyone at the time asked me just what I was so upset about, I probably would have been able only to stammer, "It's obvious, isn't it."

Without question, Course XV had a profound effect upon me but in directions entirely different from those that the designers of the course intended. When I was to meet unscientific management in the flesh much later on, as we will see, I was loaded for bear.[2]

Roethlisberger went on to receive an S.B. degree from M.I.T. There followed a period which can best be described as an attempt to find himself. He was first a chemist in El Paso, Texas, and later immersed himself in the "Bohemian" culture of New York's Greenwich Village. During this latter period, he worked as a sales correspondent for the American Book Company. The fall of 1924 found him enrolled as a graduate student in the Department of Philosophy at Harvard University. His dissertation topic required a reading of all of Descartes' letters in Medieval French. At this, Roethlisberger reports that his spirit balked and he never finished his dissertaton. He felt, "This was the end of the world. I felt deserted, forsaken, and alone. Slowly and steadily but surely I had reduced my life 'to dust and ashes.'"[3]

Somehow Roethlisberger was directed to talk with Elton Mayo, who had recently come to the business school. Mayo was curious about and somewhat amused by Roethlisberger's plight. After two interviews, Mayo offered him a job.

Why, when I was at the end of my rope and in utter despair, anyone should have wanted to throw me a lifesaver, I will never know. That is Mayo's story, not mine. But for his helping hand, I was to be ever grateful. For many years thereafter, I felt I could never cease to repay him. . . .

For the next few years I sat at Mayo's feet, spellbound by his knowledgeability, creative imagination, and clinical insights. He knew the great philosophers and the classical economists much better than I. He also knew about two areas with which up to this point I had had some acquaintance but little knowledge—psychopathology and social or functional anthropology. . . .

We read many books together—Janet, Freud, Jung, Adler, Piaget, and Durkheim, for example. I asked questions and he commented upon them. Never had I read this way before; never before had I had this kind of relation to a teacher and to an older man to whom I could state freely not only my intellectual questions but also my personal doubts, anxieties, and concerns.[4]

In Mayo, Roethlisberger found a mentor—professionally, intellectually, and emotionally—who addressed issues which, though largely unarticulated, had concerned him for years. The "elusive phenomena" that Roethlisberger was to spend a lifetime pursuing had arisen from his own personality and experiences; Mayo's concerns were consonant with his, yet were expressed more directly and decisively.

Elton Mayo

Mayo was born in Australia in 1880 and studied medicine in both that country and in England, although he never received a medical degree. Throughout his career the mark of the psychoanalyst Pierre Janet was stamped on Mayo's work. It was under Janet's influence that Mayo conducted his original work in industry in France. Even much later, in 1946, Mayo wrote in a letter: "Our work was not—and is not—modelled on the work of Pareto or Hendersen. It is after the pattern of the careful, clinical, pedestrian researches of Janet."[5]

During Mayo's lectures on human problems (Mayo did not teach a course but delivered lectures as part of a course to Harvard Business School students), Janet's basic model was almost always on the board. Mayo made frequent attacks on academia, often about "the curious inadequacy of the intellectual as a consequence of the emphasis on scientific method in modern education." His critiques of the social sciences were brutal:

> When one turns from the successful sciences—chemistry, physics, physiology—to the unsuccessful sciences—sociology, psychology, political science—one cannot fail to be struck by the extent of the failure of the latter to communicate to students a skill that is directly useful in human situations. . . .
>
> Chemistry and physics are thoroughly conversant with the materials of their study; they work in skilled fashion upon such materials every day. Economics and psychology cannot be said to be entirely innocent of skills, but such skills as they communicate seem to be at least partly dictated by a desire to give impressive imitations of physical science rather than by a determination to begin work by a thorough painstaking acquaintance with the whole subject matter of their studies. . . .
>
> The so-called social sciences encourage students to talk endlessly about alleged social problems. They do not seem to equip students with a single social skill that is usable in ordinary human situations. Sociology is

highly developed, but mainly as an exercise in the acquisition of scholarship. Students are taught to write books about each others' books. . . .

Indeed, scholarship departments by reason of their overevaluation of discursive reasoning and their under evaluation of actual skills, do much to exaggerate the individual disability and little, if anything, to remedy it.[6]

Not surprisingly, Mayo was rather unpopular among sociologists, and he seldom attended meetings of the professional sociological societies. Mayo directed his energies toward practicing managers and political leaders, those whose work involved the phenomena in which he was interested. Mayo was deeply concerned about the consequences of social maladjustment for society. He wrote:

Janet says of his patients that all, without exception, regard the world about them—especially the social world—as a hostile place, [or] *monde hostile.* There seems to be, however, a difference in type of response. Two-thirds, approximately, of the total number take the attitude "this world is dangerous, I must be careful"; the remaining third is rebellious, their attitude is "the world is hostile, let me attack it." Both attitudes are, of course, found in all instances, but one or the other will be predominantly characteristic.[7]

Mayo cited his own studies of socially maladjusted children who could not concentrate on their schoolwork and who, in private counseling, admitted they were terrified of being asked to perform in class. They feared that the teacher and other students were attempting to embarrass them publicly, and, because of their behavior, this preoccupation often became a self-fulfilling prophecy. (Mayo had formulated his basic thinking along these lines before his arrival at Harvard.)

There were obvious parallels in industry, where negative effects might result from preoccupation with and overthinking of one's personal situation. As an example, Mayo presented the case of a supervisor who moved his family east after accepting a job with greater responsibility. Because of the severe economic depression, the man's responsibilities were gradually reduced until his job was about the same as it had been prior to the job change. The way he performed his job altered significantly. His dealings with his men became increasingly acrimonious, he criticized the new location, and he repeatedly complained of his mistake in moving. Mayo observed that "his reflective thinking, originally factual and effective, had completely 'run off the rails.' He was overthinking his situation and attributing his ills to a hostile world just as a Janet patient might have done."[8]

Changes in industrial methods might evoke the same reaction. Scientific advances and new forms of organization might abolish or significantly modify trades in which someone has been involved for a lifetime, with a resulting tendency toward morbid and ineffective reflective thinking. The attitudes of such people, toward both themselves and society, would reflect a complete lack of confidence. Mayo viewed such reactions as having disastrous consequences, not only for organizations but for entire societies. In fact, he believed that such psychodynamics in Europe had contributed to the rise of Hitler.

Mayo's concerns were the concerns of a clinician. He saw in the behavior of a therapist certain social skills required of all administrators. Such skills were, in his view, necessary for dealing with the ineffective cognitive reactions that were typically triggered by organizational processes. These skills, coupled with a past history of social effectiveness, might quickly arrest employees' slippage into self-centered, debilitating preoccupations, especially those triggered by too sudden a change in their surroundings.

Such was the theoretical orientation of Elton Mayo when he joined Harvard to head the Department of Industrial Research and became a member of Harvard's Committee on Industrial Physiology. His particular task on the committee was to examine what happened to people at work from a human-social perspective. This was the Mayo who allowed Roethlisberger a "new look at the adult world of which I could make no sense and from whose nonsenses I was desperately trying to run. . . ."[9]

Fritz Roethlisberger joined the business school at Harvard as an instructor in 1927. His time was spent in counseling students who were having difficulties, some because of problems in adjusting to Harvard, others because they were not living up to their own expectations, and still others because they had been referred by faculty members. This type of helping relationship was a source of deep personal satisfaction to Roethlisberger, and soon became a focal point of his discussions with Mayo. No doubt Mayo's approach to science was bewildering to the young, systematic, engineering-trained Roethlisberger, but the two came to have a strong shared interest. Roethlisberger became familiar with the characteristics of preoccupations, including (1) how they create an inability to concentrate; (2) how they create false dichotomies; and (3) the relationships that exist between past experiences and expectations.

Following in the line of Janet, through Mayo, Roethlisberger became a student of obsessions. His work earned increasing respect from some faculty members and administrators in the business school. Three years after he began working with Mayo, he was awarded the rank of assistant professor, although Roethlisberger stated he was somewhat confused about what it was he was "professing."

Mayo and Western Electric

Mayo was never the director of the Western Electric studies, and he clearly did not view himself as such. In one letter he wrote, "It has been very difficult for me to get the leisure necessary to the proper ordering of my reflections on your interesting experiments at the Hawthorne plant."[10] In a letter three years later, he stated: "I have visited Hawthorne at frequent intervals and have endeavoured to keep myself fully posted upon the various developments by the continuous reading of available records when not at Hawthorne. This, however, is not identical with the day-to-day responsibility for the continuous direction of your inquiry. . . ."[11]

Mayo was, however, the principal source of the *interpretation* of the studies, and the source of spiritual guidance in their continuing evolution. The term "spiritual" is appropriate because Mayo did more than offer advice on methodology: he continually reassured the executives at Western Electric that the researches went beyond the pedestrian constraints of scientific inquiry. The studies, he explained, were reshaping existing paradigms.

One type of reassurance that Mayo offered is illustrated by the following portion of a letter he wrote to a Western Electric executive. Mayo was addressing a complaint about the difficulty of redefining the general objective of the experiments.

> . . . My comment is to the effect that so far as this is so it is probably a sign of health and value in the experiment. Henri Peincore in "Science and Hypothesis" points out that no science takes facts in general as its topic of study, every science selects certain facts amongst those that offer and neglects others. He further suggests that a science can do this because it takes the form of a question—and the scientist considers those facts only that are relevant to the question he studies. . . . Now a question that does not change its form and require restatement as a study proceeds is probably a question of little or no value: it is the question of a mere technician rather than a scientist. Nevertheless there are beyond doubt very awkward moments in the development of any scientific study—moments when questions need restatement and when, in consequence, the whole original method of selection amongst the facts that offer is in doubt. But that this should be so is a sign of health and not of failure. One has to welcome such moments, to "hang on" closely to the work and wait for a new illumination to reveal itself."[12]

More than a year later, Roethlisberger made basically the same point:

> . . . research should have an objective but it need not necessarily have a clearly defined objective. It starts with a vaguely defined question in a vaguely defined area, and as it proceeds it attempts to define more clearly

the question as well as the area to which it is to be limited. Your progress from the illumination experiment to the "test room" and then to the interviewing program illustrates what I mean. In each case you stated your problem a bit more precisely, but as yet you have not stated it nor answered it completely to your satisfaction.[13]

Roethlisberger went on to suggest that not all people are comfortable in such a research role, since the "flex and confusion" can often arouse "preoccupation of uncertainty and pessimism." Roethlisberger approved of the interviewing program being divided into two functions: (1) a personnel program, useful for improving the relationship between employees and management; and (2) a research program. Roethlisberger felt that the interviewers doing pure research should be as critical as they wished, either tearing down or building up current theories as their experiences warranted. He warned, however, that they should not "communicate their ruminations to the straight interviewing staff."[14]

Mayo repeatedly reminded Western Electric executives that they were pioneering a new industrial method—a way of upgrading the mediocre level of administrative practice. However, his exact role in the changing directions of the research is uncertain. His first visit to Hawthorne was on April 24, 1928, during period 10 of the first relay assembly test room. Mayo's correspondence during the summer of 1928 focused on the technical issues of measuring the impact of rest periods on fatigue and monotony. His second visit to the test room was in October 1938, during period 12 of the research. The interviewing program had begun in September of that year.

This sequence indicates that Mayo's influence was probably nonexistent in the events leading up to the interviewing program. Clearly the idea for the interviewing program preceded period 12 of the test room, which suggests that the major objective of the interviewing program was to gather facts about employees for use in the training of supervisors. Mayo did probably influence the switch from highly structured interviews to nondirective ones. He downplayed his influence, however:

> . . . it is difficult to say exactly what form the question took in the thinking of the experimenters. We know from the records, of course, what was said and the original form of the questionnaire. But the speed with which this was discarded when the work had once begun shows, I think, that a question and answer type of investigation of, for example, supervision was never regarded as relevant or important.[15]

These comments indicate a lack of involvement in the decision to adopt nondirective interviewing techniques. However, Mayo involved Roethlisberger in the training of interviewers at Hawthorne.

And Mayo, in directing Roethlisberger in his counseling work at Harvard, had already emphasized the problems of preoccupations. Further, Mayo had talked extensively with the Western Electric people about the interview as a method for dealing with excessive worker preoccupations. Mayo's influence on the studies was subtle but pervasive. His interest in obsessive thinking long predated his contact with Hawthorne, and it was from this perspective that he approached the questions posed by the experiments. Gradually, he shaped the perceptions of the experimenters as well.

Probably the most significant insight that Mayo gleaned from the relay assembly test room and the initial interviewing program was the possibility of systematically incorporating a concern with obsession into the management process. He saw interviewing programs as a potential vehicle for developing administrative skill, and felt that requiring managers to spend time as interviewers would develop in them a necessary feeling for social and psychological phenomena. Western Electric executives, as shown by their public pronouncements, clearly recognized this as the purpose and direction of Mayo's influence.

Mayo's thinking paralleled that of certain psychologists, most notably Carl Rogers. Some ten years after the Hawthorne experiments, Mayo read Rogers's *Counseling and Psychotherapy* and wrote his daughter that the book was a "pioneering effort in the pathway we have trodden these many years." Rogers, during the writing of his book, had made a few visits to Hawthorne and been startled to see work so similar to his own being done in industry.

Mayo saw Rogers's work and concerns as complementing his own, in the use of nondirective techniques to help individuals achieve insight. He viewed Rogers's work as having a limitation, however: "I think that he does not yet see the most important aspect of the problem—the question of the maintenance of communication between individuals and groups, as society grows more complex and changes more rapidly."

Mayo's Influence on *Management and the Worker*

The principal report on the Hawthorne research is *Management and the Worker* by Fritz Roethlisberger and William Dickson, neither of whom was involved in directing the studies. Dickson's role in the early stages of the experiments is unclear. Correspondence establishes that in 1929 two Western Electric executives, George Pennock and Mark Putnam, were largely running the studies. The relay assembly test room had been established by Hibarger with the approval and support of Pennock. For his part, Roethlisberger's longest visit to the plant was in 1931, when he spent the summer interviewing supervisory personnel. Prior to that summer he had made a brief visit to the plant for the purpose of training interviewers.

Originally the plan was for Mayo to sketch out an outline for a book, the details of which would be filled in by Western Electric people. However, preparing detailed research accounts was not his forte, and there were repeated delays. In the spring of 1932, Mayo, largely because he was not making much headway and because the country's economic depression was increasingly distracting to Western Electric personnel involved with the research, suggested to Pennock that Hal Wright of Western Electric spend the summer in Cambridge working with Fritz Roethlisberger on the project.

Mayo had mixed emotions about this, feeling he was abandoning the responsibility he had undertaken. However, he had to make an extended trip to England for medical treatment and noted that his absence would prevent his having access to material that might be needed should unanticipated questions arise. He said that Hal Wright and Fritz Roethlisberger "could put together a circumstantial point-by-point account of the events that happened in their appropriate sequence and order." Hal Wright stayed with the project for just six months before he was called back and reassigned. Dickson stayed for three and a half years, during which time he completed the book with Roethlisberger.

By the time Wright and Roethlisberger arrived at Harvard, Roethlisberger had decided to take a major role in writing up the studies. In his biography, Roethlisberger has frankly described his motivations in writing *Management and the Worker.* He saw the task as a chance to repay Mayo for the lifeline thrown to him five years earlier. "So help me, except for what God and the psychoanalysts know, this is the whole truth about how I got involved in writing *Management and the Worker.* I had to get a visible, tangible product—a book—that Mayo could show for his labors, whether anyone read it or not."[16]

Thus it was that two of the least senior people involved in the project became the principal authors associated with the Hawthorne research. And thus it was that, although the book was written by Roethlisberger and Dickson, the basic interpretation was Mayo's. Mayo's perspective had been internalized by both writers long before they sat down to write the book. Roethlisberger's admission of his motives shows the difficulty he would have had in arriving at conclusions contrary to Mayo's positions. In substance, whether the factors were conscious or subconscious, *Management and the Worker* became Mayo's book.

Mayo had stated the "meaning" of the studies many times in meetings with Western Electric executives, long before Roethlisberger and Dickson started writing and when Thomas Whitehead was only beginning his statistical studies. In April 1929, Mayo told Pennock that the evidence supported these conclusions:

1. Emotional instability shows itself in low and irregular production.
2. Emotional instability is associated with strong, negative preoccupations.
3. Any improvement in working conditions, and especially periodic interruption, tends to diminish morbid preoccupation.
4. With the normal person, interviews that permit expression of fears or worries similarly diminish morbidity or unhappiness.

These conclusions emerged out of conversations between Mayo and the Western Electric experimenters. The experimenters would send Mayo data, and during visits to the plant Mayo would raise questions, suggest psychoanalytical interpretations, and describe the characteristics of individuals experiencing instability. The researchers would usually verify his descriptions.

In February 1931, Mayo wrote Pennock about three observations which, he said, had "gradually emerged from the multiplicity and established their claim to be considered as important." These were:

1. The freely expressed relief of the workers at their freedom from ordinary supervision
2. The effect of personal preoccupation or misfortune on the production curve, which was observed in several instances, and the recovery of production, when the preoccupation or misfortune disappeared
3. A particular case in point—that of Operator 5 in the mica-splitting room

In actual fact, this worker's production, over a forty-six-week period, had shown approximately the same improvement—regardless of specific experimental conditions—as had the overall production of operators in the first relay assembly test room.

With regard to the first relay assembly test room, Mayo continued by pointing out "minor and major changes" that he connected with mental attitudes and preoccupations.

a) The minor changes are those mentioned which show a direct relation to obtain between preoccupation with private misfortune and a diminished production for the duration of the preoccupation.

b) The major change is that to be observed in the girls' change of mental attitude towards the Company officers, the Company itself, supervision generally and their work. They have lost all shyness and fear; they enjoy their increased earnings without any apprehension of "rate-revision," they talk freely on any subject to the official observers. *It is this major change of mental attitude which is associated with the major improvement in production.*[17]

Mayo also wrote that mental preoccupation leads to falsification of situations:

> . . . falsification is not, however, confined to supervision and personal interrelation. Interviewing has discovered that a whole department, from the supervisor down, regards itself as " side-tracked" and neglected. It is "in a backwater"; its morale and performance, under the influence of this misconception, are as poor as if the falsification were the actual truth.[18]

Mayo was of no mind to underplay to Pennock the importance of this work. "What it actually means is that *all the work* on rest periods prior to the Hawthorne inquiry, *work which has been regarded as 'scientific' and established, must be discarded as probably worthless* [italics his]. One does not want to publish such claims, since unnecessary controversy would result. But this is in effect the significance of the Hawthorne findings."[19]

Not every member of the Harvard faculty who had knowledge of Hawthorne arrived at the same conclusions. Richard Meriam, a professor at the business school, wrote that:

> . . . The test rooms are very noisy, which makes it difficult to hear the employees' conversation. Notes on the employees' conversation are not elaborate. Hibarger is interested in devising methods to control the noise, in order to study the influence of this factor.

> . . . Economic and financial factors are of considerable importance in the test room. The employees are anxious for high earnings. The test room has apparently removed the doubt in the employees' minds that the company would permit them to make very high earnings. The employees in the test rooms are peculiarly favored by being assured of a regular and adequate amount of work to do. In the relay test room there is a small group of employees under the group wage plan and the adjustment of the shares of the few employees is much more exact than in the working department. In the mica group production is held down by [a] small inaccuracy in piece rate setting that results in soft and hard rates.[20]

Meriam was not to carry the day. Tending to be somewhat pedantic in his approach, he often became locked in debate with the Western Electric researchers during his visits to Hawthorne. Writing about a visit by Meriam in 1931, Roethlisberger observed that:

> Meriam's attitude was that he did not come out here with any specialist's logic, and that he was merely looking for cold facts from a disinterested

point of view, but I think it would have been better if he had used the jargon of an economist and not tried to attack the logic of psychology and anthropology, because his attacks met with quite a bit of resistance. Meriam, I feel, made the unfortunate mistake of being a bit too patronizing with regard to the scientific and intellectual capacities of the people out here . . . there were too frequent references by first names to the vice presidents in New York.[21]

Meriam was no match for Mayo, who—as Roethlisberger more than adequately describes—was charismatic and talked comfortably with the experimenters, often over lunch in a place popular with the workers. Mayo did more than interpret the results, he gave life to them; he orchestrated his points. Although Meriam continued to have contact with Hawthorne, especially in helping to design training programs for supervisors, he was never on the same wave length with the experimenters. Nor did he ever change his conclusions about the research.

Early on, Mayo apparently had to do some selling of his interpretation to company officials in New York as well. For example, in 1931 C. W. Stoll, a Western Electric vice president, requested more specific statements concerning the pay incentive. He especially questioned Mayo's claim that an improvement of 10–15 percent might be attributable to pay incentive but that the reported 40–50 percent increase could not be. Though Stoll was inclined to be supportive, he wanted a more "extended statement and even some of the appropriate diagrams." Stoll was probably concerned primarily with how he could convince his fellow executives and wanted as much documentation as possible before publishing the results. Mayo kept Stoll informed of the progress of the research. He also wrote him from Europe to tell him that papers on management research were widely read there, and that Western Electric was frequently praised for conducting such long, varied, and continuous studies.

This was the series of events leading up to and influencing the writing of *Management and the Worker.* At Hawthorne, Mayo had come into an ongoing research project which, quite apart from his direction, had evolved in a way that lent itself to his definition of "the administrative problem." The researchers were already sympathetic to the supervisory style hypothesis, though apparently unsure what to surmise from the pattern of results they had obtained from the illumination studies and the relay assembly test room. Hibarger's modest experiment in the second relay test room had proved inconclusive.

Mayo gave the researchers a different and, for them, unique perspective on the scientific process—one that was consistent with the growing national interest in psychoanalysis and the hidden frontiers of the mind. More than anything else, Mayo was arguing for a redefinition of social science. Social scientists studied phenomena that were in many ways different from the subject matter of the physical and natural sciences: these phenomena had to be experienced to be understood. In the absence of such understanding, both armchair theories and statistical measures were likely to be devoid of meaning. Mayo's training in psychoanalysis and his experiences with political radicals in Europe had long ago convinced him of the need for an intimate familiarity with social phenomena. In Mayo's view, it was especially important for managers—who played a much more important role in society than social scientists—to acquire this familiarity. It would enable them to develop the skills that were fundamental to their jobs. For Mayo, the relay assembly and bank wiring room experiments illustrated the point. The interviewing program went even further: it suggested both the skills needed and a method for developing them.

Roethlisberger, during his apprenticeship under Mayo, had experienced "the elusive phenomena" in his campus interviewing. Among the insights he gained was an understanding of why he had rebelled against the content of the scientific management courses at M.I.T. and why his rationalistic, disciplined approach to life had let him down. Thus, interviewing was therapeutic to Roethlisberger as well as to those he interviewed. He was fascinated by the volatile nature of the phenomena he encountered. He did not have to venture beyond the boundaries of the business school to observe them: faculty members and students were a constant source of data. The human factors he observed seemed difficult to label, almost impossible to measure in the traditional sense, and harder still to control. But he saw that the factors were real enough in their consequences.

Despite the extremity of some of their statements, neither Mayo nor Roethlisberger denied that other models might partially explain the Hawthorne data. Rather, they rejected the one-dimensionality of such explanations as the wage-incentive hypothesis, feeling that such theories oversimplified the phenomena. *Management and the Worker* was not written to support what the authors viewed as the only approach to the data, but to highlight the only approach that they felt mattered. The findings were exploratory, not conclusive. Roethlisberger was interested not in refuting all the existing paradigms, but in establishiing a new one—a new vantage point from which both rational and nonrational models of management might be viewed. Rationalistic systems were part of organizational experience and managerial method, but their impact and consequences, both positive and negative, had to be understood within the framework of the subjective experiences of workers.

In reality, *Management and the Worker* was an extensive essay, written as a case study, arguing for this point of view. The conclusions it contained rested on many experiences, some of which had little to do with the data generated by Hawthorne. When Roethlisberger and Dickson, along with Wright, began work on the book, their task was not so much to test hypotheses but to descriptively illustrate the elements of their paradigm.

NOTES

1. Fritz J. Roethlisberger, *The Elusive Phenomena* (Cambridge, Mass.: Harvard University Press, 1977), p. 18.
2. Ibid., p. 21.
3. Ibid., p. 26.
4. Ibid., pp. 27, 29, 30.
5. Elton Mayo to John McDonald, 1946.
6. Elton Mayo, *The Social Problems of Industrial Civilization* (Boston: Harvard Business School Division of Research, 1945), pp. 19–20, 25.
7. Ibid., p. 27.
8. Ibid., p. 29.
9. Roethlisberger, *Elusive,* p. 27.
10. Elton Mayo to George Pennock, April 1929.
11. Elton Mayo to George Pennock, May 1932.
12. Elton Mayo to George Pennock, April 1929.
13. Fritz J. Roethlisberger to Hal Wright, September 1930.
14. Ibid.
15. Elton Mayo to George Pennock, February 1931.
16. Roethlisberger, *Elusive,* p. 53.
17. Elton Mayo to George Pennock, February 9, 1931.
18. Ibid.
19. Ibid.
20. Memorandum from Richard S. Meriam to Elton Mayo, November 12, 1930.
21. Fritz J. Roethlisberger to Elton Mayo, July 20, 1931.

8

The Legacy of Hawthorne

In 1972, forty years after the Hawthorne studies were completed, they were still being described as "the most extensive, the most significant and the most influential behaviorial science study ever conducted in a business enterprise."[1] Through their association with the Harvard Business School, Mayo and Roethlisberger enjoyed a wide and far-reaching audience. What was the message heard by practicing managers, and how was that message translated into practice? These questions are at the heart of any understanding of the human relations movement in industry. To answer them requires investigation of how the conclusions of the Hawthorne research were promoted to interested publics, such as the management community.

A logical place to begin is with the writings of Elton Mayo, who was the most visible of the Harvard Business School people associated with the studies. Mayo's books, with their extensive references to Hawthorne, argued for a point of view: Mayo used the studies to support his ideas on the nature of administrative difficulties in industrial societies. He never personally reported the research in detail; indeed, he did not believe he was close enough to the original data to do so.

Period 12 and "the Hawthorne Effect"

The foundation stone for Mayo's arguments was his discussion of the celebrated period 12 of the relay assembly test room experiment. He wrote the following in his widely referred to *The Human Problems of an Industrial Civilization*:

The history of the twelve-week return to the so-called original conditions

165

is soon told. The daily and weekly output rose to a point higher than at any other time, and in the whole period there was no downward trend. . . .

Period twelve was continued for twelve weeks and there was no downward trend. . . . The hourly output rate was distinctly higher during the full working day of period twelve than during the full working day of period three.[2]

Twelve years later, in *The Social Problems of an Industrial Civilization,* Mayo repeated his report of period 12. However, one underplayed qualification was given in parentheses. "The story is now well known. In period 12 the daily and weekly output rose to a point higher than at any other time (the hourly rate adjusted itself downward by a small fraction), and in the whole twelve weeks, there was no downward trend."[3]

Mayo claimed that period 12 "made it evident that increments of production could not be related point for point to the experimental changes introduced."[4] He thus reduced rest periods and working hours to minor importance while introducing supervisory style as the major explanatory variable. Mayo stated that the effort to hold the cooperative attitudes of the assemblers constant had unexpectedly emerged as the major experimental change that influenced the output rate.

In journalistic accounts of the studies, Mayo's comments on the twelfth period were treated as offering convincing evidence in support of the emerging human relations school. *Fortune* magazine, for example, drew this conclusion about period 12: "The workers were cooperating with the experiment and they continued to do so even when the apparent original conditions of work were restored."[5] Stuart Chase, who wrote widely about the Hawthorne studies, was also fond of Mayo's description of the twelfth period:

Remember that after almost two years of experimentation with various types of wage rates, hours, rest pauses, and working conditions, they went back to the base period of forty-eight hours, no Saturdays off, no rest pauses, no hot lunch at the company expense, no piecework incentive, nothing. They gave that test a good long time: they gave it twelve weeks. And, when they came to examine the automatic counters through which the girls dropped the relays, they found that output had jumped to an all-time high, meaning, of course, that all these various new conditions they introduced had no effect compared with certain other factors—the factors of being recognized, of being consulted, of feeling important.[6]

Chase had a flair for overstatement. (For one thing, no change in the wage-incentive structure occurred during period 12.) Chase had, however, been amply assisted in his efforts to make a good story better by his original source, Mayo.

Mayo's comments in *Social Problems* were significantly misleading;

his earlier remarks in *Human Problems* were even more so. Though total output did increase, the hourly output rate for three of the five assemblers declined, in two instances quite markedly. The output rates of the other two were erratic. During the famous period 12, four of the assemblers had average output rates lower than in the four previous experimental periods. The lone exception had an average rate only slightly higher than in previous periods, and she was one of the assemblers whose rate declined throughout the period. In other words, although total output was higher than in previous periods, the output rate (productivity) was lower than in the recent periods and showed a decline.

This suggests that Mayo's conclusion must be treated considerably more tentatively than either he or many subsequent reporters of his writing saw fit to do. While total output was higher, the women were also working more hours. Had the decline in the productivity rate continued (Mayo mentioned the decline only in his later book, without discussion), total output would have had to fall as well.

Surely it cannot be expected that, within a period of twelve weeks, both individual rates and total output would drop back to the levels of period 3. The women had become accustomed to producing higher levels of output over a period of almost two years. An immediate drop of such proportions almost never occurs, unless there is an industrial relations catastrophe. By failing to discuss the dropping productivity rate or to put the period 12 output rise in context, Mayo provided a description that is not only incomplete but deceptive as well. Thus are great stories composed and myths given birth.

In the hands of a talented storyteller like Stuart Chase, the tale gets better. After briefly discussing period 12, Chase declared in his next paragraph that economic man was made mostly of straw. The modern manager, Chase informed his audience, was one who increased output with incentives other then financial ones. Financial incentives were best given a reduced, even minor role. As we saw earlier, the Hawthorne data did not convincingly support such a conclusion. They particularly failed to do so during period 12, which was designed to test the impact of eliminating rest periods and instituting shorter working hours, and which involved no change in financial incentives.

Frederick Mosteller makes an even more dramatic assertion than Chase:

> When Roethlisberger and Dickson carried out their experiments to find conditions that would maximize productivity of factory teams at the Hawthorne Works of Western Electric, they found that every change—increasing the lighting or reducing it, increasing the wage scale or reducing it— seemed to increase the groups' productivity. Paying attention to people, which occurs in placing them in an experiment, changes their behavior. This rather unpredictable change is called the Hawthorne effect.[7]

Mosteller's proposition succeeds in generalizing the misconceptions about Hawthorne beyond period 12 in the relay assembly test room to the entire series of experiments. First, Roethlisberger and Dickson never conducted an experiment during which they reduced the wage scale. Second, as part of the bank wiring room research, the investigators tried to determine whether placing the men in the observation room had any impact on their productivity. Roethlisberger and Dickson quite explicitly stated that it did not.[8]

The list of textbook references defining "the Hawthorne effect" is seemingly endless. Many subtle variations exist, some repeating misconceptions attributable to either Mayo or the research reports, others creatively adding new misconceptions. Even simple errors of fact are rampant. Some writers report that the Harvard group designed the relay assembly test room; others described Mayo and Roethlisberger as the directors of the studies. Most accounts emphasize the discovery of informal organization and of group cohesiveness in production.

Roethlisberger and Dickson stated that they did not know who had coined the phrase "the Hawthorne effect," which to many social scientists was the major finding of the studies. None of the original researchers used the term.[9] Apart from the flaws in the Hawthorne researchers' own interpretations of the data, the extent to which respected scholars have added to the folklore by discussing "the Hawthorne effect" would make for an interesting study in the sociology of knowledge.

Nevertheless, Roethlisberger accepted at least one version of "the Hawthorne effect" as a principal finding of the studies. In an interview in 1972, forty years after the research was completed, he was asked what he felt was the most important lesson to have come out of Hawthorne. Roethlisberger responded that "what has come to be called 'the Hawthorne effect' from a scientific point of view is the most important result of these experiments—that is, the big difference that the little difference of listening to and paying attention to the employees made to them."[10] Essentially, this is a generalization about the therapeutic effect of nondirective interviewing on obsessive thinking.

For his part, Mayo promoted the idea that the increased output of the relay assemblers was caused by "the distinctly pleasanter, freer and happier working conditions, and that much can be gained industrially by carrying greater personal consideration to the lowest levels of employment." Mayo maintained that this environment had been created by an "interested and sympathetic chief observer" who "took a personal interest in her achievement. . . ."[11]

Executives at the Hawthorne plant, who from the time of the illumination studies were convinced that supervisory style somehow affected productivity, were unlikely to contradict Mayo or temper his enthusiasm. For them, Mayo's ideas were a respectable "scientific" confirmation of phenomena they themselves had observed.

Mayo's theories gained entry to *Reader's Digest,* when Chase wrote that the Hawthorne studies contained an idea "so big that it leaves one gasping."[12] This big idea was that, contrary to many of the arguments of scientific management, workers will work harder if management shows an interest in them, listens to their problems, explains things to them, and relies less on rationalistic control systems to ensure productivity. Such a managerial approach would be more powerful than financial incentives, rest periods, or the like. Many practicing managers paid attention.

It is not difficult to understand how this idea took hold. Generalizing about the Hawthorne research, Roethlisberger wrote: "In most work situations, the meaning of a change is likely to be as important as, if not more so than, the change itself. This was the great *éclaircissement,* the new illumination, that came from the research."[13] Taken alone, this is basic and sound social psychology. However, as a prescription for managerial action, it contains some potentially dangerous loopholes—loopholes that the Harvard group would have done well to anticipate. The group had long been dismayed over management's search for one simple technique that could be extracted from scientific management. They should not have been surprised to see their own ideas oversimplified.

For Roethlisberger, this great *éclaircissement* was supported by data from the interviewing program showing that workers interpreted the meaning of events according to sentiments: beliefs that were neither logical nor illogical but rather personal (and social) views of how the world works. Sentiment was the cement that held the social structure together. Many times, a worker expressed a sentiment as though it was a statement of logical fact. The supervisor who responded with a factual counterargument was missing the point and, worse, failing to understand the real problem being expressed.

Thus Roethlisberger recommended the following five rules for supervisors in handling personal relations:

1. The supervisor should listen patiently to what his subordinate has to say before making any comment himself.
2. The supervisor should refrain from hasty disapprobation of his subordinate's conduct.
3. The supervisor should not argue with his subordinate. It is futile to try to change sentiment by logic.
4. The supervisor should not pay exclusive attention to the manifest content of the conversation. There is a tendency for people to rationalize sentiments. Getting interested in the truth of the rationalization can result in missing the source of the sentiment.

5. The supervisor should listen not only to what a person wants to say but also to what he does not want to say.[14]

In other words, a supervisor should learn how to interview—and, in particular, how to listen while conducting a nondirective interview. Further, he or she should realize that employees' complaints represent the "creakings and groanings of their own social structure."[15]

It is difficult to argue with Roethlisberger's recommendations for improving communications between supervisor and subordinate. The harmfulness of an adversarial relationship can easily be verified by observing what goes on in most work organizations. And Roethlisberger's discussion of "sentiment" provides a useful insight into the sources of such a relationship.

Similarly, it is difficult to fault Mayo when he states that unfortunately most supervisors understand their work as consisting of giving orders and, if the orders are not followed, bawling out the parties involved.[16] Mayo's point that the supervisor talks instead of listening, and as a result fails to identify the real problem, is well taken. It was the attempt to relate preoccupations and sentiment directly to productivity that flew in the face of much of the observable data. The researchers, in overemphasizing this relationship, either neglected, ignored, or explained away equally significant observations.

Nevertheless, many readers were convinced. Listening became the core of virtually all human-relations-oriented management training programs. In 1929, Mark Putnam of the Western Electric Company outlined some of the positive benefits his company had derived from the nondirective interviewing method in a widely distributed talk.[17] At the top of his list was the fact that employees were getting a chance to sound off and express their problems to a sympathetic listener. Putnam stated that this, in and of itself, can improve an employee's attitude, and the technique reassures the worker of management's interest. He concluded his discussion of the interviewing program by saying, "The comments from employees have convinced us that the relationship between first line supervisors and the individual workman is of more importance in determining the attitude, morale, general happiness and efficiency of that employee than any other single factor."

What many managers took away from discussions of the Hawthorne studies was the idea that listening to and expressing interest in a subordinate can help lubricate the "creakings and groanings" of an organization's structure. This perspective led to a number of human relations programs in industry that managers hoped would result in impressive productivity gains. Many of these programs amounted to cosmetic efforts, directed toward manipulating the feelings of workers. Some managers who had been impressed by Hawthorne seemed to have gotten the message that seduction was preferable to forcible rape in gaining the victim's cooperation.

For the most part, Mayo and his associates cannot be blamed for what others chose to read into their work. Yet, the results of period 12 gave them a clear opportunity to avoid such misconceptions. The declining output rate was the red flag marking the way.

Research reports dealing with period 12 show that the test room supervisor thoroughly explained why earlier experimental conditions were being reinstated. Further, when it became evident that the women were resisting the change by purposely reducing their output rate, the observer spoke frankly with them and even promised a return to more favorable conditions in the future. The women were never pressured as they had been early in the experiment when the talking problem emerged. In short, the observer remained friendly and sympathetic, with there being no change in the supervisory style he had evolved during the course of the experiment. Yet the output rate continued its decline, and was still declining at the end of the experimental period.

Many human relations programs have failed, and it has been fashionable in some quarters to blame practitioners who sought to exploit the research of the Harvard group.[18] Yet Mayo himself supported much of the misleading publicity. After Chase's flattering article appeared in *Reader's Digest,* Mayo wrote Chase that his piece "did amazingly well express in small compass the essentials of fourteen years' rather difficult and laborious work. Since *Management and the Worker* appeared there have been many attempts to summarize, very few of which have shown any insight whatever into either the intention of the work or the rather baffling puzzles we encountered from time to time."[19] In future correspondence about upcoming Chase projects, Mayo never mentioned any need to clarify or alter Chase's representation of the studies. In fact, he remained highly complimentary about Chase's work.

Another example concerns a prepublication draft of a feature article in *Fortune.* Mayo corrected certain biographical details but proposed no changes in the description of the studies and his role in them, even though the draft suggested that Mayo had been greatly involved in the design of the studies. Further, the data were interpreted in a more confident tone than scientific prudence might recommend. Clearly Mayo was willing to live with many of the popular descriptions, and at times failed to correct misconceptions when he had the power to do so. This, we hasten to add, arose not from a desire for personal aggrandizement but from a wish to publicize the studies and what Mayo believed were their implications.

Some writers have faulted Mayo for a tendency toward overstatement while absolving Roethlisberger of responsibility for the misconceptions that emerged about Hawthorne.[20] This does not seem credible either. Roethlisberger was not inclined to place any distance between himself and his mentor when it came to describing the results of the studies.

The Hawthorne Myths

As a result of the foregoing, three popular misconceptions arose from the Hawthorne studies:

1. There were no indications that the experimental conditions were related to productivity.
2. Economic incentive is of minor importance to workers.
3. Expressing interest in the problems of workers is a major tool for increasing collaboration, and hence productivity.

All the principal books and papers on Hawthorne contributed to these myths. Consultants and practitioners of questionable motivation and abilities emerged during the heyday of the human relations movement, but these are not to be put in the same category with the researchers. The latter's conclusions were, at worst, misleading. And, while Mayo's descriptions of Hawthorne provided the basis for many of the popularized accounts, Roethlisberger and Dickson had already demonstrated a marked tendency toward a double standard by evaluating their preferred interpretation less rigorously than other, more traditional explanations. In sum, the popular misinterpretations of the Hawthorne studies stem from a variety of sources. Today, in many organizations, these misunderstandings contribute to an adversarial relationship among practitioners of different management theories.

The tragedy of Mayo's failure to follow his own advice and "pursue contradictions in our observed experiences" is that if he had analyzed why the productivity rate had dropped in period 12, he might have headed off many popular misunderstandings about the studies. Mayo was, however, caught up in a conflict between scientific investigation and the promotion of a specific perspective on industrial practice, an issue we will elaborate on in later chapters.

The Impact of the Hawthorne Studies on Management Practice

The Hawthorne studies were promoted to a wide-ranging popular audience. Through this process, the studies and their conclusions took on aspects of a social movement. They were intensively discussed in the management community. Two new strategies grew directly out of the work of Roethlisberger and Dickson: supervisory and management training, and employee counseling. A number of other human relations techniques were also born.

Supervisory and Management Training

Management training was, of course, conducted in Western Electric and in other companies prior to the Hawthorne studies. The research, however, initiated a new emphasis: employees would be interviewed in order to obtain concrete case material for training class discussion.

Prior to the interviewing phase of the Hawthorne studies, the supervisory training in the plant mainly involved teaching people company routines and policies. The researchers felt that this approach, which was typical in industry at the time, did not adequately prepare supervisors to handle the personal and social situations they would encounter on the job. Training conferences on "morale" had proved unsatisfactory because primarily the personal opinions of various executives were offered.

The Hawthorne investigators saw a need to generate facts on which training conferences could be based and develop valid principles for managing people problems. This was apparently one of the initial justifications for establishing the interviewing effort at Hawthorne. As the program proceeded, the data generated were used in a number of ways in the supervisory training meetings. Initially, selected comments that employees had made in interviews were used to generate conference discussion. After participants had expressed their opinions about the comments, the conference leader would proceed to make a number of revelant points. This was typically done by asking questions such as "How would you talk this over with a person making such a complaint?" or "What factors might be involved?" Finally, different resolutions would be discussed, with interview data used to illustrate possible results.

In later training sessions, complete interviews were discussed. Supervisors would begin by discussing any aspect of an employee's thoughts that interested them. Usually, the ensuing discussion would focus on the reasons for the employee's feelings and what could be done about the situation. Such discussion was intended to provide insight into the nature of social phenomena and individual reactions.

Another design had the training conference organized around topics such as "benefits" or "vacations," with material from many interviews presented. Comments from supervisors were also used for discussion purposes.

Many people (including M. L. Putnam of Western Electric) felt that the use of interview material in supervisory training was a principal application of the Hawthorne research. Roethlisberger did state that an ability to recognize sentiment, along with an understanding of underlying personal and social pressures, was a critical supervisory skill. Mayo went further, believing that participation in an interviewing program which generated needed data was crucial preparation for supervisory and executive responsibility. *Fortune* magazine reported his views as follows:

> The social equipment the administrator must have, according to Mayo, is wide in theoretical knowledge and the kind of clinical experience obtained by the interviews at Hawthorne. Industry must get men trained in "social skills" and bring them up as administrators through operation of a counseling program—similar to Hawthorne—among employees. This, no more, no less, is Mayo's practical program for industry.[21]

Human relations training involving case material obtained from workers became a popular technique in industry. Attention was given to the proper design of such data-generating techniques. At a conference of the Personnel Research Federation, Putnam speculated about the possibility of developing a method whereby comments could be directed from a group of employees to an interviewer back to the supervisor involved. Interviewers could then help supervisors better to understand their subordinates and their subordinates' reactions to them. Thus, contemporary organizational development techniques, such as data feedback and team-building, are traceable back to the supervisory development program at Hawthorne. Certainly, the idea of improving organizational effectiveness by altering the basic values of managers through training experiences has a heritage that includes Hawthorne.

Employee Counseling

The second application of the Hawthorne studies grew out of the first. The counseling program at Hawthorne was an extension of the earlier interviewing program. Essentially it was an effort to apply "the Hawthorne effect": the positive impact of the researcher on the subject. Roethlisberger and Dickson wrote that if the results of the illumination and relay assembly tests were partially caused by the researcher's impact on the workers in their counselor role, the company could bring about this impact throughout the plant.[22] Counselors who behaved similarly to the researchers might generate "certain beneficial effects" in affecting workers' reactions. The counseling role, like the interviewing role, was essentially noninterventionist. The counselor's job was to listen, not talk; to provide an opportunity for workers to think through their situation, but avoid giving advice;

and to describe the situations encountered through note-taking, but not change them.

Occasionally, counselors would summarize what they felt were important issues or problems in the plant, and these reports would be sent to management. Counselors also submitted reports requested by management and frequently provided input for company-wide staff conferences. In this manner the counselors were seen as facilitating communication between employees and management.

The counseling program existed at Hawthorne from 1936 to 1956. At its peak during 1948, 55 full-time counselors covered 21,000 employees in the plant. Additionally the program was packaged and transplanted to other Western Electric plants and at least two Bell Telephone companies. The program was later reduced and then terminated, having fallen victim to rising manufacturing costs and management's questioning as to whether the program's benefits could not be obtained in other, less costly ways.

In the counseling model, the limitations of "the Hawthorne effect" became apparent with time. At the time of the program's demise, the counselors themselves were beginning to question the value of performing a noninterventionist counseling role. As stated in *Counseling in an Organization,*

> It merely amounted to dealing with the constraints that the worker himself brought to the situation which prevented him from developing a better relation to it and what could be done about that. But what about the environmental constraints which prevented him from reanalyzing himself and what could be done about that? Short of doing something about that, counseling looked like a "band aid" operation.[23]

Roethlisberger and Dickson confirmed that the counselors did not view it as their mission to change the personalities or "role sets" of the workers. The counselors:

> . . . were trying to change or improve the relations of persons to each other . . . by allowing the worker to express and work through his negative feelings in the interview, he would be ready to express more positive feelings to his supervisor when he next met him, for example . . . by working on both ends of the relationship between supervisor and worker in a counseling fashion, they could improve their relations to each other.[24]

The principal tools of the counselor were interviewing skills, which were designed to help workers gain greater insight into their work relationships and have a catalytic effect on employee attitudes.

The approach certainly had some degree of effectiveness. However, in reviewing the counseling program, Roethlisberger and Dickson estimated that about 10 percent of the employees wanted and needed counseling and were helped by it. Another 25 percent of the employ-ees needed counseling but were not helped by it. The remainder did not need or want counseling and sometimes would not even talk with the counselor. These percentages place the potential of counseling in a realistic perspective: other organizations that have implemented such programs report the same degree of success. Further, being "helped" does not necessarily translate into improved job performance, al-though presumably worker cooperation was facilitated.

As the Hawthorne counseling program expanded into an accepted and packaged personnel activity, its research function diminished. This caused the program to lose an important avenue of communica-tion with management. In retrospect, Roethlisberger and Dickson con-cluded that this increased isolation of the counselors was one of the most unfortunate things that had happened to the program. The re-search aspects of the counseling program had been providing manage-ment with information for the betterment of the human aspects of the company's internal operations. Without a research role, counseling became solely an effort to ameliorate the lot of the worker through emotional measures.

Roethlisberger and Dickson clearly saw the drawbacks of a counsel-ing program that focused on the improvement of relationships with-out dealing with such problems as task specialization:

> In comparing the interviews at the beginning with those at the end, it looked as if the worker was just as much concerned with about the same sort of things today as he was yesterday. His fundamental role in terms of task specialization had not changed very much.

> We pay him more; we give him more benefits; we treat him more as a human being; he's got a union to protect him and if need be, to protest for him; we give him more information, more vacation and holiday time with pay . . . all these things have come to pass but his basic role is the same . . . in short, what we are suggesting is that the worker's concerns are implicit in his role derived from task specialization, that they can't be alleviated except temporarily with a change in this condition.[25]

Roethlisberger and Dickson reported that the dominant image of the counseling program within Western Electric was that "it just provided employees with the opportunity to get things off their chests. This was its major therapeutic effect. It was like a confessional. It was a nonprofessional psychiatric or ministerial service rendered by well-intended laymen."[26]

This image was evidently reinforced by the ways in which coun-selors explained the benefits of their activities to employees, super-visors, and managers. Roethlisberger and Dickson would no doubt have rejected such explanations as simplistic. However, the image of counseling as "therapy" is not totally out of line with the intellectual heritage that spawned the program—a heritage whose core was Roethlisberger's and Dickson's conclusions from the Hawthorne studies.

The Hawthorne counseling program conformed remarkably well to the prescriptions for supervisory practice found in Roethlisberger's writings. The practical aspects of the Mayo/Roethlisberger human relations school found almost complete expression in this program.

To the authors' knowledge, no other business organization has duplicated the AT&T commitment to counseling in terms of costs and scope. However, variations of the Hawthorne counseling approach are widespread. Today, counseling has become part of the professional personnel manager's job. Most specialists in the field would list "ability to actively listen" to employee grievances and problems as a critical skill of personnel management. A personnel manager is expected to help employees think through their frustrations and, when appropriate, make management aware of the need for corrective action in the workplace. Many plant managers even note the volume of traffic in and out of the personnel manager's office, considering frequent visits to be an indication of an effective personnel function.

Large organizations often implement formal counseling programs in an effort to reduce employee turnover. These programs often have specific focus, such as career development. The more effective programs tie counseling directly into the larger organization. For example, in the case of career development, employees are most likely to find counseling helpful if it relates to specific opportunities available in the company. Even more important is the counselor's ability to recognize policies that are preventing employees from advancing in or redirecting their careers, and to pressure management for change.

Whatever the focus of the program, follow-up is a critical part of the counselor's role. Checking to see whether an employee has resolved a particular problem, making sure a worker receives a satisfactory response to an inquiry, informing an employee of the status of a recommendation made to management—all are part of effective follow-up. The ombudsman role appears increasingly vital if a counselor is to establish credibility with a significant percentage of employees. Employees' most frequent complaint is that the counselor is ineffective in resolving the real workplace dilemmas confronting them.

Unhappily, many industrial counseling programs have the main objective of "letting employees get things off their chest." Usually the counselor's role is to help the employee talk through problems and he or she listens attentively to work-related frustrations or difficulties. The counselor has little authority to initate change in the work situation or in company practices that might be generating personnel problems. Such programs, intended as an "escape valve" for negative employee attitudes, seldom result in improved morale or improved job performance for most workers. As with the Hawthorne counseling program, employees perceive that the counselor has little power to effect change, and even workers who might be helped are disinclined to utilize the program.

Many counseling activities in organizations are either poorly or cynically conceived, with the counselors unskilled and inadequately prepared for their task. The result is frequently increased resentment, as employees react negatively to what they consider a human relations gimmick. Management's hope for "the Hawthorne effect" never materializes.

Human Relations Training in Industry: Limitations and Misuses

Just as the practice of counseling has spread beyond Hawthorne, so has managerial human relations training. Probably the most common vehicle for such training is the workshop on interpersonal skills. Some sessions deal with interviewing skills (for example, open-ended questions, acceptance, restatement, reflection, and silence) whose industrial application was pioneered at Hawthorne. Supervisors are admonished to address conflict in a nondirective manner, listening before taking action. This is, of course, the legacy of Mayo and Roethlisberger.

The advice to listen, and the skills suggested for implementing the advice, are generally sound. Skill in listening can help a supervisor avoid getting into an unnecessary adversarial posture with a subordinate over a relatively minor complaint, or can help defuse an emotionally charged situation. However, in and of itself, listening cannot resolve the many organizational sources of personnel conflict. High turnover and absenteeism, poor-quality workmanship, and similar problems are often rooted in the structure of the organization itself. Training supervisors to listen better, or to apply other human relations techniques, will not resolve these structural sources of conflict. Consultants frequently encounter companies that want to implement human relations training with the hope that supervisors and managers can be taught to finesse away deep-rooted problems. Such an attitude truly reduces training to "a 'band aid' operation."

There is another limitation inherent in human relations training: it can provide trainees with special knowledge, experience, and skills but it cannot generally provide them with motivation. The training does not guarantee that managers will use such skills once they return to their jobs. Whether the skills are actually utilized depends on the degree to which the larger organization rewards their use, the objectives of the job, the degree of follow-up after the training session, and other factors. If, for example, managers perceive that they will be rewarded for meeting certain objectives regardless of how they deal with their employees, few human relations skills are likely to be transferred.

While much of the above appears self-evident, in practice organizations often proceed as though myopic. Corporations spend considerable sums annually on training programs that they hope will curb a human resources problem which actually has nothing to do with managers' interpersonal skills. To avoid such wastes of funds, which can undercut the credibility of the entire corporate training effort, management training specialists need to have a broad-based approach to organizational problems. They should be true "organizational consultants," capable of recognizing the limitations as well as strengths of human resources approaches.

Management Training as a Direct Application of "the Hawthorne Effect"

Another curious practice is management's use of a human relations training workshop as a "motivator" for managers and supervisors. Here the training experience is seen as a potentially enjoyable break that indicates management's appreciation of a supervisor's continued good performance. The workshop is viewed as a chance to "do something" for the person. A variation of this approach is sending people to a workshop in an effort to placate them. For example, if a supervisor's performance has been dropping off, it is hoped that the training session will restore his or her enthusiasm for the job. Or, in the case of an aggressive young supervisor who wants increased job responsibility, it is hoped that the training will serve as a temporary substitute, indicating that superiors are indeed eager to promote the person's continued development.

The above applications illustrate the psychology of the Hawthorne effect carried to its logical conclusion: training becomes a vehicle for demonstrating interest in management personnel. Although it is believed that the trainees will probably learn some useful, or at least interesting, things, the primary objective is to make them feel important. At best, such "training" produces negligible results. At worst, frustrations intensify as real problems go unresolved. A basic tenet of effective training programs is: "Always train for a specific, job-related purpose." Consider, for example, an already underutilized manager whose job description is not going to be changed. The most probable outcome of generalized "training" is a more complicated morale problem as the person comes to feel even more underutilized than before.

We do not intend to suggest that management training in general, or interpersonal skills training in particular, cannot be valuable. Some organizations utilize interpersonal skills training effectively, avoiding applications that draw on the mythical "Hawthorne effect" and instead confronting difficult organizational issues. Our purpose here has been to highlight some prevalent nonproductive uses of training that stem largely from the earliest human relations orientation. Although many professional trainers are sensitive to the misuses of training, managers frequently are not—and effective corporate trainers will head off misunderstandings and preconceptions.

Other Human Relations Strategies

Beyond counseling and training, a number of other approaches have emerged as managers have grappled with putting into practice what they perceive to be the lessons of human relations.

Employee Communications

One such strategy is an increased emphasis on improved communications. To many managers, human relations has become synoymous with communications. This misconception grew out of the emphasis placed on listening techniques in many of the Hawthorne reports. Indeed, even such a sophisticated and well-trained labor relations expert as John Dunlop interpreted the human relations literature in this fashion.[27]

Such interpretations caused many companies to emphasize vehicles for communicating with employees. In this area, the Hawthorne studies had an indirect but nevertheless real influence. Though employee publications, for example, predate the Hawthorne studies, the increasing concern with human relations created an environment of expanded efforts to communicate.

The 1950s witnessed the spreading popularity of employee newspapers and house organs dealing with topics of interest to employees. At the plant level, these publications relied heavily on contributions from the workers themselves. In corporate home offices, professional journalists were often employed to produce high-quality publications. In either case, the intention was to make employees feel part of the corporate scene. In later years, senior executives began using videotapes to take their messages directly to employees.

Another idea that became more popular was for local managers to hold group meetings with employees. Again, the generally accepted purpose of such meetings was to open the lines of communication. This included giving employees an opportunity to vent their frustrations and raise questions relating to plant or office operations. At times, managers' enthusiasm for such meetings exceeded their skill in conducting them. Such meetings could be successful if the problems discussed were under the control of management, if management was open to changes that employees felt were important, and if employees and managers worked cooperatively to resolve problems of mutual interest. Without such conditions, however, there tended to be little employee participation or, worse, the sessions developed into adversarial forums as managers defended and employees resisted what they perceived to be the "party line."

One question was common to all communication efforts: How much factual information should management actually share with employees? To this day, the dilemma has never been satisfactorily resolved. There is a great tendency to dispense information selectively in order to retain influence over worker behavior. Managers who argue that sensitive information should not be shared fear that employees will misinterpret, jump to conclusions, quit, demand more benefits or security, share information with competitors, and so on. Yet withholding of information, when perceived over time by employees, has undermined the credibility of management in more than one company. Establishment of vehicles for communication creates expectations among workers. When these expectations are violated, management–worker relations deteriorate. Communications have never been easy to manage; even the simplest approach can generate unintended consequences.

"Big Picture" Programs

"Big picture" programs have long been a human relations technique in industry. While the programs vary, all involve efforts by supervisors to make employees feel that their particular tasks are critical to the achievement of much broader and more important goals. The objective, it could be said, is to get the bricklayer to see himself as building a cathedral.

In one manufacturing plant, assembly-line workers are periodically approached by foremen and told how the product they produced provided jobs for a range of workers throughout the economy. The idea is that the workers are not just manning a station on an assembly line but are making the American economy strong. Employees seem decidedly unimpressed by the argument and more concerned with their immediate work environment.

Their reaction was echoed by an air force military policeman who once informed the authors that "when you are pulling guard duty in South Dakota and up to your butt in snow, at that moment you know you aren't making the world safe for democracy. You're standing up to your butt in snow." Like the assembly-line workers, this military policeman had a rather cynical view of the "big picture" when it wasn't accompanied by solutions to his real problems.

Surveys

Opinion and climate surveys are being increasingly used in large corporations as a method for identifying and resolving organizational problems. When applied properly, the survey technology is both complex and time-consuming.

Unfortunately, the attitude persists that passing out questionnaires is an easy way to demonstrate management's interest in employees' opinions. But asking someone's opinion is a tricky business, and has traditionally been taken too lightly by managers eager to exhibit a participative style. Asking questions implies a willingness to act on the answers. Failure to treat the proffered opinions seriously often arouses anger, leaving the manager in a worse position than before the survey. Surveys should be focused on controllable problems and be accompanied by vehicles for sharing the results and acting on them.

The above characteristics of surveys are at times conspicuously absent. A new vice president of personnel at a large insurance company implemented a corporate-wide attitude survey shortly after his arrival. While it was supposed to demonstrate a new management responsiveness to employee concerns, the survey succeeded in demonstrating just the opposite. It took a broad shotgun approach that was unlikely to generate any focused, usable data. Discussions with employees indicated that the survey, and some similar efforts that had more form than substance, failed to convince employees that anything was being done for them.

Obviously, the methods we have been discussing all have potential benefits. Good communications are like apple pie—difficult to argue against. It is equally difficult to suggest that employees should not gain awareness of how their contributions relate to larger organizational purposes. A sense of mission is highly important to organized effort. The problem is the simplistic and somewhat preposterous expectation that such efforts will eliminate the need for serious examination of an organization's productive resources. If the history of management theory and practice teaches anything, it is that companies are forever ready to adopt a quick fix for what Taylor referred to as "the labor problem."

The Behavioral Science School of Management

From the 1950s through the 1970s, behavioral-science-based management theories proliferated. The qualitative aspects of life in many organizations changed significantly. Gradually the "culture definition" of a good manager was, for better or worse, altered. Among the factors contributing to the change were the increasing complexity of products, rapidly shifting markets, and substantial changes in social attitudes. The latter, along with the Hawthorne legacy, shaped new training and organizational development activities. The benefits often seem elusive, however, and the productivity gains promised by proponents of the theories have not always materialized. Nor have some of the other benefits, such as lower turnover and reduced absenteeism.

Not all of the behavioral science theories are direct descendants of Hawthorne and human relations. However, all the theories are at least second cousins. The first doctoral-level behavioral science program in a business school emerged at Harvard, the culmination of Mayo's and Roethlisberger's influence there. As applied behavioral science spread, so did the claims for it. Tentative, exploratory conclusions were exaggerated—and not always by hucksters selling snake oil. By the mid-1970s many of the internal corporate people responsible for initiating programs were trained behavioral scientists, often with doctoral degrees, trying to do their job.

When the proponents of the human resources approach increasingly suggested that behavioral research had invalidated or significantly modified traditional management thinking, the traditionalists began striking back. Often, sophisticated people trained in the behavioral sciences found themselves either defending against encroachment by these adversaries or attaining greater influence in organizations at the expense of traditional management theorists. At lower levels of sophistication, almost cult-like followings emerged around certain managerial techniques. A series of win–lose relationships had been established in "the management theory jungle."

Included in the legacy of Hawthorne are the contemporary quality-of-work-life experiments—such as the General Foods pet food plant in Topeka, Kansas, our next topic.

NOTES

1. W. Dowling, *Effective Management and the Behavioral Sciences* (New York: AMACOM, 1978), p. 203.

2. Elton Mayo, *The Human Problems of an Industrial Civilization* (New York: Macmillan, 1933), pp. 65, 67. The information in this quotation was drawn from an internal Western Electric document.
3. Elton Mayo, *The Social Problems of an Industrial Civilization* (Boston: Harvard Business School, Division of Research, 1945), p. 71.
4. Ibid.
5. "The Fruitful Errors of Elton Mayo," *Fortune,* November 1946.
6. Stuart Chase et al., *The Social Responsibility of Management* (New York: NYU School of Commerce, 1950).
7. Frederick Mosteller, "Non-sampling Errors." In D. L. Sills (ed.), *International Encyclopedia of the Social Sciences* (New York: Macmillan, 1967).
8. Fritz J. Roethlisberger and William J. Dickson, *Management and the Worker* (Cambridge, Mass.: Harvard University Press, 1939), p. 407.
9. Fritz J. Roethlisberger and William J. Dickson, *Counseling in an Organization* (Boston: Harvard Business School, Division of Research, 1966).
10. Quoted in Dowling, *Effective Management,* p. 204.
11. Mayo, *Human Problems,* p. 71.
12. Stuart Chase, "What Makes the Worker Like to Work?" *Reader's Digest,* February 1941.
13. Fritz J. Roethlisberger, *Management and Morale* (Cambridge, Mass.: Harvard University Press, 1941).
14. Ibid., pp. 41–43.
15. Ibid., p. 44.
16. Elton Mayo, "Changing Methods in Industry," *Personnel Journal,* Vol. 8, No. 5, June 1929 through April 1930, pp. 326–332.
17. M. L. Putman, "Improving Employee Relations: A Plan Which Uses Data Obtained from Employees," *Personnel Journal,* Vol. 8, No. 5, June 1929 through April 1930, pp. 314–325.
18. For example, Dowling, *Effective Management,* p. 204.
19. Elton Mayo to Stuart Chase, March 25, 1941.
20. H. Landsberger, *Hawthorne Revisited* (Ithaca, N.Y.: Cornell University Press, 1958), p. 113.
21. "The Fruitful Errors."
22. Roethlisberger and Dickson, *Counseling.*
23. Ibid.
24. Ibid.
25. Ibid.
26. Ibid.
27. John T. Dunlop, "Framework for the Analysis of Industrial Relations: Two Views," *Industrial and Labor Relations Review,* Vol. 3, 1950, pp. 383–393.

Suggested Readings for Part Two

Argyle, M. "The Relay Assembly Test Room in Retrospect." *Occupational Psychology,* Vol. 27, No. 2 (April 1953), pp. 98–103.

Carey, A. "The Hawthorne Studies: A Radical Criticism." *American Sociological Review,* Vol. 32 (1967), pp. 403–416.

Franke, R. H., and J. D. Kaul. "The Hawthorne Experiments: First Statistical Interpretation." *American Sociological Review,* Vol. 43, No. 5 (October 1978), pp. 623–643.

Kuhn, R. L. "In Search of the Hawthorne Effect." In E. L. Cass and F. G. Zimmer, *Man and Work in Society.* New York: Van Nostrand Reinhold, 1975.

Landsberger, H. *Hawthorne Revisited.* Ithaca, N.Y.: Cornell University Press, 1958.

Mayo, E. *The Human Problems of an Industrial Civilization.* New York: Macmillan, 1933.

———. *The Social Problems of an Industrial Civilization.* Boston: Harvard Business School, Division of Research, 1945.

Parsons, H. M. "What Happened at Hawthorne?" *Science,* Vol. 183, No. 4128 (March 8, 1974), pp. 922–932.

Roethlisberger, F. J. *Management and Morale.* Cambridge, Mass.: Harvard University Press, 1941.

———, and W. J. Dickson. *Management and the Worker.* Cambridge, Mass.: Harvard University Press, 1939.

———. *Counseling in an Organization.* Boston: Harvard Business School, Division of Research, 1966.

Sykes, A. J. M. "Economic Interest and the Hawthorne Researches: A Comment." *Human Relations,* Vol. 18, No. 3 (August 1965), pp. 253–263.

Wrege, C. D. "Solving Mayo's Mystery: The First Complete Account of the Origin of the Hawthorne Studies—The Forgotten Contributions of C. E. Snow and H. Hibarger." *Academy of Management Proceedings,* 1976, pp. 12–16.

PART THREE

The Topeka Plant:
Work Restructuring and the
Quality of Work Life

9

Topeka: The Gaines Pet Food Plant

In January 1971 the Gaines pet food plant, near Topeka, Kansas, began operating. Over the next several years the plant was more widely discussed and written about in management circles than any other single manufacturing establishment in the United States. In the process it became the centerpiece of the work-redesign/quality-of-work-life movement among behavioral scientists—the school of thought which, in management thinking, represents the culmination of reform based on behavioral science principles. By 1975, many regarded Topeka as a prototype of what future "humanized" plants might be like. Others saw the plant as an example of the misrepresentations and exaggerations of behavioral scientists.

Topeka is included as a landmark study because, although preceded by other job-redesign and work-culture experiments, it became symbolic of a distinct philosophy of management. Further, the principal actors in the planning and establishment of the plant clearly viewed it as a model, intended to demonstrate the feasibility of what they considered to be radical managerial positions. Finally, the Topeka approach challenged certain work-design concepts commonly associated with classic schools of management. Many people saw Topeka as a direct confrontation with ideas rooted in scientific management and related approaches.

Initiation of the Topeka Plant Design

Gaines pet foods were a product of the Post Division of General Foods. Prior to the opening of the Topeka plant, all Gaines products were produced at a plant in Kankakee, Illinois. In 1966, demand for

189

Gaines products was creating significant levels of overtime at Kankakee. Productivity problems were considered serious. Employees were frequently indifferent and inattentive, attitudes which, because of the continuous-process technology, led to plant shutdowns, product waste, and costly recycling. Employees managed to work only a modest number of hours per day, and they resisted changes toward fuller utilization of manpower. A series of acts of sabotage and violence occurred. The plant had a relatively young (over half the male and over a third of the female employees were under twenty-eight) unionized work force of approximately 1,200 people.

Lyman Ketchum was appointed manager at Kankakee in 1966. His predecessor had already initiated a consulting relationship with Richard Walton, who was at that time a professor at Purdue University. Managers at the Kankakee plant had been extensively involved in National Training Laboratory experiences and University of Illinois training programs. Ketchum wanted to continue these kinds of experiences, so he retained Walton.

Ketchum describes the developments in 1966–1968 as follows:

> During the first three years, we were successful in what we set out to do at the staff level and we were beginning to make some penetration to levels immediately below. In the economic sphere we reduced costs and met demand, but we noted some increasingly unfavorable behavioral symptoms. The paradox perplexed us. In retrospect, we can see that it is possible that one set of assumptions and values was operative at the upper levels and another set was operative at the worker/supervisor levels. Traditional assumptions have led to fractionated work and job impoverishment at the lower levels. The departmentalized structure contributed to job impoverishment at middle levels. The success of our group efforts at the top tended to coalesce upper management into a tightly knit group. The problem-solving capabilities at the upper level tended to draw the problems to higher levels for solution rather than to push them down for solution. So it would seem there were two different worlds with lower levels of the organization confused by the dissonance between values and processes articulated from the top and the characteristics of their own world.[1]

By 1968 it was clear that the continued increase in demand for Gaines products was going to require additional plant capacity. Both Ketchum and Walton strongly felt that innovation was needed in the new plant's organization. They wished to eliminate the negative attitudes, feelings of alienation, and behavior problems that existed at Kankakee, and furthermore believed that the "evolving expectations of American workers would increasingly come in conflict with the demands, conditions, and rewards of conventional organizations."[2]

Management chose to locate the new facility away from Kankakee, perhaps to avoid the types of problems experienced at the existing plant. The decision might have been affected by a desire to avoid unionization: it would be easier to obtain corporate approval to design a "humanistic" organization if employees were nonunionized.

Ketchum and Walton first advanced the idea of consciously utilizing behavioral science principles in the design of the new plant during a meeting of General Foods managers at Geneva, Wisconsin. They pointed out that a Post Division carton and container plant in Saratoga Springs, New York, had been operating in an "innovative" fashion for several years. Thus, a precedent existed within General Foods. In addition, they stated that competitor Procter & Gamble's newer plants were reputed to incorporate innovative, behavioral-science-based ideas.

In 1968 Ketchum met with his staff to determine how the new plant would be managed. There was consensus on four points:

1. An objective—lowest possible cost of goods with no sacrifice of product quality, service to the trade, or marketing flexibility.
2. An analysis—cost factors fixed by plant location and those determined by human behavior.
3. A restatement of philosophic belief—humans will best respond (be productive) where there exists a high feeling of self-worth by employee, and employee identification with success of total organization. Achievement of these response factors requires existence of other elements. None can of themselves exist but must be part of a system, and the system analysis must encompass plant design, philosophy of management, organizing, and staffing.
4. A recommendaton—the project can best be handled by a team consisting of four full-time members. . . . The project leader should report to the Kankakee Operations Manager, and the project should be separated from the Kankakee Organization. . . .[3]

Edward R. Dulworth was selected as project leader. He was an engineer by training, a member of the management team at Kankakee, and very familiar with the manufacturing processes to be employed at Topeka. Dulworth then chose Philip Simshauser as his manufacturing services manager and Robert Mech as his manufacturing manager. Mech selected Donald Lafond to assist him. These four men, along with Walton and working under Ketchum's general direction, became the team that developed the Topeka system. Walton says this about the team members:

> The strengths of the subordinates [Dulworth] selected were their technical competence, openness to new ideas, and desire to further develop interpersonal and organization skills. Significantly, Ed Dulworth selected men with whom he had worked and who had worked with each other previously. Thus, interpersonal compatability was somewhat assured.

When the team was formed in 1969, the basic technology and physical layout of the new plant had already been decided on. The team could, however, propose to alter certain features of the plant layout and technology if it could demonstrate that such modifications were required for the type of organization they were attempting to devise. With regard to management practices, the team was directed to "erase all the 'givens' and begin anew to devise a management system most applicable to today's and tomorrow's environment."

Development of the Topeka System

Over a period of about six months, the team developed what the members came to call "the Topeka system." The table they prepared describing the system offers a clear statement of their intent. The system was to maximize workers' direct participation through a team production concept, with each team given broad responsibility for work standards as well as specific production tasks. Status differentials were to be kept to a minimum. The plant also would maintain staffing at minimum levels, keep compensation above community averages to ensure employment selectivity, and rigorously screen new employees. In short, the system was designed to attract and retain above-average employees and to utilize their talents to the fullest.

Eventually, the contents of this descriptive table were disseminated rather widely. The planning team was deeply committed to its ideas and made a concentrated effort to transform them into a reality.

Recruitment and Selection

Extreme care was exercised in the recruitment process. The project team had decided that the plant supervisors (later called team leaders) would, as indicated in the table, "function as people managers rather than super-operators." Accordingly, the team developed the following profile of characteristics that they were seeking in team leaders:

> Secure—doesn't need to dominate others
> High interpersonal and group skills
> Optimistic about people
> Previous industrial supervisory experience (aptitudes for)
> Above average intelligence
> Analytical ability
> Interest in organizational approach and system
> Flexible, adaptive, and comfortable with change
> Emotionally stable

Open, honest and sincere
A leader
Perceptive
Energetic
Communication and comprehensive skills
Mechanical aptitude—potential for developing skills
Desire to grow and develop (ambition)
Comfortable/tolerant with low structure
Broad perspective—encompassing total business needs
Age, education—open.[5]

An advertisement was placed in newspapers in Kansas City and Topeka, emphasizing that "a young, new-breed idea in management" was being introduced and that the successful candidate would need "an above-average flair for working with people." Thirty candidates were narrowed down to six, partially through problem exercises and game play devised to bring out such characteristics as leadership and collaborative behavior. Once the team leaders had been chosen, an extensive skill-development program was launched for them. The program included activities designed to increase interpersonal as well as technological and administrative skills. The team leaders also became active members of the planning team and participated in the design of jobs and the compensation system.

When production workers were hired, equally selective criteria were used. The team leaders, with some help from the project team, decided on the following:

Age distribution within the team desirable
Healthy and energetic with no defects that would handicap doing any job in the plant
Schooling—practical experience and achievement instead of grade completed
Aptitude—average mechanical and numerical ability and desire to learn
Analytical ability
Comprehensive and communication abilities—above average (some members should have exceptional abilities
Responsibility—desire to accept responsibility
Social—disposition for group-oriented work environment (open, honest, sincere)
Interest in working within organization concepts [6]

Advertisements were again placed in metropolitan papers in the area. It was stated that individual potential would be emphasized and that the plant would provide "an exciting new organization concept which will allow you to participate in all phases of plant operations." Among the qualifications mentioned were willingness to accept greater responsibility and a desire to learn multiple jobs and new skills. The response was substantial.

Ketchum reports that of the 625 people who applied, 312 were eliminated by screening conducted by the Kansas State Employment Service. Testing further eliminated 76, leaving 237. A physical exam then reduced the number by 18. An in-depth, one-hour interview with each of three different team leaders resulted in narrowing the group to 98 candidates. A "selection weekend" eliminated 35 of those and the remaining 63 were offered jobs.

The Organization of Operations

The plant was organized into teams. A process (production) team and a packaging/warehouse team both reported to Robert Mech. An office team reported to Philip Simshauser. The latter team was concerned with utilities, personnel, payroll, secretarial functions, production control, purchasing and stores, cost accounting, and traffic.[7]

The processing area was a highly automated operation. Usually, it was entirely run by nine people per shift. The operation began with the receipt of raw materials (corn, soya, premixed vitamins, and meat meal). These materials were conveyed to storage, where they were weighed, moisture levels were adjusted as necessary, and the ingredients were mixed in predetermined percentages. The process was monitored by two or three team members in an air-conditioned computer control room. The team's objective was to produce a minimum of one hundred tons of dog food per shift so that the packaging/warehouse team would have a steady flow of product to work with.

The packaging/warehouse team, which usually consisted of seventeen people per shift, coated the product, placed it in bags and boxes, and moved it to the warehouse for storage. Much of this work was automated. Bags or boxes were filled automatically with preweighed amounts of dog food and placed in containers on a conveyer, where they were sealed, palletized, and stored.

In addition to performing their basic production tasks, the two teams carried out a variety of other functions that were aimed at achieving self-management. Walton wrote:

> . . . assignments of individual team members to sets of tasks are subject to team consensus. Sets of tasks can be redefined by the team in light of individual capabilities and interests. . . . Staff units and job specialties are avoided. Activities typically performed by maintenance, quality control, custodial, industrial engineering and personnel units are built into an operating team's responsibilities.[8]

The teams also coped with manufacturing problems that occurred within or between their areas of responsibility, temporarily redistributed tasks when some members were absent, chose team members to serve on plant-wide committees (such as safety and recreation), counseled employees who were not performing well, and screened and selected new team members.[9]

All of this self-management, of course, meant that the role of the supervisor, or team leader, was significantly different from that found in traditional organizations. The planning team, when conceiving of the team leader as primarily a "people manager rather than a super-operator," had left the actual responsibilities a bit unclear. But, as Walton often put it, the team leaders were largely responsible for team development and facilitation of group decision-making. They also played more specific roles, such as deciding when team members' pay should be increased and approving members' sick leave. Plant manager Dulworth described the team leader as "a kind of coach. He is a resource person rather than a governing person. He encourages independence, not dependence in team members. The more team members do on their own, the better."[10] As we will see, the somewhat vague definition of the team leader's role caused difficulty later in the plant's history.

The Pay System

One of the most innovative (and, ultimately, one of the most difficult to administer) features of the Topeka organization has been its pay system. The project team's original plan contained two specific references to pay. One was the intention to offer "above community average pay to assure employment selectivity." The other point regarding pay was expressed as follows:

Employee advancement by merit
Single job classification with grade
Level progression and above average opportunities to master multiple skills[11]

The plant established a single job classification and starting pay rate ($3.40 per hour in 1971) for all operators. Increases in pay were made when a person learned additional job skills. According to Walton, there were four pay rates in the plant: the starting rate; the single job rate, which was received when an employee mastered his or her job assignment; the team rate, which was paid when a team member learned all of the job assignments within the team's responsibility; and the plant rate, to be paid when an employee learned all jobs in the entire plant.[12] In addition, an employee could qualify for an "added-on" rate if he or she had some special trade skills, such as knowledge of electrical maintenance. The purpose of this pay system was to encourage employees to develop job skills at a self-determined pace. In addition, no limits were placed on the number of operators who could qualify for higher pay brackets. It was hoped that this would encourage employees to teach one another the various job skills.

> Employees who comprised the initial work force were all hired at the same time, a circumstance that enabled them to directly compare their experiences. With one or two exceptions on each team, operators all received their single job rates at the same time, about six weeks after the plant started. Five months later, however, about one-third of the members of each team had been awarded the team rate.[13]

By this time, some employees had expressed dissatisfaction with the pay decisions being made and the equality of opportunity to learn other jobs. Walton has pointed out that two competing feelings created difficulty for the employees and team leaders: a desire for equality, and a desire for a truly merit-based reward system. This situation, which became a chronic problem at Topeka, will be discussed later.

How Well Does the Topeka System Work?

In any ongoing activity, it is inappropriate to discuss outcomes as though they represented "final results." This is especially true in the case of the Topeka plant, since assessments of the degree of success attained there have varied greatly over time.

Early reports on the plant's progress were quite positive. One of the most widely circulated descriptions was Walton's 1972 article "How to Counter Alienation In the Plant," which probably was written a year to eighteen months after the plant's startup. Walton was very impressed with the results. Regarding the costs of operation, he noted that:

> Using standard principles, industrial engineers originally estimated that 110 employees should man the plant. Yet the team concept, coupled with the integration of support activities into team responsibilities, has resulted in a manpower level of slightly less than 70 people.

> . . . After 18 months, the new plant's fixed overhead rate was 33% lower than in the old plant. Reductions in variable manufacturing costs (e.g., 92% fewer quality rejects and an absenteeism rate 9% below the industry norm) resulted in annual savings of $600,000. The safety record was one of the best in the company and the turnover was far below average.[14]

With regard to indicators that are more difficult to measure, such as job attitudes, Walton reported that all members of the plant community—operators, team leaders, and managers—had become involved in their work and were deriving great satisfaction from it. He indicated that there was an atmosphere of openness and mutual respect, and that the plant's "participatory democracy" was spreading in the sense that team leaders and other plant managers had been unusually active in civic affairs. Finally, Walton reported that "the apparent effectiveness of the new plant organization has caught the attention of top management and encouraged it to create a new corporate-level unit to transfer the organizational and managerial innovations to other work environments."[15]

Later reports continued to be positive. In 1974, Dulworth reported savings of about $2 million a year, a quality reject rate 80 percent below that regarded as normal, an absence rate of about 1.5 percent, turnover one-third below the rate for the parent company, and continued positive work attitudes.[16] In that same year, Walton reported the same figures as he had given for 1972 and, in 1975, labeled Topeka "an unqualified success."[17] In his "after six years" assessment in 1977, Walton reported a continuation of the positive atmosphere, work attitudes, and commitment, and added that the plant had gone for nearly four years without a single lost-time accident.[18] Walton mentioned again that General Foods intended to establish similar restructuring approaches in other plants but noted that the actual diffusion of these ideas had been slow in coming.[19]

Problems and Difficulties

There was no shortage of reports describing the plant in a very positive fashion. In many of these papers Topeka was offered as a model for other organizations to follow: proof positive that innovative work organizations could succeed. There were, however, problems associated with the plant's operation.

The Team Leader Position

One of the most persistent problems in the plant related to the role of "team leader." The concept had created problems even before the plant opened, when there had been difficulty in clearly defining the role. Later shifts in the job title reflected uncertainty. At times the planning group used the term "foreman" to refer to the job; newspaper advertisements referred to a "production supervisor."

The planners had trouble drawing up a description of the exact duties and responsibilities to be performed. If planning the role proved difficult, performing it proved more so. Walton wrote that "at times team leaders provided too much structure, seeming to contradict the stated philosophy. At other times, they provided too little structure and seemed to dramatize the unpracticality of worker participation."[20] Other accounts offer a similar description and seem to emphasize that "some team leaders manifested considerable difficulty in *not* behaving like traditional authority figures."[21]

This difficulty was exacerbated by some employees' tendency to elicit and reinforce traditional authority-based behavior on the part of the team leaders. Walton recognized this situation: "In brief, the actual expectations and preferences of employees in this plant fall on a spectrum running from practices idealized by the system planners to *practices that are typical of traditional industrial plants.* They do, however, cluster towards the idealized end of the spectrum [italics added]."[22] In this connection, it is important to note that the employees (both team leaders and team members) had been carefully screened and had been selected in part because of their interest in working in an innovative plant setting. Since even some of these people found it problematic to behave in a "democratic" way, greater difficulties would undoubtedly be encountered with less carefully screened groups.

An area in which the team leader's unclear role became particularly troublesome was administration of the pay system. Published reports have varied concerning the extent to which team leaders involved their members in decisions concerning pay increases.

For example, *Business Week* reported in 1977: "As the system was set up, team members voted on pay raises for fellow employees . . . but that prerogative may be returning to management."[23] Walton reported in 1972, and again in 1975, that "individual pay decisions had been largely those of team leaders who, however, were also aware of operators' assessments of each other."[24] In 1974 he described the process this way: "Who then, decides when an employee has qualified for a higher pay bracket? In the General Foods plant, these decisions were made by the first-line supervisor usually after consultation with team members."[25] Walton's use of the term "usually," as well as "first-line supervisor" instead of "team leader," is interesting. And the quote reflects the ambiguity of the team leader's role.

Establishment of pay levels for the team leaders themselves was difficult, and was made more so by the fact that the team leader role was not well understood by General Foods managers outside the Topeka system. Ketchum described this problem as follows: "The team leader's 'freedom to act' was probably the least understood point. . . . A notion of the range of skills the team leader must possess as compared with the range in a traditional system was not accepted. . . . The idea that the team leader must assure that all the proper skills are possessed by the team members, and what this entails, was not understood."[26]

Business Week reported feelings of jealousy and competition between teams and team leaders. Walton also stated that "there was an absence of high mutual support and trust within this group." But he did not feel the problem was jealousy.

> . . . A norm of self-sacrifice seemed to apply to team leaders. Many team leaders would concern themselves with improving the work life for team members but not seek needed changes in their own lot. As one team leader said, "I never did think the Topeka system applied to team leaders themselves." The norms were that it is okay for operators to openly express strongly felt views and that team leaders will actively engage in dialogue. Some team leaders were frequently exhausted by such interchanges. It had not been made legitimate for team leaders to put boundaries on their own accessibility.[27]

Walton indicated that despite a concerted effort to improve relations among team leaders and to increase their voice over matters affecting them, by 1976 the leaders' positions were still ambiguous and unsatisfying. Their behavior continued to be marked by defensive patterns.[28]

The net effect was that the team leaders eventually began to have the same feeling as do foremen in traditional plants: that they were "men in the middle" who were neither part of management nor part of the employee group. They felt that their prospects for advancement were limited and that their current positions involved more problems than pleasures. As a result, the team leader position was unattractive to many people at the plant.

The Team Member Role

The team members also experienced some difficulty with their roles. As indicated earlier, some members wanted the team leaders to behave in a more traditional, authoritarian fashion. Those closely associated with the plant maintain that this desire was characteristic of only a small minority of team members. Still, the behavior was prevalent enough to merit discussion, especially since the workers had been carefully selected.

There were also instances when "scapegoating" behavior arose because of strong peer group pressure. Such pressure was at odds with the desired atmosphere of trust and openness.

Difficulties in Administering the Compensation System

As discussed earlier, administration of the pay system was one area in which the team leader's role remained unclear. The pay system also created problems for team members. Some difficulties stemmed from the team members' participation in pay decisions:

> For the system to work, an individual had to be . . . objective in evaluating the qualifications of peers for higher pay rates . . . . that objectivity suffered when a person feared he would be ostracized by a clique. The potential for distorting influence by cliques was related to several design factors in this new system. Influence is vested more in lateral than in hierarchical relations, which makes an operator more concerned about the judgment of his peers than superiors. There is no quantifiable, stable, automatic basis for a person's security, such as that provided by seniority in some systems. One worker explained that the tenuous basis of his security makes him continuously mindful of his relations with the many people who could help or hurt him in the future.[29]

As a result, there was a tendency toward leniency in making pay decisions. People were sometimes awarded the third pay level, or "plant rate," in the absence of a complete and objective evaluation of their actual skills.

Another problem was the way in which the pay was linked to team members' jobs. The pay system did reward learning and skill development, as had been planned. However, pay increases were seldom associated with participation in group discussion, an attitude of openness and trust, or, for that matter, continuing excellence in performing one's tasks.[30] For a variety of reasons, the pay system at Topeka has been, in Walton's words, "an important source of tension." In all the literature pertaining to the plant, no single problem has been mentioned as often.

The difficulty in administering the pay system was increased by two unanticipated events. One occurrence was that many operators felt qualified for the team rate earlier than management had anticipated. Management expressed reluctance to grant the increases, and employees who had doubted that the pay system would be administered as promised found their skepticism reinforced. Ultimately these increases were granted, which later created concerns of a different kind.

Another problem developed when management, because of increased demand for production in the plant's second year of operation, deferred the movement of workers from one team to another. Such shifts were the mechanism for advancing to the "plant rate" pay level. Workers and team leaders alike became concerned about possible inequities. Some people felt that not everyone had an equal opportunity to learn other jobs, that judgments about job mastery were sometimes inappropriate, and that team leaders were using criteria besides job mastery in promoting workers to the team rate.

Although pay increases came rather rapidly to many members of the Topeka plant, some still felt that the pay system did not provide adequate rewards for their level of involvement and their contributions. Employees were interested in some form of compensation related to plant productivity, team productivity, or both. Consequently, in 1973 a group bonus plan was considered, but it was never implemented because of resistance from General Foods.

Other Difficulties with the Topeka System

During Topeka's first few years, several other problems emerged that were largely internal to the design of the plant. One problem related to the design of jobs. The planning group had originally intended to make all jobs in the plant reasonably interesting and challenging to perform. Early reports on Topeka suggested that this had been accomplished. Walton reported, "Every set of tasks is designed to include functions requiring higher order human abilities and responsibilities, such as planning, diagnosing mechanical or process problems, and liaison work.[31]

Apparently, this was not accomplished as completely as was first thought. Robert Schrank, of the Ford Foundation, visited the plant a few years later and concluded that, while the processing team jobs seemed to offer some opportunities for planning and diagnosing, the warehousing and packaging team jobs clearly did not.[32] (It should be noted here that the warehousing and packaging team involved approximately twice the number of employees as the processing team.) Schrank observed, "All new employees come through the packaging-warehousing group, which suggests that this is the lowest status group in the plant." When he was told of management's plan to keep circulating people from one team to another for learning purposes, Schrank predicted that "eventually the processing group will become the elite and few will be willing to return to packaging and warehousing." Walton, in later reevaluating the work at Topeka, conceded that "we could not make the packaging work equally challenging with the processing work."[33]

The emphasis on participatory democracy within the teams seemed to do little to overcome dissatisfaction with problem-solving mechanisms at the plant-wide level. Plant-wide committees were formed to deal with such issues as selection of a spare parts coordinator and changes in the pay system for office employees. These committees were composed of representatives from each team, but apparently only limited confidence was extended to the representatives. As a result, committee actions received only limited support. Thus, the problem of integrating employee participation into issues affecting the entire system remain unsolved.

Topeka within the Larger General Foods System

The Topeka plant was a complex social system, and accordingly was at times frustrating to its members and difficult to administer. However, Topeka did not exist in a social vacuum; it was part of a larger, complex organization. Understanding what has happened at Topeka requires knowledge of its relationship with the General Foods organizational system.

Large corporations expect many of their members to assume new positions; indeed, mobility is often a way of life. G.F. is no different, so Topeka went through the process of manpower changes. One factor was the building of a second plant to manufacture canned pet food, adjacent to the original Topeka plant. When this plant opened, thirteen team members, two team leaders, and one manager from the dry-food plant moved over to form the nucleus of the new canned-food plant's staff.

These changes led to some difficulties in the original plant. The moves meant that relationships had to be established between new team leaders, team members, and management. Some team leaders had difficulty developing the same enthusiasm for the "team-building" tasks as they had achieved the first time around. Further, the plant was expected to maintain higher levels of production than had been true during its first year of operation. Team leaders began to hold fewer meetings. In some teams, the familiarity and mutual confidence so important to team effectiveness in the Topeka system began to erode.

The canned-food plant also created difficulty for the original plant in other ways. Walton reports that:

> . . . the canned food plant helped generate negativism in the dry food plant. Many members felt that they had been "deserted" by those who opted to go to a "more advanced rival." They also opposed the can plant's practices regarding pay and job design because a moratorium was placed on job rotation during the start up phase and pay increases were tied to more traditional criteria.[34]

The fits and starts with which the new plant was brought into production were interpreted by dry-food-plant employees as an indication that G.F. corporate leaders had a weakened commitment to the new management philosophy. This feeling was intensified when, in the summer of 1976, the new plant's product took off in the market. Production activity was rapidly accelerated in the canned-food plant, an outcome that was achieved in part because management deferred introducing many aspects of the new management system. In short, when the startup and operation of the new plant failed to duplicate the original system, morale in the dry-food plant was negatively affected.

Between 1973 and 1976, four managers left the original plant. Only one went to the canned-food plant; the other three left General Foods entirely. The reasons for their departures were difficulties with G.F. corporate management. The changes in plant management had significantly affected progress of the Topeka system. The original managers had planned and developed the system and had had a strong personal interest in seeing it succeed. Plant employees never had any doubt that these people were committed to the plant's philosophy. Some doubts were present with regard to the new managers.

The changes in management had begun with Lyman Ketchum's self-initiated move from operations manager of Gaines Pet Foods into a position on the corporate staff. Ketchum, as work on the Topeka startup progressed, had become increasingly confident about the new management approach. He decided that General Foods should implement similar approaches throughout its plant system and that he would like to spearhead such an effort. Eventually Ketchum's recommendation was approved by the operating committee, the president, and the chairman of General Foods. His appointment became official on September 1, 1971, less than nine months after Topeka had begun operations.

The Topeka plant had been the brainchild of Lyman Ketchum. He had conceived the original idea along with Walton; he had assembled the planning team; he had guided the development of the management philosophy. He had also been the key buffer between the innovative Topeka system and G.F. corporate management, had fought the battles that accompany any radical departure from usual procedure, and had therefore afforded Ed Dulworth and his management group the luxury of attending mostly to internal concerns. This helpful situation ceased to exist when Ketchum moved to the corporate staff.

The consequences of this change were significant and largely negative for the Topeka system. For one thing, Ketchum was replaced as operations manager by a man whose personal style and management philosophy were incompatible with the system.[35] Plant manager Ed Dulworth and his new boss were at odds almost immediately. This was partially because Dulworth had aspired to Ketchum's job himself, and felt that he understood the Topeka system whereas his new boss did not. The general manager of the Post Division had probably chosen Ketchum's replacement without giving serious consideration to his compatibility with Dulworth and the Topeka system. The Topeka plant represented a relatively small portion of the division's manufacturing capability, the new man offered needed engineering skills, and he was a known quantity to the general manager who appointed him.

The new operations manager's style was to "get involved" with details, and he required much more information and reporting than had Ketchum. This created significant problems for Dulworth. The Topeka plant was not generating the detailed data that the new operations manager seemed to want. As one example, maintenance costs usually appear as "fixed" costs in a traditional plant accounting system. At Topeka there was no separate maintenance function, so direct cost assessments and comparisons with other plants could not be made without modification of the plant's accounting system.

Dulworth tried to emphasize to his new boss that his plant operated differently from other G.F. facilities: while Dulworth could answer detailed questions concerning his teams' functioning and the development of his people, the financial and technical details were in the hands of his operators. The operations manager found this situation intolerable. He continued to pressure Dulworth for reporting changes, and Dulworth continued to resist; their relationship steadily deteriorated. Dulworth focused heavily on trying to maintain his system, his "fragile oasis in the General Foods conglomerate." He spent less and less time on internal plant matters.

At the same time, the elimination of the Topeka system's "buffer" when Ketchum left had opened the way for division and corporate demands that Topeka conform to the rest of the G.F. system. Not only did the new operations manager make personal demands, he also failed to protect the Topeka system from corporate pressures.

For example, members of groups such as finance, personnel, and industrial engineering were threatened by the fact that no such functions existed at the Topeka plant.[36] Perhaps they were concerned that the functions were not being performed well in the new plant; perhaps they felt that if the functions *were* being performed well, their own personal importance and job security would diminish. Members of such functional groups offered more "help" as time went by, and there was increased pressure to add such positions to the Topeka plant staff.

Another problem was the "hostile force exerted in the goal-setting process."[37] The Topeka plant had a "bottom-up" goal-setting process. In the larger G.F. organization, goals were set at the top, and falling short was considered unacceptable performance. This difference was symbolic of the gap between the plant and the rest of G.F. When any goal was missed at Topeka, this was interpreted by the corporation as a fault of the innovative system at Topeka. Without Ketchum as a buffer, the reward-and-punishment effects began to be felt more strongly by those in the plant.[38]

In 1975, nearly four years after Ketchum's departure, Dulworth arranged to meet with members of the Pet Food Division to discuss "the role of Topeka." He tried repeatedly to emphasize Topeka's role as a learning model for the corporation; stated that some divisional policies, structures, and practices might therefore not fit; and urged that such "Topeka system" differences be faced with a positive, problem-solving approach. After a number of these discussions, Dulworth concluded that the role he proposed for Topeka was not acceptable, or perhaps not even understandable, to many of those whose support he needed. Ed Dulworth left General Foods because he realized that a great irony had occurred. The Topeka planners had hoped their experiment would work so well that the rest of the corporation would want to adopt their ideas. What had evolved instead was an attitude of resistance to experimentation at Topeka.

This was, of course, not so apparent in 1971 when Ketchum set out to spread the word by becoming the corporate spokesman and change agent for new work systems. But even then some resistance was evident.

Ketchum spent his first few months in his new position gathering data on plants in the corporation and developing plans for diffusing his ideas. He then conducted a meeting on organizational development for 150 of the corporation's top operation, engineering, quality assurance, and personnel people. The session focused on five innovative management efforts under way within the General Foods organization. Ketchum reports: "Topeka was intentionally played down because it was already evident that the mention of Topeka evoked feelings of resentment on the part of many. . . . Both the chairman of the corporation in the opening keynote speech, and the vice president, Operating Services, in the conclusion, gave my new role a high level of sanction."[39] Ketchum does not suggest that these two points are related, but we believe they are.

Why would the mere mention of Topeka cause resentment? Perhaps, in part, *because* of the "high level of sanction" placed on Ketchum's new role by the corporation's top people. General Foods has a high level of internal competitiveness, and the reward it generally offers is promotion. The Topeka plant had already received much acclaim, and Ketchum as its "creator" had leapfrogged rapidly to a position of high visibility. This fact alone would have been enough to create jealousy and thus resentment on the part of some G.F. managers, directed toward Topeka and toward Ketchum himself. Such reactions were compounded by the fact that Ketchum's position did not rest on traditional systematic achievements. Instead of enforcing a conventional charter, Ketchum was about to challenge many traditional assumptions about G.F. success, doing so from a mid-level staff position.

Ketchum embarked on a mission of facilitating changeover to innovative forms of management in all of G.F.'s plants and warehouses in the United States and Canada (then 48 in number). He planned to focus first on new plants or those undergoing significant expansion, then on existing large facilities, and subsequently on progressively smaller locations. His approach was to conduct participative three-day meetings with the management group of a given plant, seeking to convert the managers themselves to change agents. His long-term strategy then involved "seeding" the General Foods organization with such managers, who had helped develop innovative work systems and believed in the new management ideas.[40]

Ketchum, however, left General Foods in 1975 without having significantly diffused his innovative management approaches in the corporation. Ed Dulworth left the same year, and for about the same reason. These men and their ideas did not fit comfortably into the management style of General Foods.

With time, it became more and more difficult for the Topeka plant to maintain its style of operation. As mentioned earlier, three managers left the plant. And the only one of the original group of managers from Topeka who ever succeeded in obtaining another position at General Foods was the manufacturing services manager, Philip Simshauser. He moved back to Kankakee as the controller there and tried for two years to institute innovative management practices. He reports that despite his best efforts to dissociate himself from Topeka, he was regarded with suspicion as "that Topeka guy" for the entire two-year period.[41] He, too, left G.F. at the end of that time.

Simshauser remains convinced that the plant was succeeding with its innovations but was foiled by corporate pressures. In 1980 he told the authors, "None of the internal problems we had at Topeka would have stopped us. Sure, we had problems, but we were overcoming them. Ketchum's move was the single most devastating blow to Topeka. We got bullied by company politics and outside pressures, not inside problems."

NOTES

1. Lyman D. Ketchum, "A Case Study of Diffusion." In L. E. Davis and Albert B. Cherns and Associates (eds.), *The Quality of Working Life,* Vol. 2: *Cases and Commentary* (New York: Free Press, 1975), p. 141.

2. Richard E. Walton, "Using Social Psychology to Create a New Plant Culture." In M. Deutsch and H. Hornstein (eds.), *Applying Social Psychology* (Hillsdale, N. J.: Laurence Erlbaum Associates, 1975), p. 140.
3. Lyman D. Ketchum, "Topeka Organization and Systems Development." Unpublished internal General Foods report, December 30, 1969.
4. Walton, "Using Social Psychology," p. 147.
5. Lyman D. Ketchum. Paper presented to the American Association for the Advancement of Science, Philadelphia, December 1971, p. 5.
6. Ibid., p. 6.
7. Ketchum, "Topeka Organization."
8. Walton, "Using Social Psychology," p. 142.
9. Richard E. Walton, "How to Counter Alienation in the Plant," *Harvard Business Review,* November–December 1972, p. 75.
10. "New Way to Run a Plant," *GF News,* February–March 1972, p. 10.
11. Ketchum, "Topeka Organization."
12. Walton, "How to Counter Alienation," p. 76.
13. Walton, "Using Social Psychology, " p. 145.
14. Walton, "How to Counter Alienation," p. 77.
15. Ibid., p. 78.
16. Reported in E. Glaser, *Productivity Gains Through Worklife Improvement* (New York: Harcourt Brace Jovanovich, 1976), pp. 61–62.
17. Richard E. Walton, "Innovative Restructuring of Work." In J. M. Rosow (ed.), *The Worker and the Job* (Englewood Cliffs, N. J.: Prentice-Hall, 1974), p. 162; Walton, "Using Social Psychology," p. 141.
18. Richard E. Walton, "Work Innovations at Topeka: After Six Years," *Journal of Applied Behavioral Science,* Vol. 13, No. 3, 1977, p. 423.
19. Ibid., pp. 423–424.
20. Richard E. Walton, "The Topeka Story: Teaching an Old Dog Food New Tricks," *The Wharton Magazine,* Winter 1978, p. 43.
21. Glaser, *Productivity Gains,* p. 58.
22. Walton, "How to Counter Alienation," p. 77.
23. "Stonewalling Plant Democracy," *Business Week,* March 28, 1977, p. 81.
24. Walton, "How to Counter Alienation," p. 76; Walton, "Using Social Psychology," p. 145.
25. Walton, "Innovative Restructuring of Work," p. 156.
26. Ketchum, "Case Study," pp. 155–156.
27. Walton, "Work Innovations," p. 429.
28. Ibid.
29. Walton, "Work Innovations," p. 428.
30. Walton, "Using Social Psychology," p. 145.
31. Walton, "How to Counter Alienation," p. 75.
32. Robert Schrank, "On Enduring Worker Alienation: The Gaines Pet Food Plant." In R. Fairfield, *Humanizing the Workplace* (Buffalo, N. Y.: Prometheus, 1974), pp. 124–127.
33. Richard E. Walton, "The Topeka Story: Part II. What's the Bottom Line?" *The Wharton Magazine,* Spring 1978, p. 40.

34. Walton, "The Topeka Story: Teaching," p. 44.
35. Interview with Philip Simshauser, October 1980.
36. Ketchum, "Case Study," p. 154.
37. Ibid., p. 153.
38. Ibid.
39. Ibid., p. 147.
40. Simshauser interview.
41. Ibid.

10

The Debate over Topeka

In our discussions of Taylorism and the Hawthorne studies, we examined how the new systems and ideas were presented in the literature and to interested constituencies. Such an examination is certainly appropriate with regard to Topeka.

Topeka has been widely viewed as a successful, plant-wide, socio-technical-systems type of innovation, a generalizable model for others to follow. It was promoted as such almost from the time the plant began operation. Although a substantial number of critics have challenged this claim, the plant is still highly touted by many behavioral scientists as a success story.

The Public Posturing of the Topeka System

Richard Walton, who wrote much of the literature on Topeka, has candidly discussed some of the difficulties associated with the plant and with the diffusion attempts that followed. However, the bulk of his writings—including those that explore problems at the plant—state that Topeka has been an unqualified success. In his earliest report on the plant, he referred to Topeka as "a prototype of change" and a "recent and radical effort which generally goes beyond what has been done elsewhere."[1] He also discussed some of the implementation difficulties, but his overall tone served his announced purpose of urging managers "to undertake the major innovations necessary for re-designing work organizations to deal effectively with the root causes of alienation."

This last point makes it evident that Walton is *not* an unbiased, scientific observer and reporter of events. He is an advocate. In 1975 he wrote, "I do not offer myself as a strictly unbiased observer. Specifically, I was deeply involved in the design effort of the Topeka plant. Moreover, generally I am committed to encouraging and improving upon innovations such as those at Topeka. . . ."[2]

Walton sincerely tried to illuminate the difficulties involved in accomplishing work restructuring. But while doing so, he continued to imply that, despite the problems, Topeka was a success. For example, to one book Walton contributed a chapter called "Using Social Psychology to Create a New Plant Culture."[3] Although by that time (1975) serious problems had emerged at Topeka, Walton described the process that he and the design team had *originally* followed in developing and implementing the Topeka system. He reported that "to date, the innovation is an unqualified success," a clearly overoptimistic assessment. He also verified his role as an advocate, writing that he had become "active in diffusing information about this particular innovation and the urgent need for similarly inspired (although perhaps formally different) social experimentation."

Some comments in Walton's article give a flavor of the widespread exposure that Topeka had received:

> As a result of efforts by Ketchum, Dulworth, and myself, the Topeka plant experiment has been on NBC's "First Tuesday" program; discussed in *Newsweek, Atlantic, Harvard Business Review, Innovation, The New York Times* and *Work in America*; has been presented at a symposium on the humanization of work sponsored by the American Association for the Advancement of Science, at conferences on changing work ethics in New York and San Francisco sponsored by the Urban Research Corporation, at a conference on the quality of working life sponsored by the Ford Foundation, at a conference on social indicators of the quality of work life sponsored by the Canadian Ministry of Labor; has been discussed with hundreds of other managers who have a particular interest in how changes might be effected in their own companies; and has been brought before a congressional subcommittee.[4]

In 1978 Walton was still proselytizing. For example, he wrote that "the Topeka organization has produced gains in the quality of worklife and productivity and has remained viable over an extended period."[5] In reality, as discussed in the preceding chapter, by 1978 the Topeka organization was in deep trouble. It was still true that "gains in the quality of worklife and productivity" had been achieved in comparison with the old plant at Kankakee, but to continue to hold this plant up as a successful prototype from which to generalize was clearly to take a position of advocacy.

Even when Walton was engaged in "explaining why success didn't take," he referred to "the strong success of the Topeka plant" and noted that it had not been matched so far by much diffusion.[6] While

Walton was indicating that the Topeka innovation was highly successful but had failed to spread, an opposite trend had set in: the larger G.F. system had begun to diffuse into Topeka! Walton was well aware that this was occurring and said that it could eventually undermine the initial project, but he still emphasized the viability of the innovation.

Ketchum and Dulworth wrote in the same vein as Walton. Behavioral scientists, including the authors of this book,[7] repeatedly cited the Topeka system as an example of a successful, innovative plant that humanized work and met the higher-order needs of workers.

A Second Look at Topeka

Although Topeka has often been referred to as a "radically innovative" plant, there are significant questions about the amount of innovation that actually occurred. Certainly Topeka was substantially different from the Kankakee plant (and from most production plants) in both climate and management methods. But exactly how extensive were the innovations that had been implemented in the course of achieving the new climate?

For one thing, the planning group that put together the Topeka system did not design the physical plant. The basic technology and the physical layout had already been decided upon by an engineering group headed by Yoval Shulman. Dulworth's team had no opportunity to design the plant so as to accommodate the semi-autonomous work groups inherent in a sociotechnical-systems approach. Rather, the team did its best to build the worker teams around existing technology.

The group did have the opportunity to request modifications of the technology if it could demonstrate a need for such changes.[8] Several alterations were made in accordance with the team's wishes. First, an effort was made to eliminate "status indicators." There was one entrance for everyone, one lunch room, a common color scheme and decor throughout the plant, and glass walls in the offices facing the plant. Second, to facilitate worker involvement in quality control, small QC labs were placed on several floors of the plant. Third, the planning team chose not to use one equipment feature that Shulman's engineers had provided. The design had called for the processing equipment to have a completely automated control system. Dulworth's team decided to start up the plant without using this system, allowing the operators to control the processing instead. The team placed a desk and clipboard in the control room and encouraged employees to use this room as a natural team-gathering point.[9]

These features, although significant, clearly constitute "tinkering" as opposed to basic design. The Topeka plant was much like any other modern processing/packaging facility. Therefore, it is not in the same category as plants *designed* to accommodate radical work innovations, such as Volvo's facilities.

Beyond the issue of technological design, there remains the question of how radically the Topeka system actually departs from conventional management practices. Walton has consistently described Topeka as extremely innovative and has said it offers "a glimpse of what may be the industrial work environment of the future," a prototype of the "more radical, comprehensive and systemic redesign of organizations" that Walton feels is necessary.[10]

Some other critical observers have not made such generalizations. Robert Schrank, for one, has said that Topeka may not be so radical after all. After his extended visit to the plant, he suggested that:[11]

1. The work of the warehousing and packaging team was "highly repetitive, with little room for autonomy and growth."
2. The work of the process team, while much more challenging and interesting, was that of "a typical operations–maintenance crew, where initiative, decision making and teamwork are essential to the smooth functioning of the process. Nothing is unusual in this type of operation."
3. A hierarchy of jobs similar to that in more traditional operations existed at Topeka.
4. There had been no worker participation in planning the new plant.
5. There was no "procedure for redress outside the existing institutional structure"; that is, there was no provision for due process.
6. The Topeka system offered no guarantee of employment security: if workers contributed substantially to improved productivity, some might become superfluous and lose their jobs.

For all of these reasons, Schrank questioned the extent to which Topeka was a radical departure from conventional practices.

Schrank also questioned Walton's claim that Topeka represented an effective way of countering worker alienation. Walton had presented six ways in which the evolving "expectations of workers conflict with the demands, conditions, and rewards of employing organizations." He argued that Topeka was a prototype of the type of organization needed to counter these six "roots of conflict."[12] Schrank, however, maintains that Topeka failed to respond, at least in part, to five of the six roots of conflict cited by Walton.[13] In Schrank's view, the only group in the plant that had any significant opportunity for challenge, intrinsically interesting work, and short-term gratification was the processing team, which involved only eight people per shift.

Thus, Schrank does not believe Topeka was all that radical a departure from conventional plants in regard to work content. He attributes the very positive early results to two factors. One is that some of the employees (specifically, the processing team members) had great freedom to circulate in the plant and to "schmooze" (socialize). The other factor is a general "open and humanistic" management style which Schrank observed at Topeka and which he describes as simply good human relations.

As is so often the case in applied behavioral science, beauty appears to be in the eye of the beholder. Walton is committed to promoting social change. Schrank is not without his biases either. He strongly believes in an interpretation of working life—one based on his own experiences and observations—in which "schmoozing," "time off," and "the need to be treated with dignity" are the primary sources of worker satisfaction. If we consider the history of the plant, and especially its interactions with the larger G.F. system, we are likely to see Schrank's criticisms of Topeka as too harsh. But his observations are not grossly misrepresentative and provide some perspective. While Topeka is not as conventional as Schrank makes it seem, neither is it as radical as Walton portrayed it. Considerable effort and planning were invested to achieve some modest yet significant changes in operating methods.

Besides the issue of the plant's innovativeness, there is the question of the extent to which Topeka operated under a number of favorable conditions that influenced results. Walton has discussed this point, listing the following relevant conditions:

1. The technology permitted and even called for effective communication between team members, as well as providing "room for human attitudes and motivation to affect cost."
2. Technical and economic conditions permitted the elimination of some of the more boring and disagreeable tasks.
3. The plant was new, was geographically isolated from other parts of the company, had a small work force, and was not unionized.
4. Pet foods are "socially positive" products, and the company had a good image. Thus employees were likely to develop positive attitudes toward the product and the company.[14]

Walton cites these factors as having influenced the success of the plant but asserts that they "are merely facilitating factors and are *not* preconditions for success."[15]

One perspective from which Walton's position can be criticized is the completeness of his list. The plant had another favorable condition going for it: the employees at Topeka had been carefully selected from a large group of applicants in accordance with certain criteria.

Mitchell Fein, among others, has commented on this fact. He believes that it explains much, if not all, of the plant's early success in terms of production. Fein offers the opinion that "comparing the performance of the Topeka workers to those of Kankakee [the older plant] is like comparing the Knicks [New York Knickerbockers] basketball team to that of a local school."[16] He goes on to say that the plant's uniqueness stems not from the management style employed but from the workers themselves, who were hand-picked. William Gomberg of the Wharton School has offered a similar criticism of Walton's representation of Topeka.[17]

We believe that still another "favorable condition" must be considered: the selection and ultimate make-up of the Topeka management group. It is rare to find an ideologically homogeneous group of managers, all holding strong behavioral-science-based values. Generally, any effort to implement a management system rooted in the behavioral sciences involves a struggle to change attitudes in the management group and thereafter to sustain the changes. The Topeka situation offers a striking contrast.

To begin with, the plant manager, Ed Dulworth, was an extraordinary manager whose talents and interests were extremely well suited to an innovative, open plant evironment. Dulworth was also able to hand-pick each member of his management team. Not only did he select individuals whose philosophies of management were consistent with his own, but he picked people whom he had worked with and whom he knew had worked well together at Kankakee.[18] In addition, during the entire planning and startup phases, Lyman Ketchum protected the operation from corporate intervention. These facts add up to a highly unusual set of circumstances—circumstances that make it very difficult to generalize from the Topeka experience to other situations.

Walton, while freely admitting that there were some conditions favorable to success at Topeka, believes that the broad principles underlying the Topeka work structure are widely applicable. Writers such as Schrank, Fein, and Gomberg obviously disagree. Fein and Gomberg, as we have seen, maintain that the nature of the work force was critical. Schrank has argued that the small plant size was an indispensable factor in allowing the openness so critical to the human-relations-oriented management style at Topeka.[19] He further questions the extent to which the Topeka system was innovative. We believe that Ketchum, Dulworth, and the management group were likewise indispensable to what occurred at Topeka.

It is impossible to know whether the various favorable conditions that existed at Topeka would be necessary to produce success in other instances of organizational innovation. However, one thing is certain: those conditions, however well they were working, were not sufficient to insulate the plant from pressure to conform to the larger G.F. system. The plant has been under consistent pressure ever since it started up. As key actors in the Topeka management group have left and new managers have entered the scene, these pressures have intensified.

The Topeka System: A Summary

What does one make of Topeka in light of the foregoing discussion? A close look at the Topeka system indicates that, like most complex social systems, it was at times frustrating to its members and extremely difficult to administer. But there are certainly positive indicators. From its inception, it apparently operated with lean staffing, productivity was good, accidents were virtually nonexistent, and, as of this writing, the plant has remained nonunion. Further, the management team sought to establish a system based on trust and the fullest possible utilization of employee talents and abilities.

Circumstances surrounding the system did not hinder achievement of these results. The plant's geographic location was favorable, and both supervisory and nonsupervisory personnel were carefully screened and selected. Members of the management team had all worked together previously and shared the same values. Certainly attitude change was not an initial problem at the plant. Although the physical plant was not initially designed to accommodate the semi-autonomous work groups, the technology does not appear to have been a problem for the planning team. Since it is generally easier to establish a social control over smaller groups of people, the size of the plant worked in the team's favor.

Even so, interesting and sometimes frustrating problems arose. The supervisory role was ambiguous and often seemed unappealing. The goal of creating challenging jobs was not completely achieved; perhaps it was significantly missed. Certainly some jobs had higher status than others. Participation in teams created some predictable problems, including scapegoating. Pay remained a source of dissatisfaction and friction within the plant.

It is easy for managers with traditional orientations to point to these problems and label the plant a failure. Such an attitude misses the point—and so does labeling the plant a success. Success or failure sets up a false dichotomy in the case of Topeka. What the plant does demonstrate is many of the consequences of attempting to implement behavioral science principles on a system-wide basis.

Difficulties emerged, but how do they compare with the problems that confront most industrial managers? (Of course, the particular characteristics of the employees must be kept in mind.) Topeka's potential contribution to behavioral science knowledge must be assessed in light of its difficulties, since these provide insight into the dynamics of the administration of social systems.

- Even in carefully selected groups, some preference for highly directive management emerges.
- Participation in group decisions can work against group members.
- Pay issues apparently shape the behavior of participants in even highly supportive and ego-gratifying environments. These issues frustrate some individuals and are a source of stress in the system.
- The ambiguous nature of the team leader's role does little to relieve the "man in the middle" syndrome that supervisors experience.

These are observations about the Topeka experience, not conclusions. Topeka offers little in the way of conclusions, despite practically everyone's tendency to identify the "explanatory factors." Topeka is not a good prototype—that is, it should not be held up as a generalized example of successful organizational innovation—for a number of reasons. The original innovations have not been completely retained. A variety of problems that developed led to significant changes in the "Topeka system," moving the plant toward a more traditional type of organization. Topeka remains, however, an organization with unusual and progressive features when compared with the original Kankakee plant or to similar G.F. facilities.

Topeka, however, did not fulfill its role as a learning model within the General Foods organization. In this respect, the experiment was unsuccessful. Rather than becoming a pilot laboratory for change, the plant became a threat to established organizational norms. Like most nonconformists, the plant has been strongly pressured to fall in line with everyone else. Thus, Walton's goal of using Topeka as a beginning point from which to diffuse organizational innovation has not been realized.

The Topeka plant is relatively unusual and is not well understood, even by its own corporate management. A number of factors may have inhibited diffusion of the Topeka ideas, such as too rapid promotion of results, too rapid changes in key personnel, and threats to other people in the organization. Thus, its limitations as a prototype are as important as the question of whether it succeeded or failed.

NOTES

1. Richard E. Walton, "How to Counter Alienaton in the Plant," *Harvard Business Review*, November-December 1972, p. 74.
2. Richard E. Walton, "From Hawthorne to Topeka and Kalmar." In Eugene Louis Cass and Frederick G. Zimmer (eds.), *Man and Work in Society* (New York: Van Nostrand Reinhold, 1975), p. 117.
3. Richard E. Walton, "Using Social Psychology to Create a New Plant Culture." In M. Deutsch and H. Hornstein (eds.), *Applying Social Psychology* (Hillsdale, N. J.: Laurence Erlbaum Associates, 1975).
4. Ibid., p. 154.
5. Richard E. Walton, "The Topeka Story: Teaching an Old Dog Food New Tricks," *The Wharton Magazine*, Winter 1978, p. 48.
6. Richard E. Walton, "The Diffusion on New Work Structures: Explaining Why Success Didn't Take," *Organizational Dynamics*, Winter 1975, p. 10.
7. David A. Whitsett, "Work Design." In L. R. Bittel (ed.), *Encyclopedia of Professional Management* (New York: McGraw-Hill, 1978), pp. 1213–1214; Lyle Yorks, *A Radical Approach to Job Enrichment* (New York: AMACOM, 1976), p. 33.
8. Interview with Philip Simshauser, October 1980.
9. Ibid.
10. Walton, "How to Counter Alienation," p. 71.
11. Robert Schrank, "On Enduring Worker Alienation: The Gaines Pet Food Plant." In R. Fairfield, *Humanizing the Workplace* (Buffalo, N.Y.: Prometheus, 1974), p. 124; Robert Schrank, *Ten Thousand Working Days* (Cambridge, Mass.: M.I.T. Press, 1979), p. 233, 235; Walton, "The Topeka Story: Teaching," p. 41.
12. Walton, "How to Counter Alienation," pp. 71–72.
13. Schrank, "On Enduring Worker Alienation," pp. 132–140.
14. Walton, "How to Counter Alienation," p. 79.
15. Ibid.
16. Mitchell Fein, "Job Enrichment Does Not Work," *Atlanta Economic Review,* Vol. 25, No. 6, 1975, p. 52.
17. William Gomberg, "Job Satisfaction: Sorting Out the Nonsense," *American Federationist*, June 1973, pp. 14–19.
18. Walton, "From Hawthorne," p. 147.
19. Schrank, "On Enduring Worker Alienation," p. 123.

Suggested Readings for Part Three

Fein, M. "Job Enrichment Does Not Work." *Atlanta Economic Review*, Vol. 25, No. 6 (1975), pp. 50–54.

Gomberg, W. "Job Satisfaction: Sorting Out the Nonsense." *American Federationist*, June 1973, pp. 14–19.

Ketchum, L. D. "A Case Study of Diffusion." In L. E. Davis and Albert B. Cherns and Associates (eds.), *The Quality of Working Life*, Vol. 2: *Cases and Commentary*. New York: Free Press, 1975, pp. 138–163.

Schrank, R. *Ten Thousand Working Days*. Cambridge, Mass.: M.I.T. Press, 1979.

Walton, R. E., "How to Counter Alienation in the Plant." *Harvard Business Review*, Vol. 50, No. 6 (November–December 1972), pp. 70–81.

―――. "Using Social Psychology to Create a New Plant Culture." In M. Deutsch and H. Hornstein, *Applying Social Psychology*. Hillsdale, N. J.: Erlbaum, 1975, pp. 139–156.

―――. "Work Innovations at Topeka: After Six Years." *Journal of Applied Behavioral Sciences*, Vol. 13, No. 3 (July–September 1977), pp. 422–433.

―――. "Establishing and Maintaining High Commitment Work Systems." In J. R. Kimberly et al., *The Organizational Life Cycle*. San Francisco: Jossey-Bass, 1980, pp. 214–245.

Whitsett, D. "Work Design." In L. R. Bittel, *Encyclopedia of Professional Management*. New York: McGraw-Hill, 1978, pp. 1213–1214.

PART FOUR

Research, Ideology, and Politics in Organization Theory

11

Taylorism, Hawthorne, and Topeka: Some Notable Similarities

What lessons are to be derived from our in-depth examinations of three classic sets of management studies? Significantly, although the studies are often regarded as contradicting one another, some remarkable similarities can be identified. An especially strong similarity can be seen in the way the studies were developed, reported on, and promoted. This chapter will look at these similarities and then at field research methods in general as they relate to the development and testing of management theory.

The Reformist Attitudes of the Theorists

In each case, the primary theorist saw his work as going beyond the specific organizational situation involved, and even beyond similar situations. The focus was on reform, in the sense of reshaping significant social institutions. For Taylor, an important issue was the resolution of conflict between management and labor: he sought a permanent, society-wide solution to "the labor problem." Basically, Taylor's system was directed toward increasing the size of the pie to be divided, coupled with a systematic method for parceling out the pieces. Taylor's goal, which was rooted in his own personal distaste for interpersonal conflict, became a reformulation of management–labor relations.

This goal evolved over time. Initially Taylor was concerned with increasing production. After repeatedly having to defend his system to a hostile public and gaining more experience in working with organizations, he came to redefine the goals of scientific management. Eventually the promotion of his ideas became a full-time vocation, and in his later years he fully believed in the necessity of industry adopting his system.

Mayo's goals were no more limited in scope. For him, the continued survival of industrial society was possible only if people developed the social skills needed to elicit cooperation. He repeatedly stressed the extent to which technological skills had outpaced the evolution of social ones. Mayo also viewed obsessive thinking as a serious threat to social institutions. As examples of destructive preoccupations, he cited the thinking of anarchists and social malcontents, whom he saw as victims of socioeconomic change. Mayo believed that World War II had occurred partially because of such displaced, obsessive thinking.

Taylor and Mayo both had a reformist zeal, but they had different patterns of involvement in their respective research studies. Taylor began with straightforward efforts to increase production, encountered resistance that he found traumatic, and gradually developed his broad views on the reshaping of the management–labor relationship. Mayo's ideas, which had been partially shaped by his confrontations with European radicals, were developed before he arrived on the scene at Hawthorne. The researchers at the plant came to Mayo with their data, and Mayo provided an interpretation. Partly because of Mayo's authoritative and distinctive guidance, management invested in further, extensive researches, giving Mayo an excellent vehicle for making his case for social skills.

For Walton, Topeka was an illustration of social change in the workplace and a learning model for society at large. He viewed Topeka as a significant and prototypical example of the direction such changes should take. The plant was not a test of hypotheses but a demonstration project. In order to capitalize on Topeka, Walton strove to maximize its visibility outside of General Foods. Ultimately, this approach conflicted with Ketchum's original goal of having the plant provide a learning experience within G.F.

Thus, Taylor, Mayo, and Walton all shared the goal of initiating broad social change. Their concerns went beyond improving efficiency. To generalize Frank Copley's descripton of Taylor, none of these men was a mere tinker of business systems. In this respect, they resemble many prominent behavioral scientists in the management field today, especially those associated with the organizational-development and quality-of-work-life movements. Such theorists, observing that most adults spend the bulk of their lives at work, believe that changing the nature of the workplace is an important leverage point for accomplishing wider social reform.

Hence *Work in America*, a task force report to the Secretary of Health, Education, and Welfare, emphasized the physical and emotional problems that are created and possibly resolved in the workplace. Applied behavioral scientists talk of humanizing organizations and label themselves change agents. Chris Argyris's comments about sociological theory are illustrative of this orientation: "In rereading the work of these authors, I became even more convinced that their theories would tend to emulate and reinforce the status quo, and if an activist were to use these theories as a basis for change, he would become an authoritarian manipulator (again, the status quo in change processes)."[1] Many management theorists, such as Chris Argyris, imply value judgments about the need for specific types of organizational change, judgments that are based more on social beliefs than on scientific evidence. Much behavioral science theory remains rooted in social philosophy, no matter how empirical the emphasis. And action- or change-oriented research always involves value judgments.

Although Taylor, Mayo, and Walton all considered themselves to be scientists, as management theorists they were reformers, advocates of a better world.

The Theorists' Humanistic Orientations

Taylor, Mayo, and Walton all justified their reforms on humanistic grounds. Of the three, Taylor had the longest journey to reach his humanistic arguments. His elitism, coupled with the harsh practical language of his times, obscured his arrival so far as others were concerned. Nevertheless, Taylor did conclude that certain humanistic factors were crucial to the successful implementation of his system. Specifically, he believed that the arbitrary power of supervisors and managers had to give way to the principles of scientific management. Clearly, a reduction of raw, arbitrary supervisory power would have great impact in human terms. Indeed, Taylor's arguments parallel contemporary arguments in favor of a management-by-objectives (MBO) appraisal process. MBO reduces a boss's subjective judgment regarding performance, clarifies performance expectations between boss and subordinate, and directs the attention of both people to specific job-related behavior.

Of course, accomplishing the type of reduction in management power that Taylor envisioned is another matter. And, ironically, scientific management has been utilized to *reinforce* management's arbitrary power and manipulate the worker. The same charge has been directed toward Mayo's human relations principles and the more contemporary intervention strategies of behavioral scientists. Critics, including some labor leaders, have labeled these approaches manipulative and elitist.

Taylor believed that the reduction of arbitrary supervisory power was an important benefit of his system, helping both the employee and the organization. Mayo and Roethlisberger were also concerned with reducing the arbitrary power of supervisors, albeit from a different perspective. Roethlisberger challenged the traditional definition of supervision as being the issuance of orders and the imposition of discipline.[2] He felt that the logic of sentiments dictated a more diagnostic approach to the problem of supervison.

Of the three traditions—scientific management, human relations, and work-life movement—the latter is the most explicitly humanistic, because of its emphasis on satisfaction of workers' higher-order psychological needs. And the Topeka system, designed to minimize the privileges of rank while maximizing workers' input into decision-making processes, sought to reduce arbitrary power associated with a position.

Though each tradition had a humanistic orientation, there were, of course, significant differences. The Topeka plant was far removed both in design and philosophy from anything Taylor had envisioned or recommended. Taylor reduced the power of line management by dividing it into staff specialties; Topeka challenged the concept of staff specialization. Taylor strove to reduce human discretion and variability; Topeka treated these qualities as potential strengths. Taylor rested everything on the concept of a one best method for doing a job; Topeka tried to let workers benefit from their individual experiences in choosing a method. Taylor was interested in eliminating soldiering; the team that designed Topeka was committed to a humanistic plant.

Thus, in many significant ways, what Taylor advocated differs from "the Topeka experiment." Yet, in the context of his times and the prevailing industrial relations practices, Taylor viewed himself as a humanistic reformer of management systems. This self-image is characteristic of today's proponents of quality-of-work-life systems.

Union Resistance and the Emphasis on Cooperation

As we have seen, hostility from labor leaders significantly contributed to Taylor's image as an anti-humanist. Organized labor directed similar hostility at the Hawthorne researchers. Both scientific management and the Hawthorne experiments were the subject of congressional hearings initiated by organized labor. In each case, labor charged that the management practices involved were exploitive.

Critics of contemporary quality-of-work-life experiments often label these as exploitive as well. Mitchell Fein makes this argument in regard to Topeka and other work-restructuring efforts, questioning the extent to which labor wants such "improvements" made in their jobs.[3] Fein argues that "behaviorists" (he uses the term in the sense of behavioral scientists with a humanistic orientation) are elitist and condescending in their approach to workers.

With certain exceptions, union leaders have been skeptical of quality-of-work-life experiments. In part this is because they believe such efforts can divert attention away from compensation, employment practices, benefits, and similar issues that unions consider to be of more direct value to their members. There is also a belief that these experiments, like the scientific management and human relations approaches, are a manipulative way for management to achieve production gains without giving tangible financial benefits in return.

Another, and more political, concern on the part of labor leaders is the fear that increased management–employee cooperation will undercut the influence of unions. Thus, one feature that occupies the battleground with labor—the search for cooperation—is found in all three of the management systems we have discussed. Taylor viewed his system as a vehicle for establishing cooperation between management and labor. For Mayo and Roethlisberger, eliciting cooperation was the essence of administration. Topeka was designed on the assumption that corporate goals and human needs were integrable. In fact, this last assumption has been at the heart of the organizational-development movement.

Taylor, Mayo, and Walton find their greatest common ground in their emphasis on the need to meet worker needs while pursuing company objectives. By taking this position, all three theorists:

1. Went counter to assumptions of many practicing managers of their times, assuming a reformist role that went beyond specific methodology to question long-held values and perceptions.
2. Contradicted a basic assumption of many political leaders and social thinkers—the idea that there is an inherent conflict of interest between economic classes—and did not feel that management should emphasize inherent conflict between its goals and those of workers.
3. Found themselves, despite the above, charged with being servants of management's interests.

The theorists did not always adhere to their positions to the point of overlooking opposing views. Walton, for example, has expressed his support of collective bargaining in a manner that recognizes the plurality of economic interests in the workplace. This position is common among quality-of-work-life theorists. However, many state that this outlook is temporary and that over the long term they wish to accomplish a significant alteration in power relations between management and workers.

Clearly, management theory has strong political aspects. When change agents try to achieve greater cooperation within a system of existing institutional arrangements, some theorists view their reforms as suspiciously designed to prop up existing power structures by co-opting workers. An effort to increase cooperation through direct confrontation with managers tends to alienate them, thereby shutting down access to the organizational settings necessary to demonstrate the practicality of the theories. The political environment in which theorists must establish their ideas pressures them to present their data in the strongest possible terms. This pressure is reflected in the ways that Taylor, Mayo, and Walton reported their findings. Their reports on field experiments were intended to *influence* practice.

Creating the Story to Make the Point

Taylor's Schmidt story illustrates how distortions can arise through a strong attempt to influence others. One point Taylor wished to make was that the person who is best suited to perform a job is precisely the one who is least likely to be able to determine how best to do it. Taylor presented a detailed dialogue of the discussion with Schmidt in order to emphasize the dynamics of explaining a job that was intellectually undemanding to a dull worker. The available evidence indicates that Taylor's story was fabricated. For one thing, it was probably Taylor's assistant, not Taylor himself, who had such talks with Schmidt. (Taylor was always careful to word his comments "Schmidt was spoken to in these words," not "I spoke to him.") At the time, Taylor was not in the loading area but was working in the machine shop on another implementation. We do not know whether "Schmidt" was actually dull, but to make his point, Taylor created a verbatim dialogue that was designed to emphasize Schmidt's dullness.

Mayo's reporting of period 12 in the relay assembly test room is of a similar nature. His discussions focused on the increase in total output and initially overlooked, and then seriously minimized, the fact that individual output rates were dropping. Mayo made no effort to hypothesize about the discrepancey between the total output and output rate curves; rather he simply labeled the declines "slight." Mayo's handling of these data is remarkable only in the context of his often stated and sincerely believed admonishment that for social science to progress it must take small initial steps and pursue the complex and messy vulgarities of the real world as observed from firsthand experience. Mayo was committed to this view of science. For him, day-to-day social science was a rather uninspiring affair.[4]

But Mayo was also a man with a mission: he wished to entirely change people's definition of administrative practice. He felt that nothing less than civilization was at stake, and therefore was given to presenting rather inconclusive findings as being of monumental consequence. He made no effort to correct journalistic misrepresentations of the Hawthorne work, and sometimes supported such presentations.

Nor was the Topeka planning team without fault. In early reports, the careful manner in which workers and managers had been selected was omitted or greatly downplayed. So were discussions of the problems that emerged during the implementation process and the limited innovativeness of the plant design. These issues surfaced after critics of the system gained access to the plant.

Why did the researchers either omit or, in the case of Taylor, fabricate events? It cannot simply be said that they were "fudging data." Indeed, Roethlisberger and Dickson made such thorough reports of the Hawthorne results that critics can easily use their data to seriously challenge the Harvard group's interpretations. There is no indication that Mayo ever tried to hide data or make them unavailable to other researchers. For his part, Walton has a track record of attempting to state his own assumptions about the phenomena on which he is reporting.

Probably most of the distortions that occurred were not deliberate. The researchers appear to have convinced themselves that the material they omitted or fabricated had no bearing on the significant results of these studies. In writing up findings in a case format, one feels pressure to elucidate one's principal point. Material is left out because it might confuse the issue. Under any circumstances, it is difficult to present complex or contradictory data. When a writer is torn between the conflicting purposes of advancing academic knowledge, achieving social reform, and immediately persuading an important audience, the priorities of the moment are likely to govern. Advocacy of the system dominates.

This mental process can occur even at an entirely unconscious level. People may re-create the events of field studies in their minds so that inconsistencies no longer exist. Greenwald has hypothesized that our ego (1) functions as an organization of knowledge, (2) is characterized by cognitive biases strikingly analogous to totalitarian information-control strategies, and (3) works to preserve its basic organization by screening out nonconforming data. In short, Greenwald suggests that in developing views of ourselves and of the world, we tend to be revisionists who will justify the present by changing the past.[5]

We all recall events selectively and in a fashion that supports our own theories about the world. For applied behavioral scientists, the problem is intensified. In action research such as that at Topeka, the researcher's relationship with the data is more personal and intense than is the case with other types of data analysis. Those involved become immersed in the management of the change process and may become personally committed to certain organizational goals, which sometimes supersede research goals. Mayo's case is somewhat different, since he had little initial involvement with the studies. But as the studies evolved, so did his personal identification with them. He saw the research findings as pointing more and more in the direction of his broader social concerns, and this made it difficult for him to remain entirely objective about the research itself.

Selling the System

Reformists who recognize the political or sensitive nature of their argument generally feel they must demonstrate their points in a clear, convincing fashion that will motivate others to action. Here Taylor, Mayo, Walton, and many other management theorists share a common ground. And when motivations converge around the need to modify the actions of others, a person can become unreliable in dealing with data.

People interested in social change have two problems. First, they must convince themselves and their colleagues that their reforms are correct. Taylor, Mayo, and Walton all believed that there was sufficient empirical support for their theoretical positions. The second problem is the promotion of one's ideas to relevant publics. This to a certain extent is a public relations/marketing task. When Taylor read newspaper accounts of Louis Brandeis's assertions that the railroads could save a million dollars a day through scientific management, he knew that there was no documentation to support such a claim and that Brandeis had significantly overstated the number for effect. Yet Taylor made no public effort to correct the claim. The publicity for scientific management was too positive for him to want to interfere with it.

Mayo probably read the effusive articles about Hawthorne not to check their scientific correctness but to see how well they captured the direction in which he wanted managers (and society) to move.

Walton showed awareness of the power of such articles when he wrote:

> Managers (action-takers, in general) do not act on new ideas on the basis of the amount of social science evidence (research findings or elaborate theory). Rather they act on the basis of the face validity of the idea, that is, its intuitive appeal to them and whether it is in line with some face experience of their own, although the idea may go beyond the experience.[6]

An understanding of the above principle is basic to success in change-oriented consulting work. As we will discuss, the principle also has an important relationship to the ways in which research has influenced the field of management.

Field Research and Management Practice

Field research has been central to the development of management theory and practice. Most prominent schools of thought have their roots in applied field experiments, written up in a case study format. Taylor's experiments and the Hawthorne and Topeka research all fall into this category. Other examples are not difficult to find.

Frederick Herzberg's motivation-hygiene theory, first presented in 1959, met with considerable interest in the management community.[7] In fact, the theory quickly became a standard part of supervisory and management development programs, and Herzberg's terminology became part of the language of management. However, application of his ideas was limited. Many companies wanted Herzberg to talk to their managers, but few budgeted money for job-enrichment efforts.

Job enrichment was originally popularized by Robert Ford and Scott Myers, who reported on application of the concept at AT&T and at Texas Instruments, respectively. The publication of Robert Ford's report[8] had a remarkable effect. Job enrichment now became a more important part of management training programs than the motivation-hygiene theory. More significantly, companies did budget money for formal job-enrichment efforts. Ford's and Myers's reports of actual field studies helped to make job enrichment a social movement in the management community—a movement so strong that it received considerable play in the popular press.

Soon there was a flood of subsequent reports of successful field applications at Bankers Trust, Travelers Insurance Company, Merrill Lynch, and similar institutions. Although the descriptions of these field applications varied in quality, a body of case literature evolved that seemed clearly to establish that "job enrichment works."

Job enrichment never established itself as an independent school of management practice along the dimensions of scientific management or human relations. However, for nearly ten years it greatly influenced behavioral-science-oriented management circles. In the process, it became a substantial part of what is now called the human resources model of management thinking. The human resources model differs from the earlier human relations theories in that it emphasizes *utilization* of people rather than the *treatment* of people.

With time, job enrichment was relabeled job redesign. It gradually merged with approaches toward work restructuring, which in turn was rooted in sociotechnical-systems theory. The history of sociotechnical-systems theory is laced with field applications. The benchmark studies were A. K. Rice's reports on new systems of working groups in the Ahmedabad Textile Mills in India and Eric Trist's studies of the Longwall system of coal mining. Jacques's book *The Changing Culture of a Factory* was a substantial contribution as well.[9]

More recent are Walton's reports on the General Foods Topeka plant and reports on the Volvo and Saab production plants, all of which have become part of a general philosophy of work restructuring. Today these efforts are seen as prototypical examples of methods that contribute to the quality of work life, an umbrella concept for many of the practices that have evolved out of a behavioral science orientation to management.

Another example of the influence of field studies is the popularization of behavior modification during the 1970s. Behavior modification rests on the principles of operant conditioning, which have been part of psychological literature for decades. The work of B. F. Skinner is well known beyond his specialized field.

Ed Feeney conducted research in container shipping departments at Emery Air Freight, essentially using Skinnerian reinforcement schedules that involved recognition and feedback. His widely reported success in altering (improving) behavior did for behavior modification what Mayo had done for human relations and what Ford and Myers had done for job enrichment.[10] The principles of operant conditioning became legitimatized as a managerial technique. Subsequent reports from Connecticut General, B. F. Goodrich Chemical, and Weyerhaeuser, to name a few, have established behavior modification as a technique of performance management. As noted earlier, one widely read article reinterpreted the Hawthorne studies as an example of behavior modification.[11]

Some people have raised questions about the scientific thoroughness of those who applied the behavior-modification principles.[12] However, the issue here is not scientific correctness but the crucial role that field applications play in establishing management theories and practices.

The Inverse Role of Field Studies

It is natural that the "field tested theory" is most likely to be accepted by the pragmatic practitioners of management. Further, the descriptive data collected through field studies are often needed at certain stages of theory development. But in management theory, field research goes beyond its usual role of generating data that may prove useful in conceptualizing and formalizing theories: field reports are used to inspire widespread change. In effect, field research and the case study method have been uprooted from their place in scientific practice. *The field application, instead of being treated as a way to generate ideas for more rigorous testing, is advanced as a role model for generalized application.* This role has been supported by both the "scientists" conducting the studies and the managerial audience.

In short, field research is used not only to generate knowledge but to promote it as well. Unfortunately, these two purposes often conflict. The dilemmas involved are well illustrated by the type of field investigation called action research.

Action Research

In action research, behavioral science principles are used in the field as a strategy for change. In its most developed form, action research is a process of joint exploration on the part of researcher and client. The researcher usually works with a certain facet of the organization and manipulates variables in the hope of achieving some positive change.

One dilemma is the fact that such a project has a dual set of objectives. The organization that is paying for or sanctioning the research wants concrete benefits. The researcher wants to learn more about the principles underlying any changes that occur. In theory, both researcher and client are committed to both goals.[13] Under such conditions, both parties have a need for the action research to produce positive results in organizational performance.

It is relevant here to consider possible distinctions between action research and consulting. In practice the line between the two is often unclear. Managers involved in action research view the researcher as someone who will provide advice; the researcher tends to think of the organization as a client that must be satisfied and given guidance.

Some writers base the distinction on the nature of the final product.[14] In this view, consultants study the organization and the final product is a report containing recommendations. Implementation of these recommendations is left to the client. Conversely, in action research the client participates as an equal partner in each step of the process, from feasibility studies to implementation of changes to final evaluation of the effort.

Many traditional management consultants concern themselves only with making recommendations. However, consulting firms specializing in the practical application of behavioral science principles often define their role differently. Many of these firms are application-oriented. Further, since the success of virtually all behavioral science strategies depends on the cooperation of management, these firms emphasize heavy client involvement and decision-making throughout the change process.

In applied behavioral science, the distinction between action research and consulting is found in the degree to which the change agent recommends a strategy. The more "programmatic" a person's stance, the more he or she is assuming a consulting role. Pure consulting involves telling the client "here's how to do it"; action research is investigative and explorative in nature. With action research the change agent brings to the organization a general theoretical framework and certain skills. Application is worked out in collaborative relationship with the client, with the change agent identifying those aspects of the work which are explorative in nature or based on uncertain knowledge. The bottom line in action research is the generation of new knowledge, not application of an existing knowledge base as is the case with consulting. Consultants define success as getting the client to some acceptable state of affairs. These differences are not always mutually exclusive; in fact, the distinction is almost always a matter of degree.

Because of the many intangible variables involved, some people would say that *all* applied behavioral science is exploratory. The difference lies in the extent to which the scientist is responsive to the need to analyze, adjust, record, and report his experiences in a manner that contributes to the scientific knowledge base. The alternative is the force-fitting of a strategy, accepting success at face value, regardless of degree, and ignoring failures.

Applications of behavioral science initiated by people in an understood consulting relationship are regularly developed as part of the management literature. Often the results are discussed in much the same manner as those of an intentionally structured action research project.

A similar crossover occurs in virtually all "pure" action research projects. Accommodation is made to meet client goals; the only question is how much. Sometimes researchers find themselves aligned with particular client personnel who feel an obligation to demonstrate the "success" of a project.

The reader can see the opportunity for much mischief here—both intentional and unintentional. Consultants may represent the certainty of a strategy's success in an effort to obtain business or relieve client anxieties. Here the consultant is attuned to the exploratory nature of what is happening, but the client is not. Often clients do their own self-protecting. They may want to spread application of a strategy to other areas of the organization and thus urge consultants to present results in the most favorable light possible. Researchers with academic affiliations are not immune to such pressures. Having positioned themselves so as to claim expertise that is valuable to the organization, they can feel as strong a need as others to report "significant findings." Since many business school professors have their own consulting practices, the business and academic pressures to demonstrate success converge.

Influences That Reinforce the Role of Action Research

There are a number of reasons why the field study in general and action research in particular are especially attractive to the behavioral scientist working in the management field.

First, such studies offer a demonstration of the utility of the knowledge base. Management is a practice-oriented discipline, so behavioral scientists must go beyond the description and categorization of data. The question always arises: How can we *use* this knowledge?

Today, of course, the line between pure and applied knowledge has become blurred virtually to the point of disappearance. As Jacques Ellul observed years ago, "scientific activity has been superseded by technical activity to such a degree that we can no longer conceive of science without its technical outcome."[15] Chris Argyris has suggested that in our society, social science research and theories will remain viable only if people can see direct applications.[16]

It is true that behavioral and social scientists in traditional academic departments often are able to do "pure" research and deemphasize the application question; application is someone else's problem. But for behavioral scientists working in professional schools, there is no someone else: the problem is theirs. In this context action research becomes attractive because knowledge can be gained while practical issues of utilization are tested.

Some argue that action research is a highly rigorous test of behavioral science knowledge. Chris Argyris writes:

> The third, and most rigorous test of a theory [in a field setting] is to be able to create the conditions hypothesized; to create the variables, and to predict a priori what should happen. The third mode is the most rigorous because it involves the researcher in generating, managing, and controlling the variables under consideration. The researcher is taking on a relationship with the noncontrived world that is similar to the one the experimental behavioral scientist takes with the experiments he plans and executes.[17]

Mayo would most likely have rephrased Argyris's statement to read "the researcher is taking on a relationship with the noncontrived world that is similar to the one the *physical* scientist takes with the experiments he plans and executes." For Mayo the principal benefit to be derived from such a relationship would be the skills the social scientist develops from working with his or her data in such an intimate, firsthand manner. To Mayo such skill was the essence of knowledge of *acquaintance,* as opposed to simply knowledge *about.*

Beliefs about the value of knowledge of acquaintance find wide acceptance in the management-oriented areas of behavioral science. This acceptance rests on the central role skill development plays in the practice of behavioral science. Many behavioral scientists who work with organizations view themselves as change agents, or professionals capable of helping an organization achieve greater "health." This application of behavioral science has been labeled organizational development.

Organizational-development specialists are application-oriented. They may use diagnostic methods, employ techniques for "unfreezing organizations," or even structure the process of change itself. Techniques associated with OD include survey feedback, T-groups, team-building, process consultation, and sociotechnical-systems design. Application of these techniques requires an intuitive familiarity with organizations, a fact that often makes OD seem more like an art than a science. In terms of the type of knowledge utilized, the behavioral scientist is more like a skilled craftsperson, or a clinician, than a scientist.

This is also true in management training and development. The design of training workshops reflects the trainer's knowledge about group processes, much of which was acquired through previous direct work with groups. Ultimately, workshop design rests on the trainer's "intuitive familiarity" with the learning process and his or her feel for "what will work with this type of group."

In short, the need for knowledge of acquaintance—that is, largely intuitive knowledge gained through past experience—is alive and well among behavioral scientists. Indeed, it is this knowledge that management wishes to obtain from the behavioral scientist. Applied field research, particularly action research, provides a supportive environment for such studies.

Another factor that has given rise to action research is the access problem. Albert Cherns has observed that "on the whole [the researcher] has to reach his fundamental data in their natural state and his problem is how to reach them in that state. His means is through a professional relationship which gives him a privileged condition. . . ."[18] Obviously, researchers who wish to study behavior in organizations must have access to those organizations. One vehicle for gaining access is the provision of professional services. By tailoring their work to meet an organization's needs, investigators gain an opportunity to research issues that would otherwise be closed to them. Thus, the notion of action research is born partially of necessity.

This alters the research process, since the problems studied are rooted not in theory but in the needs of the organization. The researcher begins with practice, works back to theory and more systematic research that may test certain tentative conclusions, and then returns to improved practice. This process does provide an opportunity to gain "knowledge of acquaintance," but many traditional social scientists criticize it on the ground that research problems should be defined by theory rather than practice.

Another important characteristic of action research is that it seems to answer the pragmatic question in which practicing managers are most interested: "How do I make it work?" The pragmatic nature of such research, as we will see, is a double-edged sword.

By its nature, action research is reported in a case study framework. This format, as Richard Walton has noted, is especially suited for generating in the reader a vicarious experience in which he or she is able to internalize the implications of a project. Action research concretely demonstrates the feasibility of a technique in a situation with which the reader can identify, such as a plant or office setting. A case report suggests a step-by-step process for putting behavioral science research into action. The reader mentally converts the phases of the research into the steps of more widespread application.

This has clearly been the experience of many management theorists with a behavioral science orientation. Robert Ford's job-enrichment experiments at AT&T provide an example.[19] The experiments involved a step-by-step process of meeting with managers, conducting a brief survey of workers' attitudes, holding a training session for supervisors and managers that culminated in a brainstorming (labeled "greenlighting") session, and editing and refining items on the brainstorming list. These steps became the basic approach to implementation of job enrichment. They also were incorporated into the theoretical explanation of job enrichment that was developed by Frederick Herzberg. The Bell System approach became widely advocated as the way to make job enrichment work.

Managers have expressed similar interest in case reports on team-production-oriented work-restructuring efforts. Managers repeatedly ask the question "What exactly did you do?" and in the case literature they seemingly find an answer.

Here the needs of manager and researcher converge. Behavioral scientists need to demonstrate the usefulness of their propositions. Action research, through the vehicle of the case report, does this convincingly. Researchers, being under external pressure to develop pragmatic solutions and confronted with a receptive audience, can easily, if subtly, develop case reports that emphasize certain steps or factors which they feel account for a project's success. Management, eager for any method that can help deal with pressing problems whose solutions appear forever elusive, selectively focuses on these same factors. Within this process lies serious potential for the misuse and misunderstanding of field research projects and resulting case reports.

Field Research and Case Studies: Their Strengths and Limitations

As tools for generating and transmitting knowledge in the behavioral sciences, field research in general, and the case study in particular, have advantages but also some important limitations. Unfortunately, case reports of field research have often been misused.

The first and foremost advantage of case reports is that they can provide insight into the dynamics of social phenomena. The records of a good field study offer precise descriptions of events, giving qualitative details not otherwise available. Such details can inspire conceptualization and suggest new hypotheses.

Field studies also serve to keep existing theories open. The rich details of a case report often provide evidence of exceptions as well as predicted occurrences, illustrating the need for theories to be more conditional.

It follows from the above that the value of a case report depends on the extent and accuracy of the detail it provides. Descriptions must be rich enough to allow independent evaluations by those with differing orientations. Evaluative or diagnostic judgments made by the researcher must be kept distinct from the descriptive data on which they rest.

These points imply a significant weakness of the case reporting method: evaluative or diagnostic judgments may continually be made, either consciously or unconsciously, about what data should be recorded. The descriptive data that ultimately become available are, of necessity, selective and subject to the perceptions of the researcher. This process is well represented in the debate over Topeka. Richard Walton and Robert Schrank, for example, might have observed the same phenomena in the plant situation but have came away with different ideas of which events and behaviors were significant. Even an observer who has been extensively trained in "objectivity" must exercise selectivity in recording events.

Another limitation of the case study is its uniqueness: a case represents a sample of one. Thus, there is virtually no basis for generalization. In interpersonal situations even small things can make a difference, a fact currently recognized by "contingency" and "fit" models of organization and management theory. In a given field investigation, specific actors, organization structures, cultural values, and environmental factors intertwine to create a unique situation. The problem is not easily resolved by carrying out additional case studies, since this usually multiplies the number of residual variables.

With the action research type of field investigation, these problems become intensified. For example, the uniqueness problem typically becomes even greater. In order to guard the integrity of the project, an action researcher will try to control the experimental environment as much as possible. This was seen in the Topeka experiment. In the design of the plant, Walton and his associates sought and largely attained conditions that made the plant highly unusual. Certainly the compatibility of values among the management group, the highly selective employment process interviews with two different members of the original Topeka management team that produced differing perspectives on the exact role of team leaders vis-à-vis workers on compensation decisions, and the "buffer" role played by Ketchum were atypical of production organizations.

The researchers wished to test the feasibility of a "countercultural" plant, but in doing so created an exceptional situation. This made any generalization of the results highly suspect. It is a perverse but logical fact that the more control researchers are able to gain over a project, the less applicable the results are to normal organizational processes.

The same point can be made about the relay assembly test room at Hawthorne. In fact, the test room had characteristics similar to those of the Topeka plant:

1. Physical segregation of the test group from other employees
2. A small, highly selective employee group
3. The presence of "buffers" between those involved in the experiment and their usual supervisors
4. The presence of an observer (supervisor) committed to maintaining positive attitudes

In the Hawthorne plant, the removal of the two problem assemblers further reinforced the selective nature of the experimental group.

Changing Research Objectives

With field research, objectives often change as a function of the research process itself. Hawthorne is a classic example. The original purpose of the relay assembly test room was to study the problem of fatigue. With time the focus of the research shifted, first toward employee attitudes and later in the direction of group processes and ways in which employees organized their knowledge. With the completion of one phase of the studies, new avenues of research suggested themselves. Mayo and Roethlisberger viewed this as a sign of the healthiness of the research. Roethlisberger wrote, "The 'Facts' you gain from research can be employed not only to answer the question that you have raised, but also to change the nature and direction of your question. In the latter case, you have a progressive research. . . ."[20]

In short, action research is open-ended in that general objectives are known at the start, but specific ones—and the methods that will be employed throughout the study—frequently are not. The changes in direction that occur make evaluation of results difficult, since conclusive scientific results cannot be obtained. Albert Cherns has written about this problem:

> "Evaluation" implies that the objectives of the research are clearly known and established in advance, and that therefore measures can be taken along the relevant dimensions to be repeated at a suitable time when the action research changes are complete. This conceptualization does not allow for the emergent nature of action research objectives. An enterprise directed toward catalyzing the release of constructive forces locked up in a situation will, as it begins to be successful, bring into play forces which will have their own hitherto unexpressed contribution to make to the determination of objectives.

> As new objectives emerge, the relevant dimensions on which their achievement can be assessed change. The dimensions on which measures were initially taken may now be of lower priority if not irrelevant. One of the traps of an "independent" evaluation is just that the selection of measures of the independent evaluators sets the seal of permanence on the objectives against which the outcome is to be evaluated. By definition, the independent evaluations cannot have any part in the emergence of new objectives or take account of them. The cautious action researcher knows that a change of objectives will ruin the independent evaluation. If he is tied to the objectives initially set, the experiment is dominated by the independent evaluator.

> It is not obscurantism or incompetence or self-serving concealment that accounts for the tendency of action research reports to offer subjective evidence of the success of the changes resulting from the research. It is the inherent difficulty associated with the partly emergent nature of research objectives. The researcher who knows from his experience of the people with whom he is working that they are now different as people from what they were when the work began finds it hard to present this convincingly; the measures available to him may be paltry by comparison. Furthermore, the capacity of the system to perform its everyday functions may have changed comparatively little; its resilience in the face of crisis may have changed . . . but he cannot provoke a crisis to demonstrate this.[21]

Unfortunately, without provoking a crisis there is no way to scientifically document an organization's improved resilience. The alternative is to accept the researcher's informed opinion as verification, a compromise that hardly conforms to the traditional demands of scientific methodology.

Field Research and the Practice of Management

For the various reasons discussed earlier, field research looms large in the evolution of schools of management practice. Although the research may be described as quasi-experimental, this is usually an exaggeration. Many decisions that affect results are not made as part of the experimental design; rather, they are dictated by organizational conditions and events that arise during the research.

In a sense, researchers cannot win. If they establish strong experimental controls, the research setting becomes atypical. If they do not establish controls, the study becomes an organizational event that can be described but that fails to meet accepted criteria for scientific explanation.

As we have seen, however, field research does have advantages: it is conducted in an actual organizational setting, and when it is successful, it is the type of research most likely to convince management. The knowledge generated, however, can only be tentative. This is not meant as an indictment of such studies; the real problem is how they have been used. Field research should be viewed as providing specific instances that suggest the importance of certain factors but raise as many questions as they answer. Yet such research reports are typically used as "classics" in management practice, as bases from which entire methodologies emerge.

Management Practice and Experimental Research

Field research, of course, is not the only type of study that has contributed to management practice. We have emphasized field studies here because of the dramatic impact they have—an impact that is in inverse proportion to their degree of rigor in comparison with other research forms.

Rigor, however, is no guarantee against misinterpretation. Field studies are not the only type of research that is loosely interpreted when results are translated into practice. For example, many researchers use college students as subjects. Usually, the degree to which results can be generalized is little better than with the field case study. The college populations that are studied bear little resemblance to any of the multitude of work populations in business and industry at a multitude of organizational levels. An experimental subject's relationship to a task (not to mention the relationship of the task to the subject's lifestyle and economic or professional prospects) is substantially different from that encountered in the vast majority of work situations. Finally, the tasks and the measures utilized in the studies are highly contrived. Yet researchers may make broad conclusions regarding goal attainment, motivation patterns, or reactions to supervisory styles in the workplace.

Experimental research conducted in work settings also has limited generalizability. Investigators often acknowledge this in their reports, but such qualifications seldom prevent theorists from extrapolating the results into a broadly stated theory with strong implications for management practice.

Experimental research lacks the surface validity that people find so convincing in field research. To convert the findings of experimental research into practice, a behavioral scientist must distill a set of general principles, relate them back to the findings, and add anecdotal examples gleaned from either field research or field experience. In the process the experimenter is converting pure research findings into prescriptions for practice. Field research expedites the process, and practicing managers generally find it the most convincing part of the presentation.

NOTES

1. Chris Argyris, *The Applicability of Organizational Sociology* (New York: Cambridge University Press, 1972), p. viii.
2. Fritz J. Roethlisberger, *Management and Morale* (Cambridge, Mass.: Harvard University Press, 1941).
3. Mitchell Fein, "Job Enrichment Does Not Work," *Atlanta Economic Review,* Vol. 25, No. 6, 1972, pp. 50–54.
4. Elton Mayo, *The Social Problems of an Industrial Civilization* (Boston: Harvard Business School, Division of Research, 1945), pp. 3–56.
5. A. G. Greenwald, "The Totalitarian Ego: Fabrication and Revision of Personal History," *American Psychologist,* July 1980, pp. 603–618.
6. Richard E. Walton, "Using Social Psychology to Create a New Plant Culture." In M. Deutsch and H. Horstein (eds.), *Applying Social Psychology* (Hillsdale, N. J.: Laurence Erlbaum and Associates, 1975), p. 149.
7. F. Herzberg, B. Mausner, and B. Snyderman, *The Motivation to Work* (New York: Wiley, 1969).
8. Robert N. Ford, *Motivation Through the Work Itself* (New York: AMACOM, 1969).

9. A. K. Rice, *Productivity and Social Organizatons: The Ahmedabad Experiment* (London: Tavistock, 1958); Eric L. Trist et al., *Organizational Choice* (London: Tavistock, 1963); Elliot Jacques, *The Changing Culture of a Factory* (London: Tavistock, 1950).

10. W. Hamner and W. Organ, *Organizational Behavior: An Applied Psychological Approach* (Dallas: Business Publications, 1978), pp. 249–258.

11. H. M. Parsons, "What Happened at Hawthorne?" *Science,* March 8, 1974, pp. 922–932.

12. J. A. Lee, *The Gold and the Garbage in Management Theories and Prescriptions* (Athens, Ohio: Ohio University Press, 1980), pp. 286–290.

13. N. Rapopart, "Three Dilemmas in Action Research," *Human Relations,* Vol. 23, No. 6 (1970), pp. 499–513.

14. For example, Albert B. Cherns, "Action Research." In L. E. Davis and Albert B. Cherns and Associates (eds.), *The Quality of Working Life,* Vol. 2: *Cases and Commentary* (New York: Free Press, a division of Macmillan, 1975).

15. Jacques Ellul, *The Technological Society* (New York: Knopf, 1964), pp. 9–10.

16. Chris Argyris, *The Applicability of Organizational Sociology.*

17. Ibid., pp. 85–86.

18. Albert B. Cherns, "Social Research and Its Diffusion," *Human Relations,* Vol. 22, No. 3, p. 210.

19. Ford, *Motivation Through.*

20. Fritz J. Roethlisberger to Hal Wright, September 11, 1930.

21. Cherns, "Action Research," p. 29.

12

Practice Theories
and Their Practitioners

Whether management is an art or a science is a question that many "principles of management" textbooks feel obligated to address. The answers cover a wide range:[1]

> Management is a young discipline, which means that it is still in the early stages of being a science. . . . Contributions to management thought come from many sources. For this reason it is considered an eclectic, or broad-based science.—Howard M. Carlisle

> In short, while aspects of management are becoming more scientific, much of management will remain an Art.—James A. F. Stoner

> The most productive art is always based on an understanding of the science underlying it. Thus, science and art are not mutually exclusive, but are complementary.—Harold Koontz, Cyril O'Donnell, and Heinz Weibrick

Obviously people disagree about the question of art versus science. One reason for the difficulty in defining management is a conflict in values between those who study management, who usually are trained as scientists, and those who practice it. John Miner clearly outlines the characteristics of science:

1. Science is directed toward increasing understanding and facilitating predictions.
2. The scientific method evolves in ascending levels of abstraction, including:
    a. Description—the classification or ordering of events
    b. Explanation—the identification of causal relationships
    c. Theory—the patterning of local constructs

3. Research should be capable of being replicated.
4. Scientific observation must be controlled.
5. Propositions must be stated in terms that make empirical testing possible.[2]

Most importantly, as Miner has observed, "Hunch and bias provide no basis for decisions, only controlled research and substantiated theory will do. 'I don't know' thus becomes not only an acceptable answer to a question, but in many cases a highly valued one."[3]

Practitioners function in a world significantly different from that of the scientist. Herbert Simon has observed that managers "satisfice" in their decision-making process, coming up with solutions that are "good enough" but far from optimal.[4] Miner makes a similar point:

> Often [the manager] must accumulate as much information as possible in the time available and then act.
>
> . . . The role of the scientist requires that he recognize what is known and is not known in order to state problems for research. He must take every precaution to ensure that his findings, once obtained, are not in error. In contrast, the managerial role does not require the advancement of knowledge but rather the achievement of organizational task and maintenance goals. Time is often a crucial factor in decision making. Risk and uncertainty are everywhere. . . .[5]

Managing is not a science, because it consists of a collection of tasks and responsibilities that vary from situation to situation. In executing those tasks, managers often use various knowledge bases, some of which have a solid scientific foundation. But managers do not practice science. Effective application of the knowledge base is at least partially a function of a manager's personality.

As for scientific replication, managers do not—indeed, cannot—duplicate the work of other managers. Their own personalities and capabilities are too much a part of the system with which they must deal. In short, managing tends to be a process of dealing with the unique and unpredictable.

Practice Theory versus Scientific Theory

In 1971, Peter Vaill became interested in the "mental set" of organizational-development practitioners when they operated within organizations. Vaill's point is that OD practitioners have ways of looking at and understanding an organizational world that many OD theorists have neglected.

Below we use the term "practice theory" to describe how managers utilize the theories of applied behavioral and organizational science to achieve their own ends. More specifically, we use the term practice theory to describe the kind of mental model that a manager uses to think about and interpret organizational phenomena. Such models are highly specific to individuals, although the general framework of a practice theory may be shared by several managers.

Some management theories that were intended as scientific statements actually function very effectively as practice theories. Indeed, they are often better practice theories than scientific ones, and practitioners may readily assimilate them. Many behavioral scientists working in industry facilitate this assimilation process by "packaging" behavioral theories in various ways.

In effect, an interactive process takes place between managers and behavioral scientists. Managers tend to alter the theories and techniques of scientists so as to make them consistent with their existing practice theories. Applied behavioral scientists, especially those who evolve effective working relationships with management, strive to convert their principles into a format that has utility for their client— in effect converting scientific theories into practice ones. Indeed, this is one skill of the effective organizational change agent.

Other factors also blur the distinction between scientist and manager. As we discussed in the preceding chapter, investigators must make accommodations in order to retain access to the client organization, and experimental approaches may have to be changed because of altered conditions within the organization. The research process moves closer to the management process as the investigator is pressured to solve problems with limited information, is told that time is a major constraint, is warned that performance targets must be met, or finds that political considerations must be dealt with if the work is to proceed.

However, the most significant occurrence from our perspective is that the behavioral scientist who writes for management tends to offer what is in effect a practice theory—while presenting the ideas in such a way that they appear scientifically validated. Managers then believe their practice theories to be scientific. Management researchers' emphasis on the scientific process has contributed to this trend.

The solution to this problem lies in the stance taken by applied behavioral scientists. They have a dual role, serving both managers and society as a whole, and they must continually distinguish between the two roles. They can continue to utilize their research skills to generate scientific knowledge that is as reliable and as valid as possible. (One aspect of their skill is recognition of the exceptional difficulties involved in behavioral science research.) At other times, such scientists can develop their practice theories and present them as such, striving to define explicitly the conditions for effective application. A clean definition is especially important when case studies and field research are used.

The pitfalls inherent in this dual role are readily apparent in the legacy of Elton Mayo. Mayo recognized the general problem when he wrote: "It would seem that some studies otherwise important . . . have proved disappointing because an enthusiast here and there has been guilty of overclaiming, giving rise to a general belief that some one remedy will cure all industrial ills."[6] Ultimately, however, Mayo's intellectual reservations were not matched by a caution in reporting and advocating his findings. He thus offers an object lesson of Miner's admonishment that: "From a scientific viewpoint the greatest error is that which occurs when inadequate or insufficient data are overinterpreted or overgeneralized, so that an unsolved problem is accepted as solved. Errors of this kind block scientific progress, because the identification of problems is made extremely difficult."[7] Mayo the scientist was aware of this problem, but Mayo the advocate of reform compromised on the issue. The Topeka plant offers a more contemporary example of this phenomenon.

The Characteristics of Practice Theories

As we have seen, practice theories evolve from management's demands that pragmatic action be taken, with some theories involving behavioral science principles. Below we speculate on the characteristics of practice theories on the basis of our observations and experiences as consultants working in organizations.

Practice Theories Meet a Need for Direction

Managers have certain needs that affect their responses to management theories. One such need, it seems, is a need for direction or policy guidance. Uncertainty is found in all organizations, and many strategies are designed to reduce its effects. Bureaucratic roles, procedures, policy guidelines, and management information systems are all efforts to reduce uncertainty and provide direction. Managers want their theories of human behavior to serve a similar purpose.

Although most behavioral scientists have been saying for twenty years that there is no one best way of managing, their practice theories have been "one best way"-oriented. Participative management, Theory Y versus X, and enriched jobs all carried with them the suggestion: "Here is how to do it right."

Contingency management has great surface appeal, but managers have difficulty operating with it. The problem with contingency theory is that when it is turned into policy, the result sounds like "our policy is to have no policy." It is even harder to turn this theory into a program. Managers want their practice theories to translate readily into the development of both policy statements and programs.

Both of the authors have had extensive experience working with groups of managers in training programs. At the beginning of a program, when the discussion tends to be intellectual and theoretical, contingency theory seems to have great appeal. Managers often argue that everyone is different, or that practices must fit the situation. Toward the end of the workshop, when managers start focusing on what they plan to do differently, the tone of the meeting changes. Faced with the reality of returning to work and its associated problems, managers want to know what, specifically, they should do. An answer such as "it depends" upsets them. They want a one best way.

Practice Theories Establish Moral Standards for Managerial Behavior

Managers often tie their practice theories to underlying beliefs, values, and philosophies. Robert Dubin has hypothesized that the popularity of certain humanistic behavioral theories (such as those of Abraham Maslow and Douglas McGregor) may partially reflect management's search for secular moral guidelines.[8] Dubin points out that Judeo-Christian theology is being used less often as a source of guidance for work decisions and suggests that applied behavioral science may afford substitute standards for the treatment of employees.

Certainly the debate over the traditional engineering view versus the newer human resources models has had moral, ethical, and even religious overtones. In 1969 The Conference Board published a list of the most widely recognized behavioral scientists in the American management literature.[9] The top six were Douglas McGregor, Frederick Herzberg, Rensis Likert, Chris Argyris, Abraham Maslow, and (collaborators) Robert Blake and Jane S. Mouton. All are humanistically oriented psychologists, and parts of their theories are more accurately described as philosophic than scientific. Rigorous empirical testing has frequently raised questions about these people's theories, but their influence in management training programs continues to be strong. Perhaps this is because, despite the many scientific difficulties with their positions, their work proves useful as a philosophical foundation for practice theories.

Abraham Maslow was surprised by the extensive use of his theories to change managerial practice.[10] The other psychologists cited were intentionally writing to inspire organizational change. All have considered their work "scientific," but their theories rest on foundations of specific, humanistic values. Empirical data are often stretched beyond their legitimate limits in an effort to support these values.

Douglas McGregor's Theories X and Y consist of statements about beliefs regarding human nature. His discussion of Theory Y rests on Maslow's hierarchy of needs.[11] Maslow himself commented:

> After all, if we take the whole thing from McGregor's point of view of a contrast between a Theory X [and a Theory Y] view of human nature, a good deal of the evidence upon which he bases his conclusions comes from my researches and my papers on motivations, self actualization, etc. But I of all people should know just how shaky this foundation is as a final foundation. . . .
>
> I am quite willing to concede this—as a matter of fact, I am eager to concede it—because I'm a little worried about this stuff which I consider to be tentative being swallowed whole by all sorts of enthusiastic people, who really should be a little more tentative. . . .[12]

McGregor asserted that his Theory Y was a challenge to management to be innovative in its practices. He strongly implied that managers had a social obligation to do so.[13]

Therein lies the problem with regard to scientific validity. The issues involved in virtually all debates about Theory X and Theory Y are largely reflective of underlying values. People make assertions and reach conclusions largely on the basis of initial assumptions. Actually, the relative merits of Theories X and Y are not easy to determine through empirical testing. Possibly one could test the degree to which such cosmologies exist in the belief systems of managers.

The two theories are, however, readily translatable into managerial practice theories. Further, the assumptions about human nature spelled out by McGregor are useful tools for getting managers to reflect upon the values they hold and the extent to which they act on those values. As such, Theories X and Y function as social philosophies. Organization theorists sympathetic to the humanistic tradition have tried to integrate Theory Y assumptions with contingency models of organizational effectiveness. Edgar Schein adopts such a posture when he writes:

> If [a manager] holds Theory X assumptions, he is not being logical or responsive to data, and will, therefore, be limited in his choices of managerial style. . . . If he holds Theory Y assumptions, he is more likely to examine the full range of alternatives available to him and choose wisely among them, taking into account the technological, economic, and group realities which face him.[14]

Schein asserts what no one has yet been able to prove: that managers holding Theory X assumptions are less logical than those favoring

Theory Y. Scientifically this is a difficult argument to sustain, especially if one wishes to continue the line of reasoning to include predictions about managerial effectiveness. Schein's argument, however, deals with much broader issues than the question of which theory brings greater success. Schein is speaking of values which, he feels, should be woven into the fabric of institutional life.

Unfortunately Maslow's need theory, which McGregor used as his primary support for Theory Y, is equally difficult to test scientifically. One problem is that Maslow defined his need categories in such general terms that measurement is difficult.[15] His categories are descriptions of related phenomena rather than discrete variables. Maslow's discussion of self-esteem, for example, is complex and includes such factors as achievement, recognition, power, and perceived difference from others. Because of the many nuances of Maslow's model, designing research to test its validity is extremely difficult. Those studies which *have* been made to test the theory have not been particularly supportive of its propositions, especially the concept that needs form a hierarchy.[16]

As John Miner has observed, Maslow's discussion of self-actualization at times becomes almost mystical and his writings take on a quasi-religious tone.[17] Here the theory clearly sounds more like a social philosophy than scientific theory.

Maslow's data were clinical in nature, and he based his theories on firsthand, intimate knowledge of the phenomena. Maslow never intended his work to be treated as definitive, but that is how it has been presented in many management training programs.

Maslow's model has had widespread appeal, despite its serious drawbacks as a scientific theory, because it has proved very useful as a practice theory. It particularly appeals to humanistically minded managers who value personal development and growth. Nevertheless, Maslow's assertion that people strive toward self-actualization once lower-level needs are satisfied appears to be untestable if conclusive proof is sought. Acceptance of this idea must rest on personal belief.

Maslow's ideas have also been reflected in the writings of Chris Argyris. In developing his prescription for achieving "social good," Argyris writes:

> One of the most urgently needed intellectual crash programs is that of developing new designs of technology, administrative controls, and leadership styles that will lead to organizations capable of being productive and self-renewing, of being effective, and of *encouraging self-actualization* among the participants. Unless research is conducted immediately and unless workable models become available, we stand a good chance of being the society who could organize to send men to the moon but could not organize so that man's highest human aspirations could be fulfilled.[18]

The prose is inspirational and the suggested standard of human conduct compelling. Scientific verification, however, remains tantalizingly elusive. Still, such ideas have led to many prescriptions for action.

Frederick Herzberg, although he proposes different strategies of intervention from those of Argyris, has similar philosophical sentiments:

> The primary functions of any organization, whether religious, political or industrial, should be to implement the needs for man to enjoy a meaningful existence. For the first time in history we have the opportunity to satisfy man's inherent wants. Yet what value to man if industry manufactures commodities to supply material comfort at the expense of human development and happiness?[19]

Herzberg also wrote: "We need to be decent, not to get something in return, not to make someone like us, but rather just to be decent. People want to be treated fairly; they do not want to do something extra in return for decent treatment."[20] In developing his motivation-hygiene theory, Herzberg emphasized that increased worker productivity and job satisfaction would not result merely from the solution of "hygiene problems" such as low salary. He repeated the point that "the job of management in hygiene areas is to be decent, not as a manipulative strategy but simply in order to be decent."[21]

In summary, each of the behavioral science theorists who have most strongly influenced managers has offered what amounts to a moral standard of behavior. As Robert Dubin has observed, the behaviors of managers are often at variance with their stated beliefs, but this is often the case in human affairs.[22]

Humanistic psychologists are not alone in developing moral philosophies as part of their theories. Behavior modification, a management practice that has become increasingly popular during the past decade, is based partially on the world view of behavioral psychologist B. F. Skinner. In *Beyond Freedom and Dignity* Skinner presents what amounts to a justification of a view of the world in which behavior is a function of consequences. Self-actualization is replaced by behavioral determinism as the central issue in social control.[23]

The appearance of social philosophy in the management literature, of course, predates the prominence of behavioral scientists. Frederick Taylor's call for a "mental revolution" and his concern with the betterment of the worker's position attest to that. Taylor's ideas of how this betterment could be achieved are echoed by contemporary proponents of the engineering view, who often bring moral issues into their arguments. They suggest that behavioral scientists are condescending toward workers, or that humanistic management practices undermine the motivation to work.

We believe that prescriptions about standards of behavior are a key component of the theories that have been most widely adopted by practicing managers. Such philosophical components are to be expected; indeed, they enhance the value of the ideas in management's eyes. Another reason moral components are valued is that their explicit nature aids in the development of practice theories—the specific guides to managerial action.

In our experience as consultants, we have found that an appeal to values is necessary if there is to be sufficient emotional and intellectual commitment to change. Those clients who internalize the philosophical components of management systems remain most committed to the methods and goals involved. Managers often seek such components to give meaning to their actions. Effective practice theories address this need.

Practice Theories Have Face Validity

Managers generally adopt practice theories only if they have face validity—that is, their content seems inherently correct and appears to match with managers' personal experiences. It is partly for this reason that field studies are so often used to support new management theories. Reports on field research have a "real world" sound to them, and managers can readily think of similar examples they have encountered. Taylor's shoveling stories, Mayo's description of the relay assembly room, and Walton's discussion of Topeka all provide much face validity.

The popular theories of humanistic psychology have face validity as well. Virtually everyone can relate Maslow's hierarchy of needs to his or her own life. A manager may recall being reluctant to take a more challenging job because it would involve less security or would disrupt current interpersonal relationships. A young employee who is eager for immediate recognition and responsibility will also see validity in Maslow's theory.

Herzberg's motivation-hygiene theory enjoys the same face validity. Nearly everyone has, with the passage of time, felt more and more dissatisfied with the salary being received. Similarly, everyone can recall good feelings that accompanied a particular job accomplishment. Although Herzberg's critical incident method of collecting data is problematic, the theory has been accepted by many managers simply because it "feels right."

The face-validity phenomenon occurs in other fields as well. A few years ago, one of the authors was making a presentation to a group of medical people from the Food and Drug Administration. One woman in the group, a nursing supervisor, argued a point about behavior that was contradicted by significant amounts of research data. Her data base turned out to be the behavior of one person she worked with. A similar occurrence was reported by a physician whose job was to visit private practitioners and present them with FDA data cautioning against the use of certain drugs. "Often," he said, "doctors reject the FDA data because of a positive experience they are having with one patient. They will say, 'Mrs. Jones has been using it for two years, and she's fine.'" Many private practitioners, despite their scientific training, apparently develop practice theories based on limited personal experience.

This human tendency is very common; as a result, no matter how convincing experimental data may be, a theory is unlikely to gain widespread acceptance if it lacks face validity.

Practice Theories Are Fudgeable

Practice theories, unlike scientific theories, do not consist of precisely defined variables and hypothesized interrelationships. Instead they involve changeable groupings of ideas and concepts that can be altered to fit a wide range of organizational situations. As Vaill states:

> In the canons of Science, a good formal theory always has its *ceteris paribus,* its other [factors] which are assumed equal. . . . To the extent that a practice theory asserts anything to be "true," the assertion is not with a *ceteris paribus* implied, but instead with a *mutatis mutandis,* that is ". . . with the necessary changes."[24]

Toward that end, most practice theories utilize terminology that can be interpreted in a variety of ways. The variables described by Maslow and Herzberg, and by Blake and Mouton in explaining their managerial grid, are easily adapted to the perceptions of individual managers.

Often the variables are applied in ways that go beyond or run counter to the intent of the theorist. An example is the way in which Maslow's needs categories are often presented in management courses. A need for "self-actualization" is used to explain the demands of young workers. Maslow, however, was skeptical of the extent to which college-age people ever truly experienced self-actualization. He used the term to describe an emerging sense of self-awareness and attainment of human potential that few people have experienced. Yet the generality of the concept has made it inviting to managers seeking cognitive maps for understanding worker behavior. In short, the same characteristic that limits a theory's scientific value (imprecise definition, causing measurement problems) facilitates its value as a practice theory.

As Vaill expressed it: "Practice theories are 'fudgeable,' as it were; that is their great utility. Formal theories, ideally at least, are not."[25]

Practice Theories Are Multifunctional[26]

Managers strive to accomplish ends on a multitude of levels. Some actions that they take are organizational, some are political, and some are personal. This mix of needs virtually always affects the ways in which managers select and present their arguments.

Once one of the authors was preparing to give a presentation on job enrichment to the president of a company in order to clear the way for implementing JE in the firm. Members of the corporate staff told him to use the phrase "management by design" at various points in the presentation to indicate that JE was consistent with a philosophy often espoused by the president. The staff also requested that the part of the job-enrichment model pertaining to complete jobs be de-emphasized, while the parts on worker control and feedback be given central stage. The purpose of this was also to make JE appear consistent with the president's philosophy that "the company designs the task, but people have a wide range of freedom in carrying it out."

Often consultants are asked to relabel concepts, discuss certain possible results more than others, or change the emphasis in a model so that it will fit the perceptions of powerful individuals in the company or convey a message to certain people. One advantage of highly general theories—such as Maslow's or Herzberg's motivation models, concepts like job enrichment, and techniques like work measurement—is that they are pliable to organizational realities. This is a role the practice theories of managers frequently play.

Practice Theories Blend Heterogeneous Phenomena

Peter Vaill summed up this characteristic of practice theories: "No matter how diverse the elements of a situation, no matter how 'logically non-comparable,' the [manager] finds some way with his practice theory of dealing with them together."[27] In other words, a manager uses practice theories to deal with the "apples and oranges" of everyday experience. This, of course, is made possible by the fudgeable nature of the theories.

In work-measurement studies, the changes in work methods that emerge usually make sense in terms of efficiency.[28] Interestingly, the changes often result from the combining of largely unrelated tasks in a manner that more fully utilizes the available time of employees. In the words of one work-measurement engineer, "Often we combine apples and oranges."[29]

Robert Ford, who was one of the main directors of the AT&T job-enrichment work, viewed H. M. Parsons's reinterpretation of the relay assembly test room results at Hawthorne as an example of job enrichment. Parsons actually was building a case for behavior modification. However, Ford merged Parsons's arguments into the feedback part of his own job-enrichment model. This willingness to integrate aspects of different techniques while ignoring theoretical distinctions is common practice among managers and many consultants.

Practice Theories Create Events through the Labeling Process

In the early stages of the development of a science, typologies are created to establish order with regard to the subject matter being studied. This also occurs with practice theories, but the labels are more flexible and often group a collection of varied characteristics into a category.

Through the process of labeling, a phenomenon is created in the mind of the practitioner. "Hawthorne effect," "Theory X manager," "9,9 manager," "self-actualizing person"—all are concepts that people regularly use as labels in their practice theories. Each is a catchy title and smooths over distinctions between events, focusing attention on the similarities. In short, labeling is a facilitating process; it appears to impose order on what may be disorder. An event, process, or type of behavior seems manageable if one knows what to call it.

Unfortunately, in utilizing practice theories, managers often do not search for what makes a situation distinctive. Two managers are labeled as "9,1" even though they are functioning in different settings, one is verbally abusive while the other is firm and highly involved in getting the work done, and one has high autonomy needs while the other seeks approval from others. Both are labeled "9,1 autocratic" and dealt with as such by other managers within the company.

Management theories that permit easy labeling are the most likely to catch on as practice theories. Here contingency theory is once again fighting an uphill battle. Proponents of this theory point to its realism in emphasizing the differences between situations and highlighting the complexity of social interactions. But to many managers, social complexity is simply confusion. Managers respond best to a labeling system that seems simple.

Practice Theories Satisfice[30]

For years the literature on decision-making has included the concept of "satisficing"—the idea that managers simply search for solutions which are good enough. Managers apply the same criteria in selecting their practice theories. Whereas scientists demand that their theories explain as much of the variance as possible, assume random influence of the residual, and hold together parsimoniously, managers demand only that their theories be "good enough." For example, managers who implement objective-based work planning and review systems generally understand that, under goal-setting theory, objectives need to be heavily influenced by subordinates. They will frequently conclude, however, that "that won't work here." They may then reason that objectives passed down from the top are better than no objectives at all, and that a modified objective-setting process is better than no process at all. In this manner they will opt for a system that is good enough.

Practice Theories: Science, Art, or Neither?

Where does this leave us? Scientific theory, while it strives to be parsimonious, also explores variance and seeks to explain as much of it as possible. Yet managers like their theories reduced to a basic common denominator. So managers do not apply scientific theories; they use practice theories. Further, many action-oriented researchers recognize this and communicate their knowledge accordingly.

In 1975, one of the authors was talking with a senior executive from a client firm. The conversation turned to projects that were under way within his division. In explaining why he had rejected help from a renowned professor at a well-known business school, the executive commented, "After several visits it became clear his primary interest was setting up experiments for his students to test his theories. . . . When I buy a stereo, all I want to know is that when I put the needle on the record, sound comes out of the speakers. I am very concerned about the quality of the sound. I don't give a damn about knowing how the speakers are wired."

A superficial thinker? Perhaps. The fact remains that this executive was responsible for many creative, complex, and successful lines of business. Neither the professor nor the executive is a villain in this scenario. They operated in different worlds; each confronted a different organizational reality. Whatever the limitations of this executive's view, it illustrates the way in which many sophisticated managers view organizational problems.

The practice of management is eclectic. It is not a young and developing science; the great limitations of our current knowledge show that it is not a science at all. Perhaps even to describe it as an art is to become too lofty and confusing about the issue. Management is a craft, trade, or practice—a collection of intuitive, social, and academic skills that are used to attain a set of situational goals.

How More Rigorous Practice Theories Can Be Developed

From the time of Frederick Taylor's studies up to contemporary work-life experiments such as the one at Topeka, investigators have presented data in a fashion that increases the likelihood of action being taken, or is aimed at social reform, but skews or misinterprets what actually occurred. This process makes the data more easily integratable into managers' practice theories.

Within organizations, we have no choice but to deal with practice theories. But this does not absolve people of responsibility for rigorous reporting. Since the process is so political, not only must reporting be more thorough, but the ways in which managers assimilate data should be analyzed more critically. We propose the following guidelines for managers who are considering the use of a given practice theory.

Articulate the Values Inherent in the Theory

Practice theories, as we have seen, are not value-free. They reflect certain assumptions about people, organizations, society, and how the three interact. Action researchers have operated under similar assumptions when carrying out their work. Unfortunately, their statements about these assumptions have often had the tone of presenting empirical facts.

Clarification of beliefs and values can eliminate significant confusion in the minds of practitioners. Management has invested much energy in arguments about people's nature, potential, and motivation to work. Invariably these discussions deteriorate into war stories: anecdotal remarks about Alice, who walked to work in the snow during the transit strike, versus Harry, who always says, "That's not my job." Broad belief or value systems are not easily subject to final verification.

One thing that a company needs is a statement of philosophy tied to its organizational goals. The assumptions held by key senior managers, with regard to the type of people the organization needs and the standards that should be adhered to in managing them, need to be explicitly stated in a philosophy of human resources. Thus, the issue becomes not "What is human nature?" but "What position does the organization take in its dealings with people?"

Does the organization assume people want to be challenged in their work and accept responsibility, or does it assume they prefer to be dependent? What are the specifics of such a position? Most important, are the current policies and practices supportive of the corporate philosophy? How does management see its policies and practices as contributing to the organization's health? Are jobs structured in such a way that people will be challenged—or will feel comfortable? What assumptions are being made about employee loyalty? (For example, is a manager expected to automatically accept a transfer?) What trade-offs is management willing to accept with regard to employee desires versus corporate objectives?

The answers to such questions relate to the degree of fit between the organization's philosophy, its business goals, the external environment (including labor unions if applicable), and management practices. Philosophy should be related to strategy. For example, if a company is designing and marketing a product whose chief selling point will be high quality, different types of people are required than if the company were pursuing some other strategy.

One consumer-oriented company implemented a goal-based performance-appraisal process tied to a concept of career development. This company regularly recruited key middle- and senior-level people from the outside. It was expected that these people would make names for themselves and move on to bigger things, usually at other companies. Replacements would be brought in from outside as the cycle repeated itself. A premium was placed on current performance. Grass roots development was never part of how this company did business, and senior management apparently saw no reason to change.

The vice president of personnel sold the new career-development system because "it was part of what was happening elsewhere." After much energy, time, and cost, the system died a quiet death. The concept just did not fit the company's style. Unfortunately, the idea of goal-based performance appraisal was lost along the way, as this concept was linked to the career-development effort. It was eight years before goal-based performance appraisal resurfaced, this time tied more closely to the company's style.

An explicit statement of philosophy could have headed off the ill-fated effort. Such a statement has implications for recruitment and hiring, training and development, compensation, promotion standards, discipline, labor practices, and so on. Policies in each area should be consistent with one another and with the overall philosophy. In short, the philosophy becomes a statement of "how to do business," not opinions about human nature.

Similarly, case reports should contain explicit statements about the values of the organization and those of the researcher. Conventional wisdom states that scientific theory is value-free; values come into play only when a user applies the theory. In the behavioral sciences, the concept of a value-free theory has always been problematic. In applied and action research, the concept is nonexistent. As Albert

Cherns remarks: "The action researcher is committed not only to research, but to action, and action which is indicated not simply by science but by values."[31] The values of the researcher come to be reflected in both the goals of the project and the interpretation of the data. (The positions taken by managers are never value-free either.) Therefore, when writing for the practitioner, a researcher should clearly delineate the scientific limits of the data. Further, when seeking to influence managers, he or she should clearly state the values involved without masking the recommendation as "scientific."

Managers, for their part, need to challenge the basic assumptions underlying their theories. There is nothing wrong with seeking to design organizational practices that are consistent with certain values; indeed, values enter into practically all policy decisions. The important thing is for managers to understand that they are not trying to apply an established "scientific principle" but are developing practical applications of a given social philosophy, a philosophy that should be translatable into an articulated vision of the organization.

A divorce of management theory from social philosophy is unlikely and, in all probability, undesirable for society. As Peter Drucker has repeatedly stated, managers fulfill a social role in our society: they determine how and where institutional resources will be directed. However, managers are constrained by the fact that they must protect the vested interests of the organizations they represent. The validity of a corporate philosophy lies in the extent to which it helps managers fulfill their organizational obligations.

Emphasize the Unique

Practice theories derive much of their content from the experience of the practitioner. They are based on firsthand observation, the internalization of other people's observations, and theoretical and philosophical positions that have seemed meaningful in relation to one's personal experiences. Managers take field studies so seriously because of values they implicitly share with the researcher, because a report seems to provide clear guidance on how to solve a pressing problem or achieve an end result, or because the language and behavior described in the report are familiar and believable. Once managers feel that a report or recommendation has face validity, they tend to minimize the differences from their own situation and exaggerate the similarities. The unique events described in the report become the basis for an entire applied methodology.

Researchers can help provide a counterweight to this phenomenon by emphasizing the unique aspects of the work situation that was studied. Such emphasis also contributes to a more complete understanding of the organizational process involved. The early reports on Topeka provide a clear example. A number of unique factors, such as the screening process for personnel and the unusual composition of the management team, can help explain why the plant developed as it did and to what extent the approach might prove feasible elsewhere.

Similarly, in the Hawthorne studies, the fact that the workers in the relay assembly test room were not representative of the workers in the general population was lost in later reports and discussions. (The massive interviewing program, which had nothing to do with the experiment in the relay assembly test room, somehow made the latter experiment seem extensive.) The one attempt to bridge the gap between the test room and the general production floor—that is, the trial with the second relay assembly test group—yielded contradictory results. Yet the contradictions were explained away rather than emphasized.

Finally, Taylor's image as a man of practical knowledge is remarkable given the limited number of implementations with which he was actually associated. The early data used to support scientific management came from tests involving carefully selected workers. Taylor's work might have been better understood if he and others had paid more attention to the specific characteristics of the work settings he was involved in.

For their part, managers who read field reports need to investigate whatever characteristics of a research setting seem unique. A preliminary list of variables to be considered would be:

- The size of the organization
- The size of the experimental population
- Geographic location
- Labor force demographics
- The technology employed
- Physical working conditions
- The demands of the external environment
- The structural characteristic of the larger organization
- The preexisting climate
- The major organizational goals
- Ways in which the organization changed as an adaptation to the research process

In addition, there is the crucial question of what variables, besides the major experimental ones, were altered during the study.

Managers' recognition of a study's uniqueness does raise the specter of their using this fact to justify the status quo. The scourge of change agents is the range of excuses managers can give for avoiding change. Attention to the unique circumstances surrounding a piece of field research is likely to generate additional excuses and intensify resistance to change. In the long run, however, this may prove to be a good thing.

Some of the most successful change interventions the authors have observed were characterized by a frank discussion of potential obstacles and the fact that existing field studies may not be generalizable. The best motivator of change is organizational need, not the excitement of embarking on a new experience. Field reports, as well as associated journalistic articles and handouts in management meetings, are best presented as examples of what *can* be done. Only by recognizing the uniqueness of such reports can management develop realistic expectations regarding change efforts.

In building a body of knowledge—scientific or otherwise—management scholars must focus on the unique. Sociologist Richard Peterson once suggested that in the social sciences, the pursuit of variance inevitably leads to history. This idea may be extreme, but it is nevertheless true that generalizations must be built slowly and that an exception often teaches more than the rule. Practitioners must understand that every implementation is a trial, no matter where else a technique has been used.

Identify Dysfunctions

For some time now, social scientists have known that the parts of organizations are interdependent and that change ripples through a social system. Some of these systemic changes are dysfunctional even when the principal change was positive. Most managers know that in order to accomplish certain goals, they will suffer costs in other areas. Their practice theories often include the sentiment "you have to pay a price."

Whenever a change is made or an experiment done in an organization, there is virtually always some dysfunctional effect. We are fortunate that Roethlisberger and Dickson, in their thoroughness, reported the problems with two of the women in the test room and the fact that the second relay test group experiment was aborted in part because other production workers wanted a similar type of incentive plan. These disclosures are important to our subsequent understanding of what happened at Hawthorne.

Similarly, the fact that the compensation program at Topeka also created pay dissatisfaction—namely, discontent over the process for learning and demonstrating team skills, which was linked with pay—is an important learning point. So too are the corporation's partial antipathy to the plant and the negative reaction of managers in the initial experimental plant when a different approach was taken in the new, canned-food plant. An awareness of these problems allows one to better assess the tensions that the plant's design created in the pursuit of other, humanistic goals.

The authors have often seen such data omitted in discussions of job-enrichment interventions. For example, taking responsibility from one set of jobs in order to increase the level of responsibility in another set can create dissatisfaction in the former jobs. And some workers do not want enriched jobs, a fact that has often been conveniently glossed over or underreported.

Here the line between academic reporting and advocacy of change must be clearly drawn. Once the researcher begins urging management to adopt strategies for change, he or she surrenders the right to be viewed as a dispassionate reporter of organizational practices and results.

Report the Duration of the Effect

This is a difficult point. Few social changes last indefinitely, and there is no specific point in time at which a change demonstrates its permanence. Still, reports on duration are important: the reasons why a given change deteriorates are often as instructive as the description of its initial success. Further, the labeling of a change as "successful" is subjective; an objective report of longevity removes the value judgment. Managers should be told the extent to which experiments have deteriorated so that they can place the achievement in perspective. This is, of course, a difficult guideline for the advocate of change. He or she is likely to view such data as "confusing the issue."

The four guidelines we have given seem basic to legitimate, critical communication of knowledge that is to be used by management practitioners and represent major questions that a practitioner should ask in reviewing any such material. These guidelines are quite similar to the rules of scientific inquiry. Yet, it must be remembered that although management interventions may contribute to social science, they are not synonymous with it.

Failure to recognize the distinctions between practice theories and scientific theories creates unnecessary confusion about the basis for managerial action. Lack of rigor—either on the part of managers who build their practice theories around "scientific" data that are not scientific, or on the part of researchers who overstate their findings— opens the door to the development of myths and unnecessary adversarial postures among schools of managerial thought.

NOTES

1. Howard M. Carlisle, *Management Essentials: Concepts and Applications* (Chicago, Ill.: Science Research Associates, 1979); James A. F. Stoner, *Management* (Englewood Cliffs, N.J.: Prentice-Hall, 1978); Harold Koontz, Cyril O'Donnell, and Heinz Weibrick, *Management* (New York: McGraw-Hill, 1980).
2. Based on J. B. Miner, *The Management Process: Theory, Research and Practice* (New York: Macmillan, 1978).
3. Ibid., p. 70.
4. Herbert Simon, *Administrative Behavior,* 3rd ed. (New York: Free Press, 1976).
5. Miner, *The Management Process,* p. 70.
6. Elton Mayo, *The Human Problems of an Industrial Civilization,* 2nd ed. (Boston: Harvard Business School, Division of Research, 1946), pp. v–vi.
7. Miner, *The Management Process,* p. 70.
8. Robert Dubin, "Theory Building in Applied Areas." In Marvin D. Dunnette (ed.), *Handbook of Industrial and Organizational Psychology* (Chicago: Rand-McNally, 1976), pp. 17–39.
9. *Behavioral Science: Concepts and Management Application* (New York: The Conference Board, 1969), p. 10.
10. Abraham H. Maslow, *Eupsychian Management* (Homewood, Ill.: Irwin-Dorsey, 1965).
11. Douglas McGregor, *The Human Side of Enterprise* (New York: McGraw-Hill, 1960), pp. 36–41.
12. Maslow, *Eupsychian Management,* pp. 55–56.
13. McGregor, *Human Side,* especially Chapter 1 and the conclusion.
14. E. H. Schein, "The Hawthorne Group Studies Revisited: A Defense of Theory Y." In Eugene Louis Case and Frederick G. Zimmer (eds.), *Man and Work in Society* (New York: Van Nostrand Reinhold, 1975), p. 84.
15. See M. A. Wahba and L. G. Bridwell, "Maslow Reconsidered: A Review of Research on the Need Hierarchy Theory," *Organizational Behavior and Human Performance,* Vol. 15 (1976), pp. 212–240.
16. Ibid.
17. J. B. Miner, *Theories of Organizational Behavior* (Hinsdale, Ill.: Dryden Press, 1980), pp. 24–25.
18. Chris Argyris, *Intervention Theory and Method* (Reading, Mass.: Addison-Wesley, 1970), p. 4.
19. Frederick Herzberg, *Work and the Nature of Man* (New York: Thomas Y. Crowell, 1966).
20. Ibid.
21. Frederick Herzberg, *The Managerial Choice: To Be Efficient and to Be Human* (Homewood, Ill.: Dow Jones–Irwin, 1976), p. 92.
22. Dubin, "Theory Building."
23. B. F. Skinner, *Beyond Freedom and Dignity* (New York: Knopf, 1971).
24. P. B. Vaill, "Practice Theories in Organization Development," p. 3. Paper

presented at the annual meeting of the Academy of Management, Atlanta, Georgia, August 1971.

25. Ibid.
26. This section is based on Vaill, "Practice Theories," p. 4.
27. Ibid., p. 5.
28. L. Yorks, M. Kaplan, and R. Ochs, "Job Enrichment and Operations Involvement," *Journal of Systems Management,* Vol. 29, March 1978, pp. 17–25.
29. Ibid., p. 18.
30. This section is based on Vaill, "Practice Theories," p. 8.
31. Albert B. Cherns, "Action Research." In Louis E. Davis and Albert B. Cherns (eds.), *The Quality of Working Life,* Vol. Two (New York: Free Press, 1975), p. 31.

13

Applied Organizational Science: Implications for Theory and Research

We have been examining in detail the process through which management research—especially that with a behavioral science orientation—is translated into action. This has included an extensive examination of three sets of research studies and a postulation of the factors that we believe are most significant in the generation and spread of this type of knowledge. Our interest was first aroused by the apparent myths that surround many prominent management theories. We saw that such myths had contributed to divisiveness within the field. Our examination of Taylorism, Hawthorne, and Topeka revealed that myths and misconceptions in the management literature have in large part resulted from the process by which social science knowledge is translated into proposals for change and promoted by researchers and others.

The development of management theory has been heavily spiced with an emphasis on reform. Taylor, Mayo, and Walton each viewed himself as a reformer of social institutions. Reform has been a theme underlying much of the organizational-development movement in industry. Advocates of OD view the changing of large organizations toward more humanistic values as a primary lever for improving the quality of life, not just for employees but for society as a whole. Actually, many OD theorists seek nothing less than radical reform of our culture, to be achieved through improved interpersonal skills and new organizational processes.

263

Chris Argyris, for example, has long advocated intervention in organizations for what amount to social reasons. He was among the first to champion sensitivity training for managers and similar experimental human relations methods. Argyris perceives our social institutions as deteriorating:

> The older and more complex organizations in our society—business firms, governmental bureaus, city governments, labor unions, churches, hospitals, schools, and universities—appear to be deteriorating. With every passing day, the human and material costs of providing a product or service seem to be going up, while the resulting quality is either wavering or going down. Organizations are becoming increasingly rigid and difficult to change; it is almost impossible to induce them to reexamine and renew themselves.[1]

Argyris predicts disaster if the situation is not corrected:

> Many of the leaders of our society's institutions realize the enormity of the problems involved in redesigning and changing complex and aging systems. They look at employee and citizen anger and impatience and they begin to despair. Some withdraw and become apathetic about the future, while others become bitter about the "sickness" among the people. This is a dangerous point in any society. When those in power become apathetic and bitter because they are being attacked by people whose major difference is that their apathy and bitterness have been fermenting for years, one has the makings of mutually reinforced despair and helplessness. The result is internal tension that predictably will be released in ways designed to hurt both sides.[2]

Ideology and Management Theories

Reinhard Bendix has analyzed the ideological function of providing justification for managerial authority and power.[3] He concludes that the theories of Taylor and Mayo, as well as the classical administrative science writers, place value on cooperative effort and on the ultimate responsibility of managerial leadership—a position that supported the emerging role of the managerial class. Bendix takes a macro view of the issue, but at the micro level, managerial theory carries ideological overtones as well. In fact, it is at the level of specific operations within an organization that the ideological functions of management theories are most pronounced.

Ideology has been described as a way of translating ideas into action: "the conversion of ideas into social levers."[4] Thus, ideology seeks to establish commitment to the consequences of ideas. We suggest that the theories of change-oriented management specialists, in effect, function as ideologies. Whereas scientists and philosophers have traditionally sought to be dispassionate, those who want to effect change develop a call to action. This is a traditional role of ideology.

Although much management research seeks to substantiate practical principles, the ideological function remains critical for researchers who hope to initiate widespread changes in institutional forms. Studies pertaining to scientific management, human relations, work restructuring, and quality of work life—all gave rise to something akin to social movements within the management community. Indeed, the studies also became popular topics of discussion in the society at large.

Daniel Bell has noted that "a social movement can rouse people when it can do two things: simplify ideas, establish a claim to truth, and, in the union of the two, demand a commitment to action. Thus, not only does ideology transform ideas, it transforms people as well."[5] This is a reasonable description of the role many management theories play, or have played. As committed proponents of a given theory or method have proselytized their position, ideological elements have become basic to their arguments.

Taylor followed Bell's definition in his use of the pig-iron and shoveling stories: he simplified ideas, established a claim to truth, and demanded a commitment to action. Taylor—along with some of his associates, such as the Gilbreths—was remarkably successful. Mayo strove toward a similar goal, as have a range of contemporary management theorists such as Walton and Argyris. The goal of substantial institutional change involves "political" action, and ideology is an important part of convincing others of a need for change.

We have stated that practice theories are not value-free. We can go further with this point: practice theories are easily transformed into ideology. Indeed, ideology—not scientific proof—is the vehicle for translation of practice theory into organizational policy and method.

Popular journalists have been important to the translation process. Stuart Chase simplified the ideas of Hawthorne in a way that demanded a commitment to action. So, too, do contemporary newspaper accounts of "Theory Z" at work. From Taylor to today, the claim that such theories are valid has rested on references to science. Yet, we have seen how questionable the "science" involved often is.

At the practitioner level, ideology sometimes develops into the "true believer" syndrome described by Eric Hoffer, in which myth is raised to the level of fact. The authors have often observed this attitude while consulting in the area of job enrichment. One executive at AT&T who was greatly committed to JE spoke cryptically of "the concept" and, by his own description, viewed himself as a Don Quixote tilting at the windmills of job fractionalization that were running rampant in the Bell System. He felt that hardly anyone understood job enrichment, which led him to present his ideas in a way that appeared to attack almost all accepted principles of management. He perceived himself as, in Hoffer's words, "the mortal enemy of things-as-they-are."[6]

Another man, who worked for a large insurance company, was very similar. However, he had the additional unfortunate habit of resorting to arguing for job enrichment because "it's the *right* thing to do." He became incensed when his efforts were resisted by line managers, who wanted "proof" that enriching jobs was economically defensible. This man had a characteristic that Hoffer says is common among true believers: he had hitched his emotional wagon to a long series of personnel fads or gimmicks. He had been repeatedly frustrated by his company's unwillingness to offer wholehearted support for any of them.

Both of these men were ideologues. Their pattern of behavior can be observed in other corporate situations and in relation to other management change strategies, including work measurement, team-building, and sensitivity training. For such individuals, managerial reform takes on an excess of passion, and theoretical purity becomes more important than the results.

While ideology can alert people to a need for change, it can also subvert scientific inquiry and obscure the importance of developing careful practice theories. Ultimately it is impossible to divorce our values from our practices. Indeed, most of us would not want to do so. We can, however, endeavor to keep ideological visions of an organization's potential from affecting the accuracy with which we evaluate organizational realities.

Normative versus Non-Normative Social Science

In view of the ideology factor, the debate over normative versus non-normative social science becomes especially relevant. Normative theory is prescriptive: it tells what types of institutional forms and practices lead to effective social organizations. Organizational development, for example, has been strongly normative in nature. The leading theorists in the field—such as Douglas McGregor, Chris Argyris, Warren Bennis, Robert Blake, and Jane Mouton—have all prescribed methods for creating and sustaining "healthy" organizations.

Many normative theories are readily translated into practice theories by managers. They are also used to cultivate ideological commitment. This ideological element is observable in humanistically based OD theories that seek to define the good or healthy organization.

Non-normative social science does not advocate; it attempts to explain existing social phenomena by describing relationships between variables. As with normative theory, the objectives are to understand and to predict. But researchers strive to suspend judgment about the consequences that are predicted. The ideal of non-normative social science is analysis without passion. However, many social scientists have found it difficult to maintain a non-normative posture because they ultimately are participants in the phenomena being studied and because few people are free of cultural bias.

In organization theory, non-normative analysis is well illustrated by the work of James Thompson.[7] His analysis of how new technology, new task environments, and increased interdependence have affected organization structure has offered a rich reservoir of hypotheses for researchers and has suggested "appropriate fit" principles for organization design that practitioners have utilized.* Thompson himself was never strongly interested in questions of applicability and had little idea of how a manager might use his work.

The tension between non-normative and normative theory can be seen in the reaction of Chris Argyris to Thompson's work. Long a pro-normative theorist, Argyris agrees that Thompson's theory predicts the serious consequences that would occur if a company's traditionally stable environment suddenly became turbulent. However, Argyris feels that the theory offers little guidance on how an organization can prepare for such an event. He challenges the "appropriate fit" model that is implied by Thompson's theory. Instead, Argyris maintains that organizations should aspire to a highly participative, organic style of organizing regardless of the environment. He states:

> . . . one has to face the fact that mechanistic systems generate internal conditions that lead to an internal environment that makes it increasingly difficult for the organization to remain in valid contact with its external environment and with its internal resources. . . . The logic of appropriate fit is basically a static model because it hypothesizes effectiveness between the internal and external environments as long as they are congruent and neither changes. . . .

> . . . The environment can suddenly change from being benign to becoming turbulent. A mechanistic organization which "fits" the benign environment is not necessarily able to change in time toward the organic structure which Thompson states is the appropriate fit for the turbulent environment.[8]

*The proponents of appropriate fit argue that for organization design to be effective, a "fit" between the organization's structure and the demands of the organization's task environment, technology, and managerial strengths and limitations must be developed. One should not speak in terms of a universally correct approach to structuring an organization.

Thompson's analysis has proved to be highly predictive of relationships between critical variables within organizations. The empirical research that has been inspired by his work, in which existing organizational forms have been studied, shows that Thompson's "appropriate fit" principles do explain much about the status quo. But it is this focus on present conditions that Argyris finds objectionable. Overall, Argyris appears more concerned with questions of what might be than with questions of what is. He tends to analyze the problems with existing organization designs and then leap mightily toward solutions.

The contributions of the two men offer an interesting perspective on contrast between normative and non-normative theories. Argyris has proposed alternative models of organizations, creating dialectic about how organizations should be managed. He has inspired innovative change, although many practitioners are rethinking the value of his methods after having difficulties over time. Thompson, who was more concerned with developing scientific theory than with suggesting practice theories, has taught us the most about how our present organizations actually work. He has been cautious as Argyris is adventuresome. Argyris inspires more speculative actions by managers, actions that periodically lead him to rework his ideas. Thompson's legacy is a sound, if incomplete, paradigm of organizational dynamics. Argyris is more likely to commit the scientific sins of Mayo.

Given the tendency of normative theory not only to suggest methods of practice but to convert theories into ideology, non-normative social science has a critical role to play: it should serve as the scientific conscience of those who advocate action. Perhaps the critical issue is not whether one normative theory is preferable to another, but whether we can manage to keep normative and non-normative theories separate. Normative theorists try to establish the usefulness of their methods; their search is for affirmation. Non-normative research, while it may suggest new methods, must also seek to disconfirm. The problem is that a given theorist may perform both roles at once.

Mayo certainly did so, and his confusion was passed on to Roethlisberger. In writing about Hawthorne, Roethlisberger and Dickson were in large part trying to confirm the value of a type of supervisory behavior. Mayo's writings were even more normative: some consisted of little else *but* affirmations of his perspective. Mayo was a man of indefatigable intellectual curiosity who respected the potential of scientific investigation. He was never, however, a likely champion of non-normative science.

Like many social theorists, Mayo tended to define his brand of social science as the only legitimate form. As a result, his legacy to organization theory was confused and remains so to this day. Although Mayo's misinterpretation of the events in the relay assembly test room does not mean his entire argument can be dismissed, the issue of how an employee's "sentiment" and nonrational thinking affect employee performance remains an open one.

Normative theories make an important and necessary contribution to management. They suggest potential methods of action that can inspire innovation among practicing managers. Often, normative theories translate existing but inconclusive empirical research into prescriptions for action. (The issue is that such prescriptions bring risks that managers should be aware of.) The body of experience accumulated by those trying to utilize such theories frequently sheds light on organizational phenomena. Further, normative models suggest hypotheses for non-normative theorists to test.

In actuality, normative theorists, regardless of their level of academic training, are the logical heirs of the practitioner/theorists of the scientific management tradition. In the fundamental aspects of their craft, the Argyrises and Waltons of contemporary normative organization theory are the descendants of Frederick Taylor.

The collection of definitive social science data is a tortuous and extended process. Field interventions are unique settings, and the pattern of events can be misleading. In laboratory studies, experimental effects cause unseen difficulties. There is no substitute for quantitative analysis coupled with thorough descriptive data on the research; there remains the danger that quantitative or qualitative data will have properties ascribed to them that they do not possess.

Given the admitted difficulty of conducting social and behavioral science research—the measurement problems, the sampling problems, the interaction between experimental design and results, the difficulty of replicating results, and the thin line between theory and philosophy—it appears that social research can aspire to recognition as a science only if the strictest standards of inquiry and reporting are observed. The maintenance of such standards is a dynamic process. Non-normative studies can provide a body of knowledge that helps balance the advocacy leanings of normative theory.

Hard, non-normative, self-critical social science can be a corrector of ineffective policy: it can contradict the beliefs of practitioners and challenge the impact of current programs, as well as suggesting new directions for action. To be credible in this role, however, social scientists must not blur the distinctions between normative and non-normative theory. They must be critically cautious rather than enthusiastic about organizational reform. Once the scientist enters the arena of practice, he or she departs from scientific concerns. The role of the normative theorist is to suggest practice theories that will improve managerial effectiveness. Even a partial blurring of the scientific role creates fertile ground for the introduction of ideology and the evolution of myth.

Action Research and Science

Field interventions are likely to remain the central vehicle for demonstrating managerial techniques. Much of this work will be designed as action research. Such research is inordinately complex, placed as it is between scientific endeavors on the one hand and policy and practice on the other. Having examined the ways in which field research results tend to be utilized, we believe it is important that action research programs emphasize their policy aspects rather than their scientific implications. Reports should not have any pretension to science except when it seems appropriate to suggest tentative hypotheses for further testing. Perhaps no action research paper should end with a section on normative recommendations; only summaries and hypotheses should be mentioned. One suspects that the patience of practicing managers is about to wear thin with still more claims about "scientific conclusions."

Most applied behavioral scientists working in industry are not primarily trying to understand the nature of motivation; they are trying to learn how to motivate workers and thereby improve their performance. The distinction is subtle but significant. The latter problem involves translating scientific knowledge into usable technique where possible, integrating it with other practices that affect workers, and developing a managerial approach that will work in a given organizational situation. The workability of an approach is determined by (1) the extent to which it will produce at least some results *if enacted*, and (2) the extent to which it is saleable to management. The latter point is important. Questions of workability—that is, whether management will even permit the trial of a method—supersede questions of science.

Taylor, Mayo, and Walton each challenged some prevalent assumptions of their time, inspiring visions of innovative organizational forms and arguing for a significant alteration in the supervisor–employee relationship. Each man knew that his ideas would win widespread adoption only if they were shown to be workable in practical settings. In the pursuit of application, each went beyond the role of the scientist. Each assumed a stance that was exciting and, in its way, legitimate—but certainly was not scientific. This trend continues today. In fact, in the field of organization theory, there has never been a greater need to distinguish between the role of scientist and the role of advocate.

Argyris's Action Science

Some indication of the direction in which field research and action research are headed can be found by examining Chris Argyris's ideas. Argyris has recently called for the development of "action science," arguing in the tradition of the organizational researchers we have been considering in this book.

Argyris is a normative theorist whose work has followed the tenets of the human potential movement in psychology. His concerns cut to the heart of power relationships in organizations. Argyris strongly criticizes traditional organizational forms and processes, arguing that they are inappropriate because of the increasing complexity and turbulence of working environments.

Above all, Argyris is an advocate of having research done in real organizational settings. He questions the very existence of non-normative data, stating that "all descriptions of reality are normative because social reality is an artifact. When we make *is* statements about the universe, they are statements about how the universe 'expects' us to behave."[9] Argyris argues that traditional empirical research (what he calls normal science) in the social sciences is flawed by its own methods. The more rigorous and precise the methodology, the more distant from the phenomena the researcher becomes. Scientific precision leads to the formulation of variables that are artificial abstractions of social reality. In the pursuit of completeness, social scientists carefully explore variance among variables, utilizing sophisticated statistical procedures to determine causality. The end result, Argyris suggests, is findings about the relationships between variables that are both valid and massive in number. Because of the latter characteristic, the findings are virtually rendered unusable.

As an example, Argyris cites a study in which researchers produced maps of several interconnected social systems in a plant. Each map contained 39 variables and over 60 different empirical relationships.[10] Argyris also points to the research literature on leadership, which increasingly reveals that a wide variety of factors contribute to the development of leadership ability. So many contingencies exist that even learning of them all is difficult or impossible; applying such knowledge to real world situations is beyond anyone's practical capacity. Argyris concludes that "as research results accumulate, their relevance and applicability seem to diminish."[11] In short, precision does not yield very useful results.

Argyris states that traditional social research has involved what he labels Model I strategies. These strategies are characterized by "single-loop learning," or learning that does not require changes in an individual's governing values. Such learning protects individuals by reinforcing their perceptions of reality. In Argyris's analysis, our social institutions, individual behavior, and research activities are governed by Model I values. So ingrained are these values that even when individuals espouse alternative models, their behavior is Model I in character. Consequently, traditional social researchers have studied only Model I organizations, and any change they have recommended has been only an alternative variation of Model I.

Argyris believes it is crucial for social scientists to demonstrate the potential of true alternative forms of social organization. To do this, they must create organizations that reflect what Argyris calls Model II values. These values involve "double-loop learning": learning in which it is most important to detect and correct any errors associated with adherence to Model I values. The establishment of Model II values requires a reprogramming of individuals and the creation and careful nurturance of supportive organizational systems. Such Model II organizations would provide a meaningful testing ground for social scientists.

Since traditional social science incorporates Model I values, Argyris proposes that a new methodology—action science—be used to establish Model II organizational forms. He argues that new organizational forms are needed if we are to gain a more thorough understanding of our traditional forms, and that action science provides a needed focus on application. Regarding the departure from strict scientific method, Argyris states:

> Because the propositions [of action science] are not highly precise, the requirements for public disconfirmability in action science must be very high. . . . If an exception is observed, it should be used to test the hypothesis. The researcher could show, for example, that the exception occurred under a different set of conditions and that the occurrence was predictable by the theory.[12]

Thus, Argyris is prepared to sacrifice precision in measuring the relationships among variables in order to develop propositions that are more applicable to the real world. He continues to say that the "accuracy" of a proposition, insofar as it produces a predefined result, should replace precision as an essential priority of social research.

Here the proposed action science becomes somewhat problematic. Variance is likely to exist between one social situation and another, whether particular propositions try to account for the variance or not. Different field applications of the same social science principle repeatedly demonstrate mixed results. Any attempt to explain such results is likely to lead one back to the need for precision. Further, the enthusiastic promotion of "applied propositions" continues to leave the door open for myth and exaggeration. Precision is the guardian against the development of excessive mythology and subjectivity in the social sciences. As Argyris himself notes, a persistent characteristic of the social scientist is self-delusion. People must be aware that action science does not rest on scientific precision; such awareness "guarantees that social scientists will not knowingly strive to kid themselves or their fellow citizens."[13]

In many respects Argyris wears the mantle of Elton Mayo. He shares Mayo's disdain for rigorous research on how organizational processes or managers' interpersonal skills can be improved. His laboratory is the real world, and he sees a pressing need for new types of organizational contexts and a redefining of effective supervisory practices. Like Mayo, Argyris seeks to alter the research practices of social science—using conversations and observations within organizations as his data—and like Mayo, he seems to be a therapist and clinician at heart.

In the early 1960s, Argyris was a prominent advocate of sensitivity training, encounter groups, and similar methods of intervention in organizations. As it became more doubtful that these approaches produced significant long-term changes in managerial performance, many behavioral scientists became more cautious in their advice to management. Findings based on contingency models cast doubt on whether management practices geared toward maximizing human potential growth were useful at all. Still, Argyris—who, like Mayo, is an intellectual adventurer—has not circumscribed his viewpoint. He believes that our entire cultural superstructure, including our social science models, are tied tacitly to the status quo. Within this context, action science contains the excitement of intellectual challenge, the adventure of new perspectives, and the pitfalls of subjective enthusiasm.

Argyris, in defending action science, asserts that applicability is an important requirement of management theories. Yet such emphasis on applicability (and on social change) is more the hallmark of a reformist than of a scientist. The fact that Argyris's notion of applicability as a scientific criterion has gained a degree of popular currency reflects, in part, the extent to which technology and science have become intertwined in our society. In effect, Argyris asks researchers and managers alike to accept as a given premise what more than twenty-five years of behavioral science research have been unable to convincingly demonstrate: that social and behavioral phenomena can be reliably and consistently "engineered."

Argyris's action science, at least in its current stage of development, might be best treated as an extension or variation of action research. The word research might be less demanding than the word science in relation to the stated goal of accuracy of application. Ideally, Argyris's proposals suggest standards that might lead to a continual challenging and tightening of practice theories, and still remain useful to managers. The results of such research could also serve to keep existing scientific theory open through the challenge of new hypotheses. Yet the precision and thoroughness of social science remain the challengers of action research; they form the conscience between what is simply useful and what can be comfortably claimed as scientific knowledge. Indeed, perhaps the problem with the social sciences is not the methodology used but the nature of the phenomena that are studied. Perhaps the management of social phenomena is inherently uncertain and fraught with risk. Social scientists could do worse than to keep reminding both practitioners and action researchers of this reality.

NOTES

1. Chris Argyris, *Intervention Theory and Method* (Reading, Mass.: Addison-Wesley, 1970), p. 1.
2. Ibid., p. 2.
3. Reinhard Bendix, *Work and Authority in Industry* (New York: Wiley, 1956).
4. Daniel Bell, *The End of Ideology* (New York: Free Press, 1960), p. 400.
5. Ibid., p. 401.
6. Eric Hoffer, *The True Believer* (New York: Harper, 1951).
7. James D. Thompson, *Organizations in Action* (New York: McGraw-Hill, 1967).
8. Chris Argyris, *The Applicability of Organizational Sociology* (New York: Cambridge University Press, 1972), pp. 31, 33.
9. Chris Argyris, *Inner Contradictions of Rigorous Research* (New York: Academic Press, 1980), p. 5.
10. F. C. Mann, B. P. Indik, and V. H. Vroom, *The Productivity of Work Groups*. Survey Research Center, Institute for Social Research, University of Michigan, Organizational Studies Series 1, Report 1, 1963.
11. Argyris, *Inner Contradictions*, p. 57.
12. Ibid., p. 132.
13. Ibid., p. 3.

14

Lessons for the Art
of Managing

The myths of management theory have had a considerable impact on corporate systems and how management is practiced. Conflicting methods are often formalized into corporate staff departments, and an ongoing battle is waged for the "soul" of the corporation. These conflicts are alive and flourishing in the attitudes and actions of line managers as well.

It is not the fact that such differences exist which is alarming. Such differences are the way of the world. Of concern is the extent to which managers work at cross-purposes because of myths that are part of the management literature. Managers who strive to be conscientious students of their field through reading, attendance at seminars, formal coursework, and exposure to the advice of experts come to think that their beliefs and methods are well substantiated, when in reality they are not.

As we have seen, the principal figures in the promulgation of management theory are not absolved of responsibility for the myths and exaggerations that have developed. Nor are subsequent theorists and practitioners who have let myths go unchallenged because they wished to convince others that a technique was valid. Meanwhile, new myths keep emerging.

We cannot expect this state of affairs to change significantly. Proponents of competing theories, each of which may contain a selective piece of useful insight, have strong vested interests. Further, complete adherence to the conservative norms of science might be not only impractical but nonbeneficial as well.

The history of behavioral science is marked by specific and useful insights, but no successfully unifying paradigm. To date, behavioral science theories have not proved to be additive in nature. Yet the managers of today's complex organizations need useful methods and technologies. They cannot afford the luxury of waiting for a theoretical position to be conclusively verified. Such a wait might prove a long one.

Management holds staggering responsibilities, both for the quality of life within organizations and for the collective effectiveness of our social institutions. Naive amateurism should not be allowed to pass for pragmatism. Ultimately, a sophisticated, critical consumerism on the part of managers is the best protection against the inappropriate application of organizational research. Managers must be willing to learn from new methods while remaining skeptical of final solutions. The acid test of a method's application is whether it enhances effectiveness in a specific situation. Generalizations come much more cautiously, and should be embraced only tentatively by managers.

Development of Diagnostic Skill

Managers who wish to critically assess the impact of various management techniques on their organizations need to develop diagnostic skill and an intimate familiarity with organizational phenomena. Elton Mayo, and later Fritz Roethlisberger, lobbied compellingly for such a skill. Mayo's view was characteristic of the subjectivity that often marks the study of management. He was convinced that a primary key to eliciting cooperation from others was the therapeutic effect of nondirective interviewing. As we have seen, there is little empirical support for such a strong assertion—especially not from the Hawthorne studies, which Mayo chose as a base for popularizing his claim.

Yet Mayo the clinician had hold of an insight that provided depth to his work beyond the specifics of his arguments concerning Hawthorne. Mayo recognized that organizational phenomena are elusive and that managers must learn to be comfortable with identifying and interpreting clinical data provided by the social universe. Although Mayo's handling and presentation of the Hawthorne data are highly questionable, today his clinical instincts seem more pertinent than ever.

Much OD intervention work has focused on the development of diagnostic skill. Unfortunately, many managers have looked for a causal relationship between application of diagnostic skill and improvements in productivity, quality, and/or personnel retention. The assumption is: "If I listen to employees, or learn what types of inter-personal processes characterize my department, performance will improve." This is how most managers have interpreted the human relations message, which was initiated in large part by the Hawthorne studies: how employees are treated determines how satisfied they are, and how satisfied they are determines productivity. The human resources model has been interpreted similarly, with the idea being that more complete utilization of employee talents will lead to more productivity. Finally, the common assumption with regard to process-oriented OD interventions is that improved group-process and inter-personal skills will lead to more cohesive work groups, and hence to higher productivity.

Diagnostic skill can contribute to managerial effectiveness, but not because it directly causes improved organizational performance. Diagnostic skill helps managers to better assess the impact of changes in their organizations, monitor fluid situations, and plan alternative interventions. However, such skill does not change the fact that results are rooted in a multitude of variables and that organizational performance will remain an uncertain consequence.

As a manager's diagnostic skill improves, it is likely that he or she will have a less programmed approach to the implementation of management strategies. Diagnostic skill involves listening to and observing both individuals and organizational processes, with the goals of interpreting events and developing better practice theories. The manager has essentially a clinical relationship with the organization, learns to make firsthand observations in precise and descriptive form, and often develops a spirit of discovery and investigation. If, in contrast, a person applies a management theory mechanically—whether it involves a human relations, quality-of-work-life, or conventional management approach—the implementation will be mindless and flawed.

The authors have found, in dealing with managers and supervisors on human resources problems, that impatience soon emerges if a basic diagnostic approach fails to result in a linear, relatively immediate result. Let's take a rather basic example:

A first-year staff accountant for a prestigious big-eight firm is given un-challenging work on an audit and hands in appallingly sloppy work papers. This is especially shocking because he is a recent M.B.A. graduate of an equally prestigious business school. When confronted about his poor work by the senior-in-charge of the audit, the staff accountant replies: "It doesn't make that much difference anyway. I don't know why I'm doing this cleri-cal work." Continued discussion elicits several comments about the work being "dumb" and "a gross underutilization of my education."

We have observed a pattern in the way a senior reacts to this type of problem. First, he or she will alternately point out specific incidents of sloppiness in the work papers and then attempt to convince the staff accountant that all big-eight careers begin this way because such experience is necessary to fully understand the problems associated with real world auditing. Neither argument tends to make much headway with the staff person, and the discussion may grow heated to the point where disciplinary action is threatened.

This situation offers a classic example of Mayo's distinction between statements of sentiment and statements of fact. The staff accountant is expressing sentiment: no work is actually "dumb," but there is the meaningful issue of whether the staff person wishes to do it. The senior responds with statements of fact; specific examples of sloppy work, and the reality that all members of the firm begin as staff accountants doing similar work. Unfortunately, as Mayo observed, sentiment is not easily altered by arguments of fact. Both parties become frustrated, and disciplinary action may be imposed. Usually, the outcome is either that the accountant begrudingly works at a performance level vacillating between acceptable and unacceptable standards, or that the person leaves the assignment and probably the firm. Either outcome means more stress and overtime work for the senior.

An alternative handling of the situation would begin with the senior first being skillful enough to distinguish between sentiment and fact. The senior should also be able to listen and respond in a fashion that allows the accountant to make the same distinction and then to choose between his or her options. Careful listening would also enable the senior to gain a better understanding of what factors gave rise to the accountant's sentiment.

Such an approach requires a degree of skill that can come only from repeated application of listening and counseling techniques, coupled with careful assessment of the responses these techniques have elicited. Only through experience can one acquire an intimate familiarity with the phenomena of feelings and how they interact with organizational systems.

Unfortunately, application of diagnostic skill cannot guarantee that the final result will be any different from the one described in the staff accountant example. There lies the rub. If a senior tries careful listening but finds that this does not cause the staff accountant to improve the work papers, he or she concludes that taking a diagnostic approach is not worth the effort. In short, most managers want a high degree of certainty that "treating" the staff person differently will result in desired organizational outcomes. If such a linear connection cannot be demonstrated, they tend to reject the idea of trying to improve diagnostic skill.

Such a rejection has two major consequences. First, managers who have had training in diagnostic skill continue to handle situations in a traditional fashion, seeming to have taken little away from the experience except an intensification of their own initial reflex responses. Second, they remain insensitive to the range of reactions people have to the firm. This lack of awareness makes them less likely to think of useful solutions to organizational problems that they will encounter as they advance in the firm. Diagnostic skill will not make them good managers, but it appears to be a prerequisite for their having an indepth understanding of problems that must be dealt with repeatedly. Managers with diagnostic skill have heightened sensitivity to the ebbs and flows of sentiment and the interconnectedness of the various dimensions of organizational life.

Different management theories and practices should not be evaluated in terms of being either right or wrong; rather, managers should assess their degrees of appropriateness to a given situation. When a certain method or procedure has unanticipated, negative consequences, the manager with a diagnostic approach does not ask who or what is at fault, but what has happened and how it can be modified. The diagnostic perspective begins with an awareness that organizational systems constitute an attempt to impose an artificial rationality on highly nonrational phenomena. Thus, these systems will always be characterized by continual trial-and-error learning. The Catch 22 of applied management research is that the more controlled the research is, the more contrived and unrepresentative will be the situation; the more natural the research setting is, the greater will be the uncertainty about what caused the results. Nevertheless, the investigator and the practitioner break new ground with each experiment or application.

Process, Not Technique

The history of American management practice is characterized by the search for technique. Perhaps this is because our culture places a high value on pragmatism; perhaps it reflects the extent to which we have been socialized to perform in bureaucratic organizations. Whatever may be the roots of the phenomenon, American managers have often been quick to adopt techniques with little consideration of what organizational processes are needed to support them. This has been particularly true with regard to work measurement, management by objectives, T-groups, job enrichment, and quality circles. Each of the above techniques has at one time enjoyed almost fad status in the management community. Managers who have applied a given technique have been primarily concerned with the specific methodology of "making it work," usually giving little attention to whether the technique is consistent with the organization's general system of management. Certainly all responsible theorists from Taylor on have appreciated the systematic properties of organizations and have recognized that no single technique will resolve the problem of effectively managing people. Taylor said that a mental revolution was needed if scientific management was to be implemented in a meaningful way. More than half a century later, the terminology used by behavioral scientists does indicate that a degree of revolution has occurred. The term "project" is used less often in referring to interventions. Instead, behavioral scientists speak of their methods as ongoing, continuous processes that must become part of the culture of an organization.

Although people have become more aware of the limitations of any specific technique unless it is well integrated into a system of management, management theorists have still tended to promote what "sells" in the short term. As theorists and researchers seek audiences for their ideas, they tolerate, and sometimes support, fads that arise around a given technique. The best check on this process seems to be rebuttals by other theorists. In view of the long history of distortion in the way management theories are promoted, practicing managers must develop personal knowledge of organizational processes. Unfortunately, most managers are so results-oriented that they take little time to focus on process. As a consequence, many lack knowledge about both interpersonal group processes and broader organizational processes.

To obtain such knowledge, managers must become directly involved with organizational phenomena and develop the diagnostic skill discussed earlier. Knowledge of process cannot be memorized or intellectualized; it must be experienced. People tend to approach management training as a problem of obtaining information. Although experiential learning has become widely utilized in recent years, it is still difficult to persuade managers to invest their time in such efforts. Instead, executives say: "Give me a program and the steps to make it work." Such an attitude reflects a mode of thinking that is highly susceptible to misrepresentation of techniques.

Another problem is the way in which organizations tend to assess the payoffs of experiential training. Traditionally, the focus has been on whether such training has the long-term effect of causing executives to trust others more when engaged in activities such as coaching or delegating. Another criterion has been whether the training has improved specific facets of organizational effectiveness, such as profitability, turnover, product innovativeness, or organizational climate. These measures may be, at the same time, too ambitious and too short-sighted. A meaningful outcome might be one in which a manager leaves experiential training with a subtly improved feel for the dynamics of organizational processes. Such an outcome is not readily measurable or even immediately usable, but it nevertheless may prepare the manager to assess intelligently different management techniques that could be applied to a given situation.

Managers as Integrators

In this book we have proposed that actual management research findings do not justify the extent to which groups within organizations sometimes "go to war" over management methods. Such battles are beneficial in forcing theorists and consultants from various camps to address issues that they would prefer to avoid. However, organizations can save much wasted energy if they stop asking "Which method is correct?" and instead look for the combination of methods that is likely to maximize organizational effectiveness. Managers will benefit most from theories if they recognize the uniqueness of their situation and creatively seek to integrate methods rather than conform to one school of thought.

The road to integration is made easier if managers recognize two important points. First, *managerial methods must support organizational goals and strategies.* A company whose strategy is to protect and further penetrate a relatively narrow market confronts different issues than one attempting to enter a variety of new markets.[1] The former must adopt methods of operation that will increase efficiency and reduce costs. Typically there is a high degree of centralization, standardization, and formalization. However, behavioral-science-based approaches should not be rejected out of hand because superficially they seem less pertinent to the company's situation than "engineering" approaches. The objective should be to make meaningful choices among a variety of methods that might be *potentially adaptable* to the organization's needs.

For example, the company seeking to protect a relatively narrow market might have to emphasize these management approaches:

- Work measurement of jobs
- Automation wherever possible
- Centralized goal-setting
- Selection of employees willing to work in a highly structured environment

- Specific behavioral approaches to job training, coupled with a participative approach to the identification and achievement of goals
- Identification of practices that cause redundancies in the work flow, perhaps resulting in more complete jobs or "nested" teams of workers[2]
- A practice of retraining displaced managers and workers

Because corporate strategy involves moving in a more centralized direction, a totally participative approach is not feasible. In explaining specific participatory approaches to employees, managers would have to avoid setting unrealistic expectations by speaking of flexibility and worker discretion in job performance, participation of subordinates in setting work objectives, and rapid development of human resources. However, the various management approaches can be explained in the context of the organization's current situation and strategy. This affords a greater sharing of information than is typical in many centralized organizations.

By contrast, a company active in a range of markets must be able to utilize the talents of individual contributors in a very flexible manner. Again a mixture of "behavioral" and "engineering" methods might be required:

- Identification of critical dependencies between organizational units and the use of appropriate structures (such as special integrator roles or task forces) to manage these dependencies[3]
- Identification of the appropriate mode of operation for each unit of the business (degree of structure and centralization, and accompanying use of either traditional efficiency-oriented approaches or innovative work-structuring techniques such as job enrichment or team production)
- Training and development techniques designed to foster "generalists" at relatively low levels of the organization

Such variation in approaches brings up the second point crucial to integration: *management methods must be congruent throughout the organization.* The approaches used—such as compensation methods, work structuring, problem-solving vehicles, and management development activities—must be mutually reinforcing and encourage people to behave in consistent ways.

Managers must avoid simply imitating other organizations and instead seek opportunities to integrate various methods. In the application of managerial techniques, ideological purity is no virtue. There are abundant opportunities to integrate a range of theories, but some specialists wear "one best method" blinders. One-best-method stances were first taken by innovative practitioners who were confronted with operational problems and had no meaningful maps to guide them. Eventually, practitioners might also develop important guidelines for *integrating* management theories.

The Ability to Assess Field Reports Realistically

The examples in this book have, we hope, brought home the risk of accepting a theory simply because it has face validity. True, some of the theories that have helped practicing managers most are presented in oversimplified, pragmatic terms that many researchers and theorists consider "sloppy" and unscientific. But reports of field studies should be read with a sensitivity to the differences between one situation and another and with an understanding of the likelihood that not all the data have been presented. A manager might ask:

- What are the similarities between our situation and theirs? The differences?
- At what points does it appear that problems might have developed?
- What counterproductive outcomes might have occurred along with the favorable outcomes?
- What unique factors might have contributed to the success of the effort?
- How would we have to do things differently here, and how might these changes affect the results?
- How consistent are the suggested methods with our organizational strategy?
- If we apply similar methods here, what support systems will have to be developed?

The Example of Japanese Management

The early 1980s have witnessed a widespread interest in Japanese management.[4] Fascination with Japanese methods had been building for some time. Peter Drucker, Richard Pascale, William Ouchi, and Ezra Vogel were among the authorities writing for the practitioner throughout the 1970s.[5] Interest was further heightened when Japanese businesses obtained significant shares of the U.S. and world markets in a number of industries, most visibly automobiles and electronics. Many managers saw the "Japanese challenge" as threatening the growth, profitability, and employment potential of American firms. The perceived challenge was as ominous as the American challenge had seemed to Europeans when Servan-Schreiber penned his political-economic manifesto for European industry in the 1960s.[6] Such a difference a decade makes.

The success of Japanese industry has sparked research into the employer–employee relationships in that country. Two communities of interest presently exist. One is the scientific community, in which it is felt that many interesting issues have been raised with regard to social organization. The other group consists of practitioners who are looking for ways of meeting competitive pressures. The former has time to speculate and await the accumulation of data; the latter interest is immediate (and possibly transitory). Over the next five years, opinions about Japan's management methods are likely to vary with the country's position in world markets; the topic may eventually draw yawns as a training conference topic. The scientific questions will, of course, remain.

Overall, interesting insights have been gleaned from Japanese methods. But people's enthusiasm has far exceeded the insights. The reason for this is rooted in an old view of what confronts management: "the labor problem." A group of American managers, in discussing their difficulty in competing with the Japanese, will continually refer to labor costs, employees' commitment to product quality, company loyalty, and so on. The terminology may be different, but the issue is the same one that Taylor addressed almost a century ago. Management thinkers—from Taylor to Mayo to the contemporary quality-of-work-life theorists—have clearly indicated some bafflement about how the labor problem is to be solved.

As Americans have come increasingly to regard the land of the rising sun as the land of business success, they have also attached considerable face validity to a new management approach, usually called Theory Z. Many managers are already applying this label to a range of different phenomena.

The current interest in Japan holds both promise and a significant trap. The promise is that the phenomenon of Japanese business may have dramatically demonstrated that American organizational forms are social artifacts. That is, there are effective models or organizational processes other than the ones historically inspired by our Western bureaucratic tradition. It is not surprising that Japanese methods differ from American ones, since Japan's industrial organizations are embedded in a socioeconomic structure and cultural tradition that differ significantly from our own. It is a favorable sign that American executives are willing to reflect on these differences. A complete commitment to the status quo is the most dangerous attitude that can exist within an organization.

Thus the promise is that Japanese methods hold new opportunities; the trap is the common assumption that the methods largely hold the solution to our managerial problems. Comparisons between companies such as ITT and Matsushita provide many instructive insights, but significant questions remain. Some crucial points raised by Edgar Schein include the fact that corporate indoctrination practices are likely to be less effective in our society, where resistance to conformity is often strong; that the paternalistic aspects of holistic management may clash with American values of individualism and self-determination; that the macrostructure of Japanese industry differs from our own; and that, if the circumstances are otherwise similar, there is no convincing evidence that Theory Z organizations are more effective than our traditional American organizations.[7] William Ouchi characterized the latter as governed by "Theory A," "a form where people link tenuously to one another and rarely achieve intimacy."[8]

The popular, application-oriented books on Japanese management rely heavily on case and anecdotal examples. Interestingly, different authorities distill somewhat different lessons for the American manager.[9] Ouchi suggests more openness, clarity, and explicit feedback; Pascale and Athos argue for the skillful use of ambiguity and subtle messages.[10]

There is also the very real possibility that the Japanese success is attributable to a variety of other factors, such as application of robotics, more attention to long-term management of production resources, and reliance on senior managers who are as skilled in production needs as they are in the arts of management. In sum, just because Japanese organizations differ from those in the West, the differences do not necessarily account for Japan's industrial success.

The Management Theory Jungle: Is There a Way Out?

Out of frustration with such uncertainties, the practicing manager might decide to ignore the "authorities" and rely simply on common sense. Today's professionals, however, are unlikely to find such an approach satisfying. Solutions are to be found in a more careful examination of the management literature, rather than in reliance on instinct.

The contradictory explanations for the Japanese success that are offered by Ouchi and by Pascale and Athos illustrate that theories based on field research or observation of an application cannot be taken at face value. They represent the position of the author on what ought to bring results, not necessarily what *does* bring results. Good conceptualization, useful insight, thoughtful analysis, and anecdotal evidence cannot be confused with empirical data.

Management remains a creative process, in which analysis of the strengths, weaknesses, and future direction of one's own organization must be combined with insights gleaned from other sources and forged into a tool appropriate for specific situations that arise. New ideas must be evaluated from a range of perspectives, with recognition that every method will have pros and cons.

It is also important that senior management present new ideas as offering a possible learning experience, rather than as an implied criticism of individuals who hold opposing views. Unfortunately, new ideas are often introduced into organizational training programs in the form of a tight presentation based on one theorist's views. This is not so much training as indoctrination. A series of presentations in which managers are encouraged to examine an argument from different sides is generally more beneficial in the long run. Managers have too often been made to feel that training and development programs must teach them to "do something" back on the job. An excessive focus on technique impoverishes the presentation of conceptual issues and reinforces people's tendency to perpetuate oversimplified, anecdotal evidence as providing support for their approach.

Technique is obviously necessary. Less obvious to many "pragmatic" managers is the periodic need to be a good theorist, to examine ideas and data thoroughly, and to assess the evidence without continually thinking: "How will I use this knowledge?" Organizational researchers have become very skilled in presenting knowledge in formats that are conducive to application. However, managers need to recognize the importance of moving in the opposite direction as well, dealing with the data on which arguments for application rest. Professionalism demands no less.

Once an organization has developed a program for implementing a new approach, managers do need specific skill training. But differences in individual perspectives need to be acknowledged and respected, not papered over. Any other approach simply encourages exaggeration and the perpetuation of myth.

NOTES

1. R. Miles and C. Snow, *Organizational Strategy, Structure and Process* (New York: McGraw-Hill, 1978).
2. See R. N. Ford, *Motivation Through the Work Itself* (New York: AMACOM, 1969).

3. See P. R. Lawrence and J. W. Lorsch, *Organization and Environment: Managing Differentiation and Integration* (Homewood, Ill.: Irwin, 1969).

4. Two particularly popular books are W. Ouchi, *Theory Z* (Reading, Mass.: Addison-Wesley, 1981); and R. T. Pascale and A. G. Athos, *The Art of Japanese Management* (New York: Simon & Schuster, 1981).

5. See especially Peter Drucker, R. T. Pascale, and W. Ouchi, "Made in America (Under Japanese Management)," *Harvard Business Review,* March–April 1978; and E. F. Vogel, "Meeting the Japanese Challenge," *The Wall Street Journal,* May 19, 1980.

6. J. J. Servan-Schreiber, *The American Challenge* (New York: Atheneum, 1968).

7. E. H. Schein, "Does Japanese Management Style Have a Message for American Managers?" *Sloan Management Review,* Fall 1981.

8. W. Ouchi, *Theory Z,* p. 67.

9. Schein, "Does Japanese Management?"

10. Ouchi, *Theory Z.;* and Pascale and Athos, *Art of Japanese Management.*

Suggested Readings for Part Four

Argyris, C. *The Applicability of Organizational Sociology.* New York: Cambridge University Press, 1972.

————. *Inner Contradictions of Rigorous Research.* New York: Academic Press, 1980.

Bell, D. *The End of Ideology.* New York: Free Press, 1960.

Cherns, A. B. "Social Research and Its Diffusion." *Human Relations,* Vol. 22 (1969), No. 3. pp. 210–218.

Clark, A. W., ed. *Experimenting with Organizational Life.* New York: Plenum Press, 1976.

Dubin, R. "Theory Building in Applied Areas." In M. D. Dunnette, *Handbook of Industrial and Organizational Psychology.* Chicago: Rand McNally, 1976.

Lee, J. A. *The Gold and the Garbage in Management Theories and Prescriptions.* Athens, Ohio: Ohio University Press, 1980.

Miller, L. "Hard Realities and Soft Social Science." *The Public Interest,* Spring 1980, pp. 67–82.

Rapopart, R. "Three Dilemmas in Action Research." *Human Relations,* Vol. 23 (1970), No. 6, pp. 499–513.

Vaill, P. B. "Practice Theories in Organization Development." Paper presented at the annual meeting of the Academy of Management, Atlanta, Georgia, August 1971.

Epilogue

This book began with an interest in the myths that surround many prominent management theories. We wondered about the extent to which these myths were contributing to the divisiveness that marks the field. Through a detailed examination of this issue, we concluded that the heart of the issue was the process through which social science knowledge has been translated into proposals for change and promoted by its advocates.

The line from Taylor to Walton is one of increasing humanism. Taylor's humanistic concerns emerged as he developed his theoretical position and began to promote it. However, his attitude remained colored by a strong sense of elitism and condescension, directed toward managers and workers alike. And he regarded efficiency as the primary goal, not a positive consequence of workplace reform. The latter position is taken by Walton, who began his professional career in the humanistic tradition.

The three major theorists whom we have discussed share a common assumption: that cooperative effort between labor and management is the key to organizational effectiveness. Taylor and Walton have explicitly stated that organizational goals and employee needs can be congruently satisfied; Mayo has implied this. However, the three offer different prescriptions for achieving cooperative effort. Taylor felt that the answer was to integrate substantial economic rewards with production goals and to demonstrate the methods for and feasibility of attaining goals. Mayo believed the key was interviewing, as a method for dealing with employee sentiment. Walton emphasizes constructive, joint problem-solving approaches that utilize the suggestions of employees, a position contrary to Taylor's.

Nevertheless, the philosophical frameworks of the three theorists are more similar than is commonly assumed. For example, Taylor

289

would have agreed with Walton's argument that underutilization of talent destroys motivation. Taylor would not have predicted success for his system at a plant such as Topeka, in which highly capable and talented employees had been recruited. The idea of deliberately recruiting such production workers probably was foreign to him; if it was not, he may have doubted that such employees were available on a widespread basis. As we have seen, Taylor believed that the employee best suited to perform a job at a given level generally had limited ability to conceive how the job should best be organized. Taylor would have never advocated recruiting highly talented people with strong credentials and placing them in routine, fragmented jobs—which is what many contemporary organizations do. He was aware of the need for "fit" between employee, job, and the larger organizational control system.

Taylor, Mayo, and Walton each used field studies to illustrate principles that they believed would significantly reform organizations for the better. In general, these principles rest as much on the perceptions of the theorists as on the evidence generated by the studies. This is characteristic of much management theory. Because of organizational problems, innovative ideas—with supporting evidence that is often intriguing and persuasive, if soft—are pressed into service. Evaluating the new theories is difficult because scientific verification cannot keep up with managers' creative adaptations of the ideas or with the shifting economic scene.

It appears that one reason Taylorism and human relations, for example, have often been represented as opposites is that parties *need* to present them that way in order to facilitate a dialectic. In part, this reflects the dichotomous nature of Western thinking—the belief that attitudes must be polarized if people are to be galvanized into action. Within organizations, staff specialists use polarized positions to attack straw men while trying to create a need for their preferred techniques. "War stories," anecdotal evidence, and the myths of the literature are important weapons in this process. In short, myths emerge not only because there are inevitable distortions in the communications process but because there is a political need for them.

In view of this tendency, managers should be flexible in their approach and be prepared for the instances when reality falls short of a theory's promise. When the latter occurs, the baby should not be thrown out with the bath water. Management should adopt a balance-sheet approach, identifying as much as possible the assets and liabilities of the method, on the basis of personal experience.

Organizations are technological, monetary, social, psychological, and political entities. In the studies we examined in this book, each of these dimensions affected results. When a particular dimension is given excessive prominence over the others by a theoretical school, the nature of organizations is being distorted.

An important characteristic of organizations is that collaborative effort is needed if they are to be effective. Cooperation is the essence of organization, but the methods of obtaining it appear to be diverse. Scientifically, we have only begun to learn the range of possibilities. In practical terms, the search for cooperation is an elusive and ongoing challenge that never really ends, since conditions are continually changing employees' perceptions of whether and how they should cooperate. Thus, management must learn to patiently observe and acquire knowledge about this phenomenon, resisting a "single school of thought" solution.

Index

action research, as type of field research, 231–236

Adams, Brooks, *Theory of Social Revolutions,* 93

Ahmedabad Textile Mills in India, and working groups, 230

American Federation of Labor (AFL), and Taylor system, 60, 61, 62

American Institute of Industrial Engineers, and Taylor, 78

American Management Associations, Gantt Memorial Medal presented by, 78

Applied Time and Motion Study (Holmes), 79

Argyle, Michael, on Hawthorne studies, 134, 139, 145–146

Argyris, Chris
and field and action research, 271–274
and intervention for social reasons, 264
and Maslow, 248–249
Model I of, 271–272
Model II of, 272
as normative, 266, 267–268, 271
on sociological theory, 223
and social science research, 233
on Taylor, 69
as widely known behavioral scientist, 246

AT&T
and employee counseling, 177
and job enrichment, 229, 235, 252–253, 265

Athos, A. G., on Japanese management, 285

Babcock, George, as manager of Franklin Auto Company, 52

Bankers Trust, and job enrichment, 229

bank wiring observation room, in Hawthorne studies, 117–121

Baritz, Loren, on Taylor, 82–83

Barrett, G., on Taylor, 69

Barth, Carl
and Franklin Auto Company, 52
and pig-iron studies, 29–30
after Taylor, 77

Bass, B., on Taylor, 69

Bayha, F. H., *Engineered Work Measurement,* 79

behavioral science school of management, 1, 4–5, 183, 230

Bell, Daniel
on Taylor, 71–72
on social movements, 265

Bell System, and job enrichment, 235, 266

Bell Telephone, and employee counseling, 175

293